The Beauty of Holiness

The Beauty of Holiness

Re-Reading Isaiah in the Light of the Psalms

Joseph Blenkinsopp

LONDON • NEW YORK • OXFORD • NEW DELHI • SYDNEY

T&T CLARK
Bloomsbury Publishing Plc
50 Bedford Square, London, WC1B 3DP, UK
1385 Broadway, New York, NY 10018, USA

BLOOMSBURY, T&T CLARK and the T&T Clark logo are trademarks
of Bloomsbury Publishing Plc

First published in Great Britain 2019

Copyright © Joseph Blenkinsopp, 2019

Joseph Blenkinsopp has asserted his right under the Copyright,
Designs and Patents Act, 1988, to be identified as Author of this work.

Cover image: King David. Drawing for the rose window of the Cathedral of Leon,
14th century. Photo by PHAS/UIG via Getty Images.

All rights reserved. No part of this publication may be reproduced or
transmitted in any form or by any means, electronic or mechanical,
including photocopying, recording, or any information storage or retrieval
system, without prior permission in writing from the publishers.

Bloomsbury Publishing Plc does not have any control over, or responsibility
for, any third-party websites referred to or in this book. All internet addresses
given in this book were correct at the time of going to press. The author
and publisher regret any inconvenience caused if addresses have changed or
sites have ceased to exist, but can accept no responsibility for any such changes.

A catalogue record for this book is available from the British Library.

Library of Congress Cataloging-in-Publication Data
Names: Blenkinsopp, Joseph, 1927- author.
Title: The beauty of holiness : re-reading Isaiah in the light
of the Psalms / Joseph Blenkinsopp. Description: 1 [edition]. |
New York : Bloomsbury Academic, 2018. | Includes bibliographical
references and index. Identifiers: LCCN 2018000629|
ISBN 9780567680297 (hpod) | ISBN 9780567680303 (pbk.)
Subjects: LCSH: Bible. Isaiah–Criticism, interpretation, etc. |
Bible. Psalms–Criticism, interpretation, etc. | Intertextuality.
Classification: LCC BS1515.52 .B439 2018 | DDC 224/.106–dc23
LC record available at https://lccn.loc.gov/2018000629

ISBN: HB: 978-0-5676-8029-7
PB: 978-0-5676-8030-3
ePDF: 978-0-5676-8032-7
eBook: 978-0-5676-8031-0

Typeset by Deanta Global Publishing Services, Chennai, India

To find out more about our authors and books visit www.bloomsbury.com
and sign up for our newsletters.

'O *worship the Lord in the beauty of holiness*'.
Ps 96:9, King James Version.

For Jean with Gratitude and Love.

CONTENTS

Foreword viii
List of abbreviations x

1. Re-reading Isaiah in the light of Psalms 1
2. The Psalms and their authors 11
3. Psalmody and prophecy 27
4. Psalmody in Isaiah 1–39 37
5. Prophecy and Psalmody in Isaiah 40–55 57
6. Prophecy and Psalmody in Isaiah 56–66 75
7. Zion as reality and symbol in Psalms and Isaiah 87
8. The two ways in Psalms and Isaiah 107
9. The Servants of the Lord in Psalms and Isaiah 121
10. The repudiation of sacrifice in Isaiah and Psalms 135
11. The beauty of holiness 147

Subject Index 163
Author Index 171

FOREWORD

In the present work, I want to present, as a supplement to my three-volume Anchor Bible commentary on Isaiah, an intertextual reading of Isaiah and Psalms, two of the most substantial compilations in the biblical archive, as if one literary work with two interconnected components. I argue that, read in this way, they can be shown to coalesce in a religious vision, a way of experiencing and articulating a commitment to the fundamentals of the faith of Israel, with its own distinctive character over against, but not inconsistent with, torah religion in its major formulations. The emphasis is on affect and emotion, the expression of joy and sorrow articulated in music, singing, and dancing; in praise, thanksgiving, and lament. In the context of world religions, this emphasis may be read as of the same general type as the Hasidic movement in Judaism, the Sufi schools in Islam, Pietism in German Lutheranism, and Pentecostalism and the charismatic movements in the modern period, to mention only the better-known religious variations of this kind. An initial clue to this distinctive character comes to light when we take note of terms and names of primary importance in the scriptural texts as a whole which are either absent from, or of rare occurrence in, or used with a different emphasis in Isaiah and Psalms. In the first chapter, this is shown to be the case with *torah*, Moses, and Sinai. In Isaiah/Psalms, *torah* proceeds most frequently not from Sinai but from Zion, the dominant religious symbol in these two texts; it is mediated primarily through prophetic channels, not by promulgation from Sinai (named only in Ps 68 but not as the site of the giving of the law); and, most importantly, it is available to all peoples.

To establish this proposal something must first be said about the Psalms component and its authors (Chapter 2) and the relation between psalmody and prophecy, including a critique of the cult prophet hypothesis associated primarily with Sigmund Mowinckel (Chapter 3). This will prepare for a survey of the place of psalms and psalm fragments in the three main sections of Isa 1–39, 40–55, 56–66 (Chapters 4, 5, and 6). There follows a study of Zion as a central symbol in both components (Chapter 7). Starting out from a reading of Ps 1, Chapter 8 deals with the practice of displaying moral character in terms of contrasting categories familiar from the teaching on the Two Spirits in the Qumran Community Rule and the *Didache* (*The Teaching of the Twelve Apostles*) in early Christianity, the most basic form of which would be the righteous – the wicked. This provides a starting point in Chapter 9 for presenting the evidence, meagre and insufficient as it is, for the formation of conventicles or self-segregating groups under such titles as the Poor (*'anawim*), the Devout (*ḥāsîdîm*), and especially the Servants of the Lord (*'abdê YHWH*). In these groups, the distinctive vision of Isaiah/Psalms was cherished and promoted. There follows a special test case, namely, the critique of temple sacrifice and the priesthood which controlled it, an important aspect of priest-Levite hostility in evidence in both Isaiah and Psalms, of obvious relevance to the Levitical singers and musicians (Chapter 10). The last chapter deals with the importance of the temple as the place of encounter with God, the place where one might expect a more intense experience of the divine presence. This expectation is well attested in Psalms but also in Isaiah, most clearly in the prophet's vision in the temple (Isa 6:1–13). This last chapter will also explain the title I have given the book.

LIST OF ABBREVIATIONS

AB	Anchor Bible
ABD	D. N. Freedman (1992), ed., *The Anchor Bible Dictionary* (6 vols). New York: Doubleday
ANET	J. B. Pritchard (1969), ed., *Ancient Near Eastern Texts Relating to the Old Testament* (3rd edn). Princeton: Princeton University Press
Bib	*Biblica*
BK	*Bibel und Kirche*
BN	*Biblische Notizen*
BZ	Biblische Zeitschrift
CBQ	*Catholic Biblical Quarterly*
DDD	K. van der Toorn, B. Becking and P. W. van der Horst (1999), eds, *Dictionary of Deities and Demons in the Bible* (2nd edn).Leiden: Brill
EDSS	L. H. Schiffman and J. C. VanderKam (2000) *Encyclopedia of the Dead Sea Scrolls* (2 vols). Oxford: Oxford University Press
ErIsr	*Eretz Israel*
ET	English Translation
HTR	*Harvard Theological Review*
ICC	International Critical Commentary
JAAR	*Journal of the American Academy of Religion*

JAOS	*Journal of the American Oriental Society*
JBL	*Journal of Biblical Literature*
JCS	*Journal of Cuneiform Studies*
JJS	*Journal of Jewish Studies*
JNES	*Journal of Near Eastern Studies*
JPS	Jewish Publication Society translation of the Hebrew Bible
JSJ	*Journal for the Study of Judaism in the Persian, Hellenistic and Roman Period*
JSOT	*Journal for the Study of the Old Testament*
JSOTS	Journal for the Study of the Old Testament Supplement Series
JSP	*Journal for the Study of the Pseudepigrapha*
JTS	*Journal of Theological Studies*
KTU	M. Dietrich, O. Loretz and J. Sammartin (1976), eds, *Die keilalphabetischen Texte Ugarit* (Alter Orient und Altes Testament 24/1). Neukirchen Vluyn: Neukirchener Verlag
LCL	Loeb Classical Library
LXX	Septuagint
MT	Masoretic Text
NEAEHL	E. Stern (1993), ed., *The New Encyclopaedia of Archaeological Excavations in the Holy Land* (4 vols). Jerusalem: Magnes
NCB	New Century Bible
NRSV	New Revised Standard Version
NTS	*New Testament Studies*
OCD	S. Hornblower and A. Spawforth (1996), eds, *The Oxford Classical Dictionary* (3rd edn). Oxford: Oxford University Press

Or	*Orientalia*
OTS	Oudtestamentische Studiën
RB	*Revue Biblique*
REB	Revised English Bible
TDNT	G. Kittel and G. Friedrich (1964–76), eds, *Theological Dictionary of the New Testament* (8 vols). ET by G. W. Bromiley. Grand Rapids: Eerdmans
TDOT	G. J. Botterwick and H. Ringgren (1974–), eds, *Theological Dictionary of the Old Testament* (8 vols). ET by J. T. Willis, G. W. Bromiley and D. E. Green. Grand Rapids: Eerdmans.
UF	*Ugarit-Forschungen*
VT	*Vetus Testamentum*
VTSup	Supplements to *Vetus Testamentum*
WBC	Word Bible Commentary
ZA	*Zeitschrift für Assyriologie*
ZAW	*Zeitschrift für die alttestamentliche Wissenschaft*

1

Re-reading Isaiah in the light of Psalms

The book of Isaiah has much more in common with Psalms than might appear at first reading. Both are compilations put together over several centuries by multiple authors, almost all unidentified. If we were to take them together, as if one literary work with two components – an experiment which I will attempt in the following chapters – they would add up to one of the largest literary units in the Hebrew Bible, more, calculating by the Masoretic verse count, than all the other prophetic books (3,818 verses against 3,723) and more than the Deuteronomistic History in the books of Samuel and Kings (3,818 verses against 3,070). What, therefore, I wish to argue is that Isaiah and Psalms, when taken together and read intertextually, coalesce in a religious vision, a way of experiencing and articulating commitment to the fundamentals of the faith of Israel, which has its own distinctive character vis-à-vis torah religion whether of the Deuteronomistic (D) or Priestly type (P), a fortiori with respect to the didactic and reflective compositions in the Writings (*ketuvim*) comprising the third part of the tripartite canon.

We can obtain an initial sense of the distinctive character of this putative Isaianic-Psalmodic corpus by noting the incidence of undoubtedly significant terminology throughout the biblical texts in general which is absent from our corpus, of rare occurrence in it, or used in it in a different way. This exercise will obviously not settle the matter but it may at least motivate us to pursue the proposal further. The key term *torah* used with reference to the Mosaic-Sinaitic law is the first and most significant example. The word *torah* occurs twelve times in Isaiah – seven times in Isa 1–39, five times in Isa 40–55, and not at all in Isa 56–66, but never expressly as the law of Moses and never as *torah* given at Sinai.[1] In Isa 1.10 and 2.3, *torah* is in parallelism with 'the word of the Lord' with reference to a prophetic oracle, and in 5.24, it is identified with 'the word of the Holy One of Israel', meaning, again, the prophetic word. The entire section 8.16–22, in which *torah* occurs twice, deals with the passing on of the prophet's teaching to posterity, and the *torat YHWH* ('the law of the LORD') of Isa 30.9 must likewise be committed to writing as testimony to the obduracy of the prophet's contemporaries. In Deutero-Isaiah, especially Isa 40–48, *torah* generally has the sense of the imposition of law and order to be brought about by Cyrus, founder of the Persian-Achaemenid empire, called by the God of Israel to world rule (Isa 42.4, 21; 51.4). This *torah* corresponds more or less to what today is known as international law. I do not find this limited usage an adequate basis for the hypothesis that the book of Isaiah, as a book of Jewish Scripture, has the Mosaic torah as its principal subject matter,[2] or that the book has undergone a thorough torah revision,[3] or that the Isaianic author is in debate with the 'wisdom tradition'.[4]

The name *Moses* (Moshe), intimately linked with *torah*, occurs only once in Isaiah, where he is presented as guide out of Egypt and through the wilderness but not as lawgiver (Isa 63.11–12).[5] On the other hand, David's name appears ten times. In Isaiah, *torah* signifies predominantly the instruction from God mediated through

---

[1]Isa 1.10; 2.3; 5.24; 8.16, 20; 30.9; 42.4, 21, 24; 51.4, 7. In Isa 24.5, the word occurs in the rare plural *tôrôt*, elsewhere only in Lev 26.46; Ezek 43.11; 44.24; Neh 9.13.
[2]Gerald T. Sheppard, 'The "Scope" of Isaiah as a Book of Jewish and Christian Scriptures', in *NewVisions of Isaiah*, ed. Roy F. Melugin and Marvin A. Sweeney (Sheffield: Sheffield Academic Press, 1996), 257–81.
[3]Ronald E. Clements, 'The Meaning of תורה in Isaiah 1-39', in *Reading the Law. Festschrift Gordon J. Wenham*, ed. J. G. McConville and Karl Möller (New York & London: T. & T. Clark, 2007), 59–72.
[4]Joseph Jensen, O.S.B., *The Use of tôrâ by Isaiah* (CBQMS; Washington, DC: Catholic Biblical Association, 1973).
[5]*mōšeh 'ammô* (Isa 63.11), absent from LXX, is probably a gloss.

a prophetic source, the prophetic 'word of Yahweh', rather than a written law. Moreover, this instruction proceeds not from Sinai, which is not even mentioned in Isaiah, but from Zion and, most importantly, it is destined for all people or, in other words, it is internationalized:

> In days to come
> the mountain of the Lord's house
> will be set over all other mountains,
> raised high above the hills.
> All the nations will stream towards it,
> and many peoples will go and say,
> 'Let us go up to the mountain of the Lord,
> to the house of the God of Jacob,
> that he may teach us his ways
> and that we may walk in his paths.'
> For instruction (*torah*) comes from Zion,
> the word of the Lord from Jerusalem. (Isa 2.2–3)

What this means is then spelled out in the following verses: arbitration rather than conflict between nations, the abolition of war – the ultimate horizon of prophetic teaching – and an end to the manufacture of armaments. The same vision of the future is stated more succinctly in Deutero-Isaiah:

> Instruction (*torah*) will shine forth from me,
> and my judgement will be a light to peoples. (Isa 51.4)

So much, then, for Isaiah.[6] The situation in Psalms is similar. *Sinai* occurs only once, in one of the most ancient psalms but not as the

---

[6] On this topic, see further Irmtraud Fischer, *Tora für Israel – Tora für die Völker* (Stuttgart: Katholisches Bibelwerk, 1995); Marvin A. Sweeney, 'The Book of Isaiah as Prophetic Torah', in Roy F. Melugin and Marvin A. Sweeney (eds), *New Visions of Isaiah* (JSOTSup 214; Sheffield: Sheffield Academic Press, 1996), 50–67. I have also profited from a hand-out of Jaap Dekker, 'The Concept of Torah in the Book of Isaiah', a paper delivered at the Joint SOTS-OTW meeting in Edinburgh on 22 July 2015.

place where the law was given to Moses but as the place of origin of the 'God of Sinai', literally, 'The One of Sinai' (*zeh sinai*):

> There were myriads of God's chariots,
> thousands upon thousands,
> when the LORD came in holiness from Sinai. (Ps 68.18)

The law in the more familiar sense of a written law is referred to occasionally in Psalms, but never as given to Moses at Sinai.[7] Ps 90 is presented in the rubric at the head of the psalm as 'a prayer of Moses, man of God' but the psalm itself contains no reference to the law. The law achieves prominence only in Ps 1, generally read as introduction to the collection understood as a guide to the moral life; in Ps 19, which contemplates the glory of God revealed in the heavens and in the moral law – reminiscent of Kant's famous dictum about the starry skies above and the moral law within; and, finally, in Ps 119. In this mega-psalm of 176 verses, an anomaly among psalms in both length and theme, which has been described as a proto-rabbinic composition,[8] the word *torah* occurs 25 times. Elsewhere in Psalms, Moses is presented as a guide in the wilderness, as he is in Isa 63.11–12,[9] a priest together with his brother Aaron in Ps 99.6, and a prophet who intercedes and performs miracles,[10] but not as lawgiver. In Psalms, as in Isaiah, he is far less prominent than David, whose name appears in the initial rubrics of seventy-four of the psalms, in several of which his exalted status is affirmed.[11] The closest we come to the giving of the law is the statement in Ps 103.7 that God made known 'his ways' to Moses.

We note further that even where the law is the principal theme in Psalms, as in Ps 19, the language has its own distinctive character. Rather than being simply imposed, or a threat to human freedom, the law of God revives the spirit, gives joy to the heart and light to the eyes. It is more to be desired than gold; it is sweeter than honey

---

[7]Pss 37.31; 40.9; 78.1, 5, 10; 89.31; 94.12; 105.45.
[8]Yehoshua Amir, 'Psalm 119 als Zeugnis eines proto-rabbinischen Judentums', in idem (ed.), *Studien zum Antiquen Judentums* (Frankfort and New York: Peter Lang, 1985), 1–34.
[9]Compare Pss 77.21; 106.23, 32.
[10]Pss 103.7; 105.26; 106.16, 23.
[11]Pss 2, 89, 110, 132.

extracted from the honeycomb (vv. 8–11). This is the language of the mystics, 'hasidic' language, far removed from formalism and legalism. It seems to have inspired the language of a well-known Hasidic song, the final verse of which, in addressing God as Father and the Merciful One, affirms that 'your friendship gives him (the Hasidic author) greater pleasure than honey from the honeycomb or any taste'.[12] On the other hand, the language most characteristic of the temple musicians – language about joyful singing accompanied with instrumental music as the medium of praise and thanksgiving addressed to God – is found in narrative texts only where a song attributed to Moses or David has been inserted.[13]

This brief survey of the incidence of these key terms in Isaiah and Psalms supports an at least preliminary assumption that our Isaiah-Psalms text is distinctive but not oppositional vis-à-vis the Deuteronomistic and Priestly orientation to the written law delivered to Moses at Sinai. This conclusion is reinforced by a reading of psalms attributed, in the introductory rubrics, to the temple musicians guild named for Asaph, instituted by David, where they record or simply refer to the traditions of national and ethnic origins (Ps 50.73–83). The fullest version of these historical traditions is to be found in Pss 78 and 81. Psalm 78.5 refers to a decree established in Jacob and a law in Israel, and v. 10 of the same psalm rebukes Ephraimites for violating God's covenant and law. In neither case, however, is there reference to Moses or Sinai/Horeb, and the law and covenant in question do not seem to fit the place in the sequence of events occupied by the Sinai narrative in Exodus 19 to Numbers 10. Hence it seems unlikely that Ps 78.5 is an insertion in the style of the Deuteronomists, as some commentators have proposed.[14] In the context of Ps 81.1–5, the statute, ordinance, and

---

[12] yĕdîdût
[13] Exod 15.1–18; Deut 32.1–43; 2 Sam 22–23. The terms most frequently occurring are *šîr*, *šîrāh* (song, singing), *rānan*, *rinnāh* (shouting for joy, rejoicing), *zimmēr*, *zimrāh*, *niggēn* (instrumental music, playing a musical instrument).
[14] Ps 78.5 reads, 'He established a decree in Jacob/ and appointed a law in Israel'. Harry P. Nasuti, *Tradition History and the Psalms of Asaph* (Atlanta: Scholars Press, 1988), 81–93, ascribes the verse, and much else in the psalm, to an Ephraimite-Deuteronomic tradition. Frank-Lothar Hossfeld and Erich Zenger, *Psalms 2. A Commentary on Psalms 51-100* (Minneapolis: Fortress, 2005), 295, find in v. 5 what they call 'The culture of memory in Deuteronomic-Deuteronomistic circles'.

decree – good Deuteronomistic terminology – refer not to the law given at Sinai but to the obligation to praise God with music and singing in the liturgy.

> Sing out in praise of God our refuge,
> acclaim the God of Jacob,
> raise a melody, beat the drum,
> play the tuneful lyre and harp...
> this is a statute for Israel,
> an ordinance of the God of Jacob,
> laid as a solemn decree on Joseph
> when they came out of Egypt.

According to the author of Chronicles, this obligation was imposed not by Moses but by David (1 Chr 15.16; 16.4–6, etc.).

In summary, we may be sure that the Mosaic law was known to the authors of the book of Isaiah and Psalms, but the emphasis has changed in significant ways: *torah* proceeds not from Sinai but from Zion, it is mediated through prophetic instruction rather than by the promulgation of a collection of laws and, most significantly, it is now available for people from all nations.

However, the psalms in which *torah* is a central theme, Pss 1, 19, and 119, are of a different kind from the psalms intended for liturgical performance; they belong to the category often referred to imprecisely as 'wisdom psalms', understood as intended not for liturgical performance but for private or group prayer and reflection. Hence it is understandable that none of them is attributed to one or other of the liturgical singers guilds. A detailed study of these psalms lies beyond the scope of my enquiry.

It will be evident after a close or even a not so close reading of Isaiah in the light of Psalms that one of the central themes of both is Zion. The ark tradition, which is constitutive of the Zion theme, was transmitted by inspired individuals – Samuel in relation with Saul (1 Sam 15.2), Nathan with David (2 Sam 7.8), Elijah with Omri and Ahab, rulers of the northern kingdom of Israel (1 Kgs 18.15), and finally Isaiah with Hezekiah (2 Kgs 19.31; Isa 37.32). But this prophetic genealogy cannot be dissociated from the cult of successive sanctuaries beginning with Shiloh in the Central Highlands (1 Sam 1–4), then Bethel (Hos 12.6; Amos 3.13–14), Beth-shemesh (1 Sam 6.19–21), Kiriath-jearim (1 Sam 7.1;

2 Sam 6.1–2), and finally Jerusalem/Zion. The Zion tradition is therefore in its origins basically both prophetic and cultic. But apart from the texts which profile the prehistory of Zion, to be discussed in a later chapter, the name *Zion* is conspicuously absent from the mainline historical record (1–2 Samuel, 1–2 Kings), now generally referred to as the Deuteronomistic History, with the exception of 2 Kgs 19.21 and 19.31, which correspond respectively to Isa 37.22 and 37.32. Zion is also absent from the early traditions of Priestly origin in Exodus and Leviticus, as it is from Ezekiel, Haggai, and Malachi, notwithstanding that all these prophetic books are much concerned with the temple and its personnel. On the other hand, the name *Zion* appears forty-six times in Isaiah and thirty-eight times in Psalms, and the only other biblical books in which it reaches double digits are Jeremiah (seventeen) and Lamentations (fifteen).

These humble statistics, which are no more than indicative but will be given substance in the following chapters, support the proposal that Isaiah and Psalms, read intertextually, represent a distinctive modality of religious experience and expression. This proposal should not be difficult to accept or at least ponder. While there are fundamental and indispensable elements in every religion which all who confess it must accept, there is more than one way of experiencing and giving expression to this basic religious commitment. Such variations have arisen in the course of time in most if not all religions in reaction to a dominant way of thinking inculcated by the leadership of the religious group in question, or an undiscriminating and one-size-fits-all legalism, or contemporaneous cultural influence from outside, or a combination of the above. Examples abound. In Islam, the Sufi orders (*tariqas*) associated with Rumi, the great mystic and poet, engaged in prayer, chanting, singing, dancing, and silent meditation. In Judaism, the Hasidic movement of the Baal Shem Tov in eighteenth-century eastern Europe combined strict fidelity to the laws with ecstatic prayer and song. Pietists in seventeenth-century Germany, who emerged in reaction to the formalism of orthodox Lutheran theology, often shared their religious enthusiasm in small conventicles, ecclesiolae within the ecclesia, a religiosity which found expression in the hymns of Paul Gerhardt and the cantatas of Johann Sebastian Bach. The Pentecostal movement of the early twentieth century in the United States, and the Catholic charismatic movement which came to a head in the 1960s, had their own unique way of expressing their Christian commitment. It is difficult to see why such distinctive approaches could not have arisen during the centuries covered by the biblical texts, perhaps in reaction to legal formalism or prophetic pessimism, but especially in the post-collapse period following on the obliterating catastrophe of the early decades of the sixth century B.C.E. with the destruction of Jerusalem and its temple and the subsequent deportations. In the following chapters, we shall try to fill out and give substance to this claim in greater detail with special reference to the liturgical psalms, that is, those adapted to, and actually performed in, the temple liturgy and the book of Isaiah. This will entail the following: discussion of the close relations between visionary prophecy and psalmody (Chapters 2 and 3), the extensive use of psalm material in the three principal sections of the book of Isaiah (Chapters 4–6), Zion as present reality and future ideal in Isaiah and Psalms (Chapter 7), the formation of conventicles, *ecclesiolae*, most clearly attested in Psalms and Isaiah (Chapters 8 and 9), the critique of the prescribed sacrificial system attested in both compilations, pointing to a situation of conflict among temple personnel, which influenced Levites and therefore the singers guilds (Chapter 10). The final chapter will explain and comment on the title I have assigned to the book, followed by a brief summary of what is most distinctive about Isaiah and Psalms when read intertextually in the way I have suggested.

By way of footnoting, I emphasize once again that we will be concerned in the first place with the liturgical psalms in the sense explained above, including those assigned in the initial rubrics to one or other of the singers' guilds, and less so with psalms which seem rather to be designed for prayer and meditation. Another disclaimer: It goes without saying – but let us say it – that the demonstration of close intertextual linkage between Isaiah and Psalms rests primarily on evidence internal to the two compilations, but the question inevitably arises, and is currently being addressed, whether it may also be accounted for by actual contact between the temple singers who are the presumed composers of psalms – for who else but these members of professional musician guilds would be the composers? – and those circles of learned and devout scribes who carried forward and expanded the message of the great prophet of the second half of the eighth century B.C.E. over a period of more than four centuries down into the Hellenistic period. To address this further issue adequately would call for a thorough account of the formation of the two compilations which cannot be undertaken here. We will nevertheless maintain that the Babylonian diaspora situation and the repatriations which followed provided a favourable occasion for such an encounter.

2

The Psalms and their authors

Liturgical music in the Near East and Israel

We must now try to say something about these liturgical poems and their putative authors, the singers and instrumentalists, co-founders with David of the temple liturgy and thereafter responsible for liturgical music. For information on the temple musicians, we depend exclusively on Chronicles and Ezra–Nehemiah together with what can be gleaned from the psalms themselves and the rubrics attached to most of them. In the first place, we know no names of individual composers of any of the 150 psalms, unless it be Heman and Ethan, the Ezrahites whose names appear in the rubrics to Pss 88 and 89 respectively. The religious poem cited in Isa 38.9–20 is attributed to king Hezekiah after his recovery from a dangerous illness (Isa 38.9), but this may simply mean that at some point a redactor decided to insert a psalm, like Ps 102 described in the rubric as 'a prayer of one afflicted, when faint and pleading before the Lord'. There is no evidence of any great interest in individual authors. For the most part, the rubrics indicate the temple musician guilds, whether Asaphite (Pss 50, 73–83), Korahite (Pss 42–49, 84–88), or Ezrahite (Pss 88, 89), in which the psalms were thought to originate, and probably did originate. Psalms of a more reflective or didactic nature, suitable for private or collective prayer and meditation or otherwise unsuitable for liturgical use, would have originated outside of the guild environment and would have been included at a later stage in the formation of the collection, perhaps at the final stage.¹ Rubrics attached to psalms which carry the name of one or other of the eponyms of the singers guilds – Asaph, Korach, Ethan – indicate the origin of the psalm in question in the designated guild. The place, time, and circumstances of the final editing of the collection are disputed. Much depends on whether it is thought to have taken place before or after the final destruction of the temple and cessation of its liturgy. The debate will no doubt continue, but the most probable hypothesis is that the collection of liturgical psalms, in the process of formation through several phases over a long period of time, was essentially complete before the destruction of Herod's temple by the Romans in 70 C.E., and was the work of singers and instrumentalists co-opted into the ranks of the Levites, those, in other words, who actually 'performed' these psalms.²

In all parts of the Near East and Levant, and at all times, music played a major role in worship and public ceremony. Music was essential for creating a shared mood of joy or sorrow, depending on whether the ritual in question was one of praise and thanksgiving or lament and commination. The creation of this shared mood was not, however, left to the spontaneous reaction of those present. It called for a trained class of professional musicians – singers and instrumentalists – as a permanent category of the personnel of the temple or sanctuary to which they belonged. Such musical specialists are attested at all times throughout the history of the Near East, whether Sumerians, Hurrians, Hittites, Babylonians, Assyrians, or Egyptians. One example: the Babylonian *nāru*, a professional singer, was responsible for the rendition and probably also the

---

¹Christoph Levin, 'Das Gebetbuch der Gerechten: Literargeschichtliche Beobachtungen am Psalter', *ZTK* 90 (1993): 355–81, maintained that the book of Psalms, in its final form, was the prayer book of a community of the *saddîqîm*, but he leaves many questions unanswered.

²The most recent contribution to the discussion on origins and authorship, with documentation and bibliographies, is Susan Gillingham, 'The Levites and the Editorial Composition of the Psalms', in *The Oxford Handbook of the Psalms*, ed. W. P. Brown (Oxford and New York: Oxford University Press, 2014), 201–13; also 'The Psalms and Poems of the Hebrew Bible', in *The Hebrew Bible. A Critical Companion*, ed. John Barton (Princeton and Oxford: Princeton University Press, 2016), 219–24.

composition of hymns. These would be sung, with instrumental accompaniment, in processions and in temple liturgies, especially on the occasion of sacrificial offerings and meals and during the great *akitu* New Year festival.[3]

To repeat, what we know about the temple musicians and singers in Israel derives exclusively from Chronicles and Ezra–Nehemiah together with what can be reasonably deduced from Psalms.[4] These texts confront us with many problems, one of which is to determine the status of this class of temple personnel, especially as they relate to Levites. In the most basic genealogical sense, 'Levite' means a descendant of Levi the proto-parent, son of Jacob and Leah, and in this sense all temple personnel with the exception of the lowest categories, including slaves, are represented as Levites, that is, descendants of one or other of the three sons of Levi: Gershom, Kohath, and Merari (Gen 46.11; Exod 6.16; Num 3.17, etc.). For priests, legitimacy was established by the claim to belong to the lineage of Aaron, grandson of Kohath, second son of Levi (1 Chr 5.27–41 (Eng. Tr. 6.1–15)). The different categories of assistants to the priests known as Levites are also represented as descended from the three sons, depending on the functions ascribed to them, not all of which are liturgical (6.4–15 (Eng. Tr. 6.16–30)). The same applies to the founders of the temple musician guilds: Heman through Kohath, Asaph through Gershom, and Ethan through Merari (1 Chr 6.16–32 (Eng. Tr. 6.31–47)). Since, according to Chronicles,

---

[3] On Near Eastern liturgical music, see F. W. Galpin, *The Music of the Sumerians* (Cambridge: Cambridge University Press, 1937); Gilbert J. P. McEwan, *Priest and Temple in Hellenistic Babylonia* (Wiesbaden: Franz Steiner Verlag, 1981), 67–120, 159–82. On Egypt see Jan Assmann, *Ägyptische Hymnen und Gebete* (Zürich: Artemis, 1975); on liturgical music in the Hittite empire: Enrico Badali, 'La musica presso gli ittiti: un aspetto particolare del culto in onore di divinità', *Bibbia e Oriente* 28 (1986): 55–64; and for music in the ancient Near East and ancient Israel in general Claus Westermann, 'Musik III. Instrumentale Musik, Gesang und Dichtung in Israel', *RGG* IV cols. 1201–5; V. H. Matthews, 'Music in the Bible', *ABD* 4: 930–4; A. D. Kilmer et al., 'Musik', *Reallexikon der Assyriologie.8*. (Berlin and New York: de Gruyter, 1995–7), 463–91; J. Braun, *Die Musikkultur Altisraels/ Palästinas: Studien zu archaeologischen, schriftlichen und vergleichenden Quellen* (Freiburg: Universitätsverlag/ Göttingen: Vandenhoeck & Ruprecht, 1999).

[4] I refer to them as 'singers' which is a correct rendering of the Hebrew *mĕšōrĕrîm*, though in reality it corresponds to both singers and instrumentalists, and to both the composition and performance of temple music.

these three eponyms of the guilds were appointed by David to serve in his temporary ark shrine (1 Chr 6.16), and since for the author of Chronicles everything of note to do with the temple is derived from David as founder of temple worship even before the temple was built, the space between Levi and David is filled in with some twenty generations.[5] As we first encounter them, the three founding fathers of the singers guilds are clearly distinct from Levites who are assigned other responsibilities (1 Chr 6.33 (Eng. Tr. 6.48)). At a later point, however, in preparation for the transfer of the holy ark to Jerusalem, David instructs the Levites to commission singers and instrumentalists *from their own ranks*, to participate in this solemn act, and therefore the same three musicians, equipped with the standard repertoire of musical instruments, namely, lutes, lyres, and cymbals,[6] are appointed once again and placed under the baton of the precentor and master-musician Chenaniah (1 Chr 15.16–22). The procession then takes place accompanied by loud music, percussion, and a liturgical dance performed by David (15.25–29). On arrival, there is a further appointment, this time with Asaph rather than Heman in the leading position, and it is he who initiates the liturgical praise of Yahweh in Jerusalem which, here as elsewhere, accompanies sacrifice (1 Chr 16.4–7).

Beginning with this solemn *translatio* of the holy ark from the house of Obed-edom and its *depositio* in the temporary shrine prepared for it in the City of David, the Chronicler highlights the role of the temple musicians at several defining moments in the history of the Judaean monarchy, passing in silence over the kingdom of Israel, of tainted origins in this author's view. He gives

---

[5]There are four genealogies in 1 Chr 5.27–6.33 (6.1–48); 5.27–41; 6.1–4a; 6.4b–15; 6.16–33. As to their authenticity and correct transmission there are serious questions which need not be pursued here. The author had difficulty tracing the descent of all types of temple personnel from the three sons, and in the first of the four lists, dealing with the Levitical descent of the Aaronite–Zadokite priesthood of the Chronicler's own day, at least four names are repeated.

[6]On musical instruments, see J. Rimmer, *Ancient Musical Instruments of Western Asia in the Department of Western Asiatic Antiquities* (London: British Museum, 1969); J. W. Kleinig, *'The Lord's Song': The Basic Function and Significance of Choral Music in Chronicles* (JSOTSup 156; Sheffield: JSOT, 1973), 77–89; J. Montague, *Musical Instruments of the Bible* (Oxford: University Press, 1997); V. H. Matthews, 'Music in the Bible', *ABD* 4 (1992): 930–4; J. Braun, 'Musical Instruments', *OEANE* 4 (1997): 70–9.

his own version of a military crisis during the reign of Jehoshaphat in the mid-ninth century in which an Asaphite Levite features prominently (2 Chr 20.1–30), an incident to which we shall return. He describes the coup organized by the priest Jehoiada with the support of Levites, followed shortly afterwards by the deposition and execution of Athaliah, the only female Judaean ruler, in which distressing event temple musicians also participated (2 Chr 23.1–15). More than a century later, the guilds are reconstituted during a religious revival by Hezekiah in obedience to the mandate of David (2 Chr 29.25–30). Finally, the guilds of Asaph, Heman, and Jeduthun (the last-named replacing Ethan)[7] play a prominent part in Josiah's reforms culminating in the celebration of Passover (2 Chr 35.15).[8]

It will be obvious that in several respects, the Chronicler's account of the origins and early history of the liturgical music guilds is confused and self-contradictory. As he comes to the end of David's reign, he presents a list of temple personnel including 38,000 Levites divided according to their different functions into four divisions: 24,000 in charge of temple management and administration, 6,000 officers and judges, 4,000 gatekeepers, and 4,000 who 'are to offer praise to the Lord with the instruments I have made' (1 Chr 23.2–6). Temple musicians therefore constitute a category of Levites, but the author then goes on to relate how David, assisted by his military officers, appointed Asaph, Heman, and Jeduthun as founders and leaders of guilds of liturgical musicians, with no mention of their Levitical status or descent from Levi (1 Chr 25.1–31). The patrons and founders of the guilds of liturgical musicians during David's reign are, in one place, Heman, Asaph, and Ethan (1 Chr 6.18–33), elsewhere Asaph, Heman, and Jeduthun (1 Chr 25.1); the liturgical musicians are appointed with the cooperation of Levitical leaders (1 Chr 15.16–22) but elsewhere David is assisted by army officers (1 Chr 25.1). The author is clearly not writing history for its own sake. The reconstruction of the past, especially the heroic age of David, is everywhere in the service of the author's own agenda and reflects the vicissitudes of history and the conditions of his

---

[7] Jeduthun makes a textually uncertain appearance in the rubrics to Pss 39, 62, and 77.
[8] A detailed study of these episodes involving liturgical music must be left to the commentaries.

own place and time.⁹ This is most transparently the case with the liturgical role of the Levites and the guilds of musicians which assume such prominence in the author's work as to suggest to some commentators that he himself belonged to one of those guilds.¹⁰ On this subject, at any rate, he is not writing primarily as a historian. He used historical sources, the books of Samuel and Kings in the first place, but makes adjustments, omits, and inserts to suit his own purposes. Here and elsewhere he traces everything of significance in the institutional life of the people back to the heroic figure of David, but in doing so inevitably reflects the many vicissitudes to which these institutions were subject over the centuries.¹¹

---

⁹On the date of Chronicles, or the dates of successive editions and expansions of Chronicles, there is an ongoing debate which practically defies documentation. Convenient surveys along the way in David L. Petersen, *Late Israelite Prophecy* (Missoula, Mont.: Scholars Press, 1977) with special reference to our subject; Hugh G. M. Williamson, *1 and 2 Chronicles* (NCB; Grand Rapids: Eerdmans, 1982), 15-17; Sara Japhet, *I & II Chronicles* (OTL; Louisville: Westminster/John Knox,1993), 23-8. Since the terminology and thematic of the author of Chronicles are found throughout Ezra–Nehemiah, and some parts of Ezra–Nehemiah postdate the time in which the activities of the principals are placed, that is, the mid-fifth century B.C.E. - for example, Nehemiah's *amanah* (agreement made under oath; Nehemiah 10) – I assume a broad span of time for the composition of Chronicles, allowing for some authorial or editorial expansions, from the last decades of Persian rule to the first decades of the Hellenistic era.

¹⁰Samuel Rolles Driver, *An Introduction to the Literature of the Old Testament* (Cleveland and New York: World Publishing, 1956; original date 1897), 518-19: probably a Levite, perhaps a member of the temple choir; Robert H. Pfeiffer, *Introduction to the Old Testament* 2nd edn (London: Adam & Charles Black, 1948), 797: he may have belonged to the guild of Asaph: Hugh G. M. Williamson, *1 and 2 Chronicles* (NCB; Grand Rapids: Eerdmans, 1982), 17, claims that this opinion is out of favour but tends to favour it himself; Jacob M. Myers, *1 Chronicles. Introduction, Translation and Notes* (AB; Garden City and New York: Doubleday, 1965), LXXXVII, describes the author as an ecclesiastical official, a churchman of the highest order. According to an older view, represented by C. C. Torrey, *Ezra Studies* (Chicago: Chicago University Press, 1910), 242-51, and William Foxwell Albright, 'The Date and Personality of the Chronicler', *JBL* 40 (1921): 104-24, Ezra was the author of Chronicles, a view no longer in favour.

¹¹On liturgical music and musicians in Chronicles see, in addition to the commentaries, H. Gese, *Zur Geschichte der Kultsänger am zweiten Tempel. Von Sinai zum Zion* (Munich: Kaiser, 1963), 147-58; J. W. Kleinig, *The Lord's Song: The Basis, Function and Significance of Choral Music in Chronicles* (JSOTSup 156; Sheffield: JSOT,

The temple musicians in Ezra–Nehemiah

The situation becomes more clearly defined when we turn to Ezra–Nehemiah which takes over the historical narrative from the Chronicler at the point of the accession of the Persian Cyrus II (2 Chr 36.22–23 repeated in Ezra 1.1–3). Unlike the references to liturgical musicians in Chronicles, where they are more often than not presented as Levites, the singers and instrumentalists in Ezra–Nehemiah are almost invariably a class of temple personnel distinct from Levites.[12] They appear as a separate category in Ezra 2.41 (variants in Neh 7.44 and 1 Esd 5.27), which records the names of those who returned to Judah from exile in Babylon following on the rescript of Cyrus II in the first year of his reign (539/538 B.C.E.). There is broad agreement, however, that the numbers – 49,897 in Ezra, 49,942 in Nehemiah and 1 Esdras – are far too high for any one migration of this kind; the logistic problems involved can only be imagined. There is therefore something close to a consensus that the list must either come from a later time and have a different function, perhaps a census of the province of Yehud from no earlier than the mid-fifth century, or be the result of conflating several repatriations beginning with the fall of Babylon in 539 down into the reign of Darius I (522–486 B.C.E.). Among temple personnel, it lists the four 'families' of priests, 4,289 in all, who vastly outnumber the lower orders of clergy. Exclusive of slaves, these subordinate classes comprise three categories: 74 Levites, 128 Asaphite singers (148 in Neh 7.44), and 139 gatekeepers (138 in Neh 7.45). The figures are consistent with other indications in Ezra–Nehemiah of this imbalance between priests and lower-order personnel. Levites were missing from Ezra's caravan about to leave southern

---

1973); S. deVries, 'Moses and David as Cult Founders in Chronicles', *JBL* 107 (1988): 619–9; T. Willi, '*Leviten, Priester und Kult in vorhellenistische Zeit. Die chronistische Optik in ihrem geschichtlichen Kontext*', in *Gemeinde ohne Tempel: Community without Temple*, ed. Beate Ego et al. (Tübingen: Mohr Siebeck, 1999), 75–98.

[12]The only exception is the list of those who, we are told, 'volunteered' to live in Jerusalem after the return from exile (Neh 11.1–19), followed by a list of temple personnel (Neh 12.1–19). These lists are parallel with 1 Chr 9.3–44, and the presentation of these people as 'volunteers' (*mitnaddĕbîm*) is language characteristic of the Chronicler (1 Chr 29.5–17; 2 Chr 17.16).

Mesopotamia for Judah in the seventh year of Artaxerxes I (458 B.C.E.) until Ezra recruited about forty individuals belonging to the same class from 'Casiphia the place' (Ezra 8.15–20). This must have been a place of worship frequented by Judaean deportees, a kind of proto-synagogue, perhaps the place referred to by Ezekiel as *miqdaš me'at*, 'a sanctuary for a little while' (Ezek 11.16). Iddo is a priestly name, and a cultic establishment is suggested by the expression 'Casiphia the place' occurring twice in this short passage, 'place' (*māqôm*) being a familiar synonym for 'temple'.[13] We would hardly expect to find a clergy training centre without a place of worship at that time in southern Mesopotamia. Later still, Nehemiah the governor had to complain about the lack of material support for Levites and singers, which led them to walk off the job and go home (Neh 13.10–14). At the time of Nehemiah's term of office as governor of the province, the liturgical musician guilds therefore formed a distinct class of temple personnel operating independently of Levites in temple worship, a situation no longer assumed to be the case in the Chronicler's work. It would therefore be reasonable to conclude that in the interval between the events recorded in Ezra–Nehemiah in the middle decades of the fifth century B.C.E. and the composition of Chronicles in the late Persian or early Hellenistic period, the temple musicians, originally a distinct category of temple personnel like their counterparts in Mesopotamian temples, were co-opted into the ranks of the Levites coincident with the gradually lowered age for entry into the Levirate: from thirty (Num 4.2–3, 47) to twenty-five (Num 8.24–25), and eventually to twenty years of age.[14]

Liturgical music in Solomon's temple

Our need to rely on Chronicles and Ezra–Nehemiah for information on temple musicians and temple music should not mislead us to think exclusively in terms of the temple rebuilt under Persian rule,

---

[13]For example, Deut 12.5, 14, 18; 1 Kgs 8.29; Jer 7.3.
[14]Ezra 3.8; 1 Chr 23.24, 27; 2 Chr 31.17. For a somewhat different reconstruction of the history see Helmut Gese, 'Zur Geschichte der Kultsänger am zweiten Tempel', in *Vom Sinai zum Zion* (Munich: Kaiser Verlag, 1963), 147–55.

according to Ezra 6.15 in the sixth year of the reign of Darius I, therefore 516 B.C.E., seventy years after its destruction by the Babylonians. Music and singing must also have been an essential element in Solomon's temple since, without music and singing, liturgy is inconceivable, especially as accompaniment to the prescriptive sacrifices. Though they are not mentioned explicitly, temple singers must have been among those carried off to Babylon together with other temple personnel in the deportations of 597 and 586 B.C.E.,[15] 128 of whom were among those said to have been repatriated in the early Persian period.[16] In all probability, singers were the ones asked to entertain their Babylonian captors by singing 'the songs of Zion', in other words, psalms, by the waters of Babylon (Ps 137.3). Evidence for liturgical music and song in the first temple is not abundant, to put it mildly, but we recall Amos' curt dismissal of liturgical singing:

Spare me the sound of your songs,
I shall not listen to the strumming of your lutes. (Amos 5.23)

The songs are certainly psalms or hymns, in this instance accompanying the sacrificial cult, as was generally the case. The reference to music and singing no doubt referred to Bethel, principal sanctuary of the kingdom of Israel,[17] but it would apply equally to eighth-century B.C.E. Jerusalem, its temple liturgies, and its temple personnel.

In pronouncing doom on his contemporaries in the kingdom of Israel, Amos made a prediction which quite accidentally raises the gender issue, of such consuming interest today, with respect to the temple singers and instrumentalists. Amos 8.3 reads as follows in the Hebrew: *helilu širot hêkāl bayyom hahu'*. NRSV translates as follows: 'The songs of the temple shall become wailings on that day', and REB has 'On that day the palace songs will give way to lamentation'. The first problem is that the Hebrew verbal stem in question – *yll* in the Hiphil theme is active ('howl, lament') requiring

---

[15] 2 Kgs 24.14–16; 25.11–12; Jer 52.15–16.
[16] Ezra 2.41; 1 Esd 5.27; 148, exactly twice as many as Levites, according to Neh 7.44.
[17] Amos 3.13–14; 4.4–5; 5.5–6; 7.10–13.

a subject – and songs do not howl and lament; people do. In that respect the JPS version, 'the singing women of the palace shall howl on that day', is preferable. But there is still the problem that *hêkāl* can be translated as either 'palace' or 'temple', so the issue must be decided on a basis other than textual. In any case, the temple in question was in Bethel not Jerusalem. Another text to reckon with respecting the same issue is Ps 68.25–26, which reads as follows: 'Your processions, God, come into view/the processions of my God, my King, in the sanctuary/ in front the singers with minstrels following/ and in their midst girls beating tambourines' (REB). Who these girls entrusted with the percussion were, and whether this was a regular feature or a special occasion, we are not told. A final observation on this issue: We must conclude that the male and female singers listed among those repatriated from Babylon in Ezra 2.65 = Neh 7.67 were for secular entertainment not temple service since the temple singers are listed separately in the roster (Ezra 2.41 = Neh 7.44). On the whole, regretfully, the evidence does not favour gender equality among the ranks of the temple singers.[18]

Taking all this into account, we acknowledge that much about the history of this class of temple personnel remains obscure. Unlike the rich artefactual and literary source material available for Mesopotamian temples during the Neo-Babylonian, Achaemenid, and early Hellenistic periods, the sources for Jerusalem, limited as they are to a few biblical texts, leave us in no position to write a history or even present a rounded account of the liturgy of either the first or the second temple and their personnel. But we must do the best we can with what we have.

The Edomite connection

The encomium on Solomon in the historical record of the two kingdoms (1 Kgs 5.9–14 (Eng. Tr. 4.29–34)) reports that his wisdom surpassed the wisdom of all the people of the east and all

---

[18] It would have been interesting to know what the Qumran *pesher* on Ps 68.26 had to say about these tambourine-playing girls, but unfortunately the passage in question (1QpPs. frag. 8) is too fragmentary to permit a reading.

the wisdom of Egypt; in fact, he was wiser than anyone,[19] including Ethan the Ezrahite and Heman, Chalcol, and Darda, sons of Machol. It was this wisdom which enabled him to compose 3,000 proverbs and 1,005 songs (5.10–12); no mean achievement, but not nearly as many as David, at least according to the colophon to the Qumran Psalms Scroll where he is said to have composed 4,050 songs through the spirit of prophecy which was given to him by God (11Q5 col. XXVII). Ethan, first of the five sages named, is identified as an Ezrahite only here and in the introductory rubric to Ps 89, the prefixed *lamed* probably indicating authorship. He is a liturgical musician; indeed, according to 1 Chr 15.16–17, he is one of the three musical guild leaders – Heman, Asaph, and Ethan – appointed by David for service in the temple yet to be built. The gentilic *Ezrahi*, which further defines him, cannot be dissociated from the name Zerah, son of Reuel and grandson of Esau (Gen 36.13), a name attached to both an Edomite clan (Gen 36.17) and the early descendants of Judah and Tamar his daughter-in-law (1 Chr 2.4–6).[20] The list of the male descendants of Judah with Zerah their son and Zerah's five sons is too close to the list of easterners, in effect Edomites, in 1 Kgs 5.10–12 to be coincidental: The Judahites are Zimri, Ethan, Heman, Chalcol, Darda; the Edomites are Ethan, Heman, Chalcol, Darda, Mahol. An Edomite-Judahite link should not surprise given the evidence for the origins of Judah as a member of a tribal league, closely related to Edomites, Kenites, Kenizzites, and other north-west Arabian tribes to the south and south-east of the future kingdom of Judah. The link is reflected in the relations, both intimate and contentious, between Jacob (Israel) and Esau

---

[19] Several commentators read *mikol hāʾĕdômîm* ('than all the Edomites') for *mikol hāʾādām* ('than anyone'). This would make good sense in the context, but there is no textual support for emendation; see Mordechai Cogan, *I Kings. A New Translation with Introduction and Commentary* (AB 10; New York: Doubleday, 2001), 222.

[20] The gentilic *ʾezrāhî* cannot be interpreted as 'native' or 'indigenous' (*ʾezrāh*), and therefore either Israelite or Canaanite, as William Foxwell Albright, *Archaeology and the Religion of Israel* (OTL; Louisville: Westminster/John Knox, 2006 [1942]), 127, and Roland de Vaux, *Ancient Israel* (London: Darton, Longman & Todd, 1961), 182, trans. of *Les Institutions de l'Ancien Testament* (Paris: Editions du Cerf, 1957), 157.

(Edom) in the biblical texts[21] and, less obviously, in the primaeval history of Cain, ancestor of the Kenites.[22]

Heman, first of the three sons of Machol in 1 Kgs 5.11 and third son of Zerah in the Judahite genealogy in 1 Chr 2.6, is also Ezrahite, therefore Edomite. If we may read *hêmān* with LXX for MT *hêmām* at Gen 36.22, he is assigned a different father as the son of Lotan and grandson of Seir the Horite in the land of Edom.[23] He is also listed as first of the three founders of liturgical musical guilds – Heman, Asaph, Ethan – appointed by David, and is given an impressive Levitical genealogy through Joel, yet another father (1 Chr 6.18–24; cf. 15.16–17). Like Ethan, Heman the Ezrahite is also assigned a psalm in the canonical collection (Ps 88.1).

With Ethan and Heman, we see how, by means of genealogical manipulation, the Chronicler has indigenized these two Edomites, assigning them positions of the greatest importance in the liturgy of the second temple. With the remaining names the situation is not so clear. Albright identified the name Chalcol with *kurkur*, a hieroglyphic name on one of the Megiddo ivories, originally *kulkul* in Egyptian, a name belonging to a female singer of the god Ptah worshipped in thirteenth-century B.C.E. Canaanite Askelon.[24] Darda, in 1 Kgs 5.11 and – following the Syriac version, the Targum and some LXX mss – also in 1 Chr 2.6, is of unknown origin. All four are 'sons of Machol', a substantive meaning 'dance' rather than a personal name, permitting the inference that they are members of a

---

[21]Gen 25.21–26; Num 20.14; Deut 23.8; Amos 1.11; Mal 1.2.
[22]On the relations between Judaeans and Edomites, see Roland deVaux, O.P., 'The Settlement of the Israelites in Southern Palestine and the Origins of the Tribe of Judah', in *Translating & Understanding the Old Testament*, ed. H. T. Frank and W. L. Reed (Nashville: Augsburg, 1970), 108–34; C. H. J. de Geus, 'JUDAH (PLACE)', *ABD* III 1033–6; Joseph Blenkinsopp, 'The Midianite-Kenite Hypothesis Revisited and the Origins of Judah', *JSOT* 33, no. 2 (2008): 131–53. On the basis of these onomastic data together with a broad catchment area of texts and hypotheses, Nissim Amzallag, *The Rise of a Seirite Religious Elite in Judah at the Persian Period* (Pende: Gabalda, 2015), has constructed an interesting theory about these Edomite singers, the details of which will no doubt call for close scrutiny.
[23]Most recent commentaries shy away from analysis of the numerous names in Genesis 36; not so John Skinner, *A Critical and Exegetical Commentary on Genesis* (2nd end, Edinburgh: T. & T. Clark, 1930), 432–4.
[24]*Archaeology and the Religion of Israel*, 127 and notes 97, 98. Albright took this, rather hastily, as evidence of the Canaanite origin of the temple musician guilds.

guild of liturgical musicians. Dance was part of religious celebration for Mediterranean and Near Eastern people from ancient times. Examples abound: We hear of young women celebrating the great autumn festival at Shiloh with dancing (Judg 21.19–24), and the prophets of Baal performing their limping dance around the altar of sacrifice (1 Kgs 18.26), a practice perhaps associated with a spring festival, to which we shall return. It was no different in ancient Israel. Miriam and the women joyfully celebrate the rescue at the Papyrus Sea with singing and dancing to the beat of the tambourine (Exod 15.20–21). The psalmists affirm that God's name is to be praised with singing and dancing (Pss 30.12; 149.3; 150.4). As the learned Qoheleth teaches us, dancing is the antithesis of mourning, and there is a time and place for both (Qoh 3.4). For the psalmists, the time was the festive gatherings for offering praise and thanksgiving to God, and the place was God's temple in Jerusalem.[25]

Another Edomite subject to thorough indigenization by the Chronicler is Korah son of Esau and Oholibamah, second of Esau's three wives, and eponym of an Edomite clan (Gen 36.5, 14, 16, 18). He too is given a Levitical pedigree as the grandson of Kohath, second son of Levi (Exod 6.21; 1 Chr 6.1–8, 22–23). He was the leader of the rebellion of Levites in the wilderness against Moses and Aaron, in effect against the preponderant role of the priesthood, an incident which may be taken to reflect conflict between priests and lower-order temple personnel during the period between the destruction of the first and the building of the second temple and for long afterwards (Num 16.1–35; 17.1–5). Korah is said to have perished in the suppression of the rebellion, but his sons, Assir, Elkanah, and Abiasaph (elsewhere Ebiasaph, 1 Chr 6.8; 9.19) survived (Num 26.11).[26] In this way, the Edomite Korahites were transformed into a Levitical clan or family (Num 26.58), and though some of them are said to be gatekeepers (1 Chr 9.19; 26.1, 19) and even bakers (1 Chr 9.31), their primary status as liturgical

---

[25] See the informative essay of John Eaten, 'Dancing in the Old Testament', *Exp. Times* 86 (1975): 136–40. He cites the poet Heine: 'Tanzen war ein Gottesdienst, war ein Beten mit den Beinen' ('Dancing was a form of worship, a praying with legs').
[26] On this episode see, in addition to the commentaries, George W. Coats, *Rebellion in the Wilderness* (Nashville: l968). The name of the third son, suggestive of the guild eponym Asaph, may hint at either ambiguity in the composition of the singer guilds or in the compilation of these lists.

musicians is never lost from sight, and twelve psalms attributed to them are preserved in the canonical collection.²⁷

Something, finally, should be said about Obed-edom, whose name would suggest Edomite origin notwithstanding the fact that the Obed-edom, in whose house-shrine the ark was deposed and from which it was transported by David to Jerusalem, is described as a Gittite, in all probability therefore from Gath in Philistine territory.²⁸ The Chronicler's description of this event (1 Chr 15.16–28) is not entirely perspicuous. Preparatory to the transfer of the ark, David tells the Levitical leaders to appoint some of their fellow Levites as singers, one of whom was Obed-edom. But this Obed-edom is also one of the gatekeepers, meaning presumably a kind of security officer for the duration of the transfer (15.24). Then, on arrival, he resumes his function as liturgical musician under the leadership of Asaph (16.4–5). This incident during David's reign, evidently a creation of the Chronistic author, seems to be a reflection of an event narrated by the same writer and assigned to the reign of Amaziah in the early decades of the eighth century. His account of this reign in 2 Chr 25.20–24 follows his source (2 Kgs 14.11–14) in recording a disastrous defeat at the hands of Jehoash, ruler of the northern Israelite kingdom, after which the victor seized all the gold, silver, and precious vessels in the temple and palace treasuries. Chronicles, however, adds one further detail: that a certain Obed-edom was one of the hostages carried off. The most probable assumption is that this Obed-edom was responsible for the security of the temple treasury; he was therefore an important functionary among the temple hierarchy similar to that of gatekeeper. This episode may have suggested the name of the person under whose

---

²⁷Pss 42–49, 84–85, 87–88. Note that Pss 42 and 43 were originally one psalm, as the refrain common to both shows. On the Korachite psalms see, in addition to the commentaries, M. J. Buss, 'The Psalms of Asaph and Korah', *JBL* 82 (1963): 382–92; G. Wanke, *Die Ziontheologie der Korachiten* (BZAW 97; Berlin: de Gruyter, 1966); Michael D. Goulder, *The Psalms of the Sons of Korah* (JSOTSup 20; Sheffield: JSOT, 1983); Erich Zenger, 'Zur redaktionsgeschichtlichen Bedeutung der Korachpsalmen', in *Neue Wege der Psalmenforschung*, ed. Klaus Seybold and Erich Zenger (Freiburg: Herder, 1994), 175–98.

²⁸See Henry Preserved Smith, *The Books of Samuel: A Critical and Exegetical Commentary* (ICC; Edinburgh: T. & T. Clark, 1904), 293–5; P. Kyle McCarter, Jr., *II Samuel. A New Translation with Introduction and Commentary* (AB; Garden City, New York: Doubleday, 1984), 170.

protection the precious ark was placed for a time during the reign of David. We may therefore conclude that, in spite of the sometimes fierce hostility to Edom in prophetic writings and psalms, the silence of the biblical texts on any particular affinity for music and singing among Edomites, and the obscurity surrounding their contribution to the liturgy of the temple, it seems that Edomites made their not insignificant contribution to the service of music and singing in the Jerusalem temple.

3

Psalmody and prophecy

The link between psalmody and prophecy

As a preface to our discussion of the close affinity between Psalms and the book of Isaiah in the following chapters, something should be said about the close affinity between psalmody and prophecy in general. One aspect of the profile of these temple musicians which cannot be ignored is their prophetic and oracular character. This should not surprise us since the affinity between prophecy and music has a lineage going back into ancient times, into the mythic past. One thinks of Orpheus son of Apollo whose singing charmed animals, plants, and rocks and could even summon the dead in Hades back to life with its more than human power. Even after death, his severed head, carried by the sea to Lesbos, continued to utter oracles. Or consider Pan, son of Hermes, in Arcadia, the sound of whose pipes inspired both panic fear and ecstatic trance. His biblical equivalent would be Yuval son of Lemech and Adah (the Dawn?), ancestor of all who play lyre and pipe. Like Pan, he and his brother Javal are tent dwellers and shepherds, and his pipe, the most primitive of all instruments, matches Pan's syrinx. Levi son of Jacob, the genealogical ancestor of the temple musicians, is not so primordial, but the deathbed blessings of Moses on the twelve tribal ancestors assign a kind of prophetic power to him through his control of the oracular Urim and Thummim (Deut 33.8), a power later limited to the high priest, beginning with

Aaron.[1] According to the author of Chronicles, Levi is ancestor to all classes and grades in the service of the temple and its liturgies, and his prophetic gift is therefore, so to speak, in the DNA of all his descendants in one way or another.

For the temple musicians, at any rate, David came to assume a much larger role. In the firmament of great figures from the past, David outshines not only Levi but Moses in the Chronicler's history, in which his name appears thirteen times more often than that of Moses. In the first of several accounts of David's entry into public life recorded in the Deuteronomistic History, he is anointed by the prophet Samuel as successor to king Saul, whereupon the spirit enters into him with power (1 Sam 16.13). Like the god Pan, David is both shepherd and musician; his music could both exorcize the evil spirit which came upon Saul and induce a fit of manic violence (1 Sam 16.14–23; 18.10–11). We are reminded of his inspired, prophetic status at several points during his career and, at the end, he is identified, and identifies himself, as a prophetic figure in his last words recorded in 2 Sam 23.1–7 (my translation):

> The oracle of David, son of Jesse,
> oracle of the man set on high,
> the one anointed by the God of Jacob,
> the favourite of the songs of Israel.[2]
> The spirit of the Lord speaks through me,
> his word is on my tongue.

This image of David is confirmed by the occurrence of his name in the headings to seventy-four of the canonical psalms, and his

---

[1] Exod 7.1; 28.30; Lev 8.8; Ezra 2.63; 4QpIsa^d 1.5–6 (a pesher on Isa 54.12). The prophecy of Caiphas about Jesus' imminent death, pronounced by virtue of his priestly office, points in the same direction (Jn 11.49–51). On the claim to prophetic as well as priestly status of the Hasmonaean rulers see Josephus: *Ant* 11.327; 13.282–3, 299–30, 322; *War* 1.68–69. On this issue in general see my 'Prophecy and Priesthood in Josephus', *JJS* 25, no. 2 (1974): 239–62.

[2] The phrase *nĕʿîm zĕmirôt yiśrāʾēl*, 23.1c is patient of more than one interpretation. Cf. LXX: *euprepeis psalmoi Israēl* ('the splendid psalms of Israel'), Vulg: *egregius psalta Israel*, 'the excellent musician of Israel'). Among modern translations one may choose among NRSV 'The favorite of the Strong One of Israel', JPS 'The favorite of the songs of Israel', REB 'The singer of Israel's psalms'.

prophetic endowment is explicitly recognized in the colophon to the Qumran Psalms Scroll:

> David, son of Jesse, was wise … . He wrote three thousand six hundred psalms and three hundred and sixty-four songs to be sung in front of the altar over the perpetual daily offering for all the days of the year, all three hundred and sixty-four. He also wrote fifty-two songs for the sabbath offering, and thirty songs for the offerings of the first days of the months, for all festival days, and for the Day of Atonement. All the songs which he uttered were four hundred and forty-six, not counting four to intone over the possessed. The total was four thousand and fifty. All these he uttered through the spirit of prophecy given to him from the Most High God.[3]

David's prophetic authorship of psalms and his role as mouthpiece of the Holy Spirit were also recognized in early Christian communities (e.g. Acts 1.16–20; 4.25–26).[4]

This gift did not remain with David but was passed on to those responsible for liturgical music as master-cantors and instrumentalists, founders of the guilds of liturgical musicians. All three of these – Asaph, Heman, and Jeduthun – received the prophetic gift as seers or visionaries, and they and their associates 'prophesied' with lyres, lutes, and cymbals, the instruments in general use in liturgies (1 Chr 25.1–8).[5] The verb used here refers not to prophecy as generally understood but to the behaviour characteristic of a condition of high emotional excitation, even

---

[3] 11Q5 col. XXVII. J. A. Sanders, *The Psalms Scroll of Qumrân Cave 11 (4QPs*ᵃ*)* (Oxford: Oxford University Press, 1967), 91–3.

[4] On David as psalmist and prophet see Nahum Sarna, 'The Psalm Superscriptions and the Guilds', in *Studies in Jewish Religious and Intellectual History presented to Alexander Altman*, ed. S. Stern and R. Loewe (Tuscaloosa: University of Alabama Press, 1979), 281–300; Simon de Vries, 'Moses and David as Cult Founders in Chronicles', *JBL* 107 (1988): 619–39; Martin Kleer, *Der liebliche Sänger der Psalmen Israels: Untersuchungen zu David als Dichter und Beter der Psalmen* (Bodenheim: Philo, 1996); James L. Mays, 'The David of the Psalms', *Int* 40 (1996): 143–55.

[5] 2 Chr 29.30 (Asaph), 1 Chr 25.5 (Heman), 2 Chr 35.15 (Jeduthun). Ethan is one of the three original founders (Heman, Asaph, Ethan, 1 Chr 6.16–32; 15.16–22), but with the passage of time he appears to have been supplanted by Jeduthun, and the Asaphites took the place of the Heman group as the leading guild.

mental dissociation, provoked by singing, music, percussion, and, at times, dancing. The Chronicler provides an example from his record of the reign of Jehoshaphat (2 Chr 20.1–30; mid-ninth century B.C.E.). Under attack by a coalition of the Transjordanian kingdoms – neighbours, hence enemies of Israel – the people assembled around their king in the temple precincts and, after Jehoshaphat had offered a prayer, the spirit came upon a certain Jahaziel ben Zechariah, an Asaphite singer, in the midst of the assembly. So inspired, he uttered an oracle assuring those present of a successful outcome and even giving them precise information on the movements of the enemy. This comforting prediction was greeted by an outburst of loud acclamation and singing from Kohathite and Korahite Levitical singers. The next day, the army took to the field with the singers appointed 'to sing to the Lord God and praise him in holy splendour'. They continued singing and making music as the oracle was fulfilled while their enemies, no doubt confounded by the music, conveniently destroyed each other, thus rendering further fighting superfluous. After viewing the many dead bodies and collecting the booty, the king, his army, and his attendants returned to the city and the temple, the musicians still singing and playing on harps, lyres, and trumpets (20.27–28).[6]

The close affinity of oracular and prophetic speech with music is also well illustrated by accounts of prophetic activity in the early period of Israel's history, comparable to similar phenomena among neighbouring peoples. We come across small colonies of self-sustaining 'prophets' associated with local hill sanctuaries, who had their own traditions about attaining and maintaining a state of high emotional excitement, or ecstasy, or mental dissociation, under the guidance of a shamanistic master-ecstatic, by singing accompanied by lute, lyre, and flute, percussion with drum or tabor, and ecstatic dancing and whirling.[7] Samuel tells Saul that

---

[6] The trumpet was generally reserved to the priests, perhaps on account of its use to issue commands. A great variety of priestly trumpets, or trumpet calls (*tsotsĕrôt*) is in evidence in the fantastic account of warfare in the Qumran War Scroll (1QM). On this episode in 2 Chronicles 20 see, in addition to the commentaries, Petersen, *Late Israelite Prophecy*, 68–77.

[7] On early Israelite group prophecy see my *A History of Prophecy in Israel* (2nd edn, Louisville: Westminster/John Knox, 1996), 48–64, with bibliography to the time of writing. For an anthropological treatment of these phenomena and interesting

he will encounter a band of prophets coming down from a hill shrine at Giv'at Elohim with harp, tambourine, flute, and lyre in a state of prophetic rapture, and so it comes about (1 Sam 10.5, 10). Somewhat later, Saul's servants, and eventually Saul himself, come upon such a group under the leadership of Samuel in a state of transformed consciousness; the experience proves contagious, and they too are drawn into it (1 Sam 19.18–24).

The contest between the Israelite prophet Elijah and the prophetic devotees of the Baal associated with the ancient sanctuary of Carmel provides an especially interesting example since it accompanied a sacrificial ceremony (1 Kgs 18.20–40), always an important occasion for liturgical music. The ritual conduct of these prophets of the local Baal is described as a desperate and unsuccessful attempt to provoke a miracle, but the actions themselves are not of unique occurrence: ecstatic and prolonged invocation of the god, the performance of a limping dance around the altar[8] accompanied by singing, music, percussion, and self-inflicted lacerations.[9] The cult of the calf deity at Sinai also involved singing, certainly accompanied by musical instruments and percussion, dancing, and acclamations loud enough to be heard at a good distance (Exod 32.17–19).

Prophets and temple worship: The cult prophet hypothesis

The link between psalmody and prophecy in its different manifestations is therefore well founded, and provides the necessary background and basis for the affinity between the book of Isaiah and the book of Psalms, which will be exemplified in the following chapters. According to the author of Chronicles,

---

comparative material see I. M. Lewis, *Ecstatic Religion. A Study of Shamanism and Spirit Possession* (3rd edn, London and New York: Routledge, 2003).

[8] On the limping dance and the episode in general see, in addition to the commentaries, Roland de Vaux, *The Bible and the Ancient Near East* (Garden City and New York: Doubleday, 1971), 238–51.

[9] For another example of self-inflicted wounds associated with ecstatic prophecy see Zech 13.6.

Isaiah was the author of a vision, and he therefore belonged to the same category of visionary or seer as the temple singers (2 Chr 32.32), one of whom listed by the author of Chronicles also bore the name Isaiah (1 Chr 25.3, 15). It is also important not to make too much of the distinction in the history of prophecy in Israel between the earliest prophetic figures mentioned above – more expressive in their behaviour, more subject to trance states and influenced by music – and the prophets to whom books are attributed. In his early public activity, Isaiah was influenced by Amos in the Kingdom of Samaria, and may even allude to his preaching without naming him.[10] Amos himself was born during the lifetime of Elisha disciple of Elijah, in the early years of the eighth century B.C.E. The relatively few biographical or autobiographical passages in Isaiah reveal a seer on whom 'the hand of God' was laid (Isa 8.11), therefore subject to prophetic seizure. He was therefore consulted by kings (7.1–17), worked miracles (38.7–8), healed (38.21–22), carried out public sign-acts (20.1–6), and had his disciples, in all these respects not unlike Samuel and Elijah (Isa 8.16).

The association of these early prophetic figures and their conventicles with local sanctuaries, noted earlier, makes it natural to enquire whether one or other of the prophets to whom books are attributed, including a prophet like Isaiah and, in addition, the anonymous continuators of the Isaianic tradition in the book, had any connection with the temple and its worship. The idea that some of these prophets, especially those who seemed to be more directly concerned with temple worship, Joel and Habakkuk in particular, not only borrowed from the Jerusalem temple cult but were involved directly in it was first clearly enunciated by Sigmund Mowinckel almost a century ago.[11] In retrospect, this hypothesis has appeared to some to be a typical product of the characteristically Scandinavian

---

[10]'The Lord sent a message against Jacob, and it will fall on Israel. The entire people will experience it – Ephraim and the people of Samaria' (Isa 9.7–8). See my *Isaiah 1-39. A New Translation with Introduction and Commentary* (New York: Doubleday, 2000), 217–18.

[11]Sigmund Mowinckel, *Psalmenstudien III: Kultprophetie und Prophetische Psalmen* (Oslo: Jacob Dybwad, 1923). See also his more discursive account in *The Psalms in Israel's Worship* (Nashville: Abingdon, 1962, reprinted Sheffield: JSOT Press, 1992), 2.53–73; original Norwegian version 1951.

emphasis on the primacy of cult,[12] but Mowinckel did his graduate studies with Hermann Gunkel, and the formulation of his theory was much influenced by Gunkel's trailblazing work on literary genres (*Gattungen*), more often than not based on oral tradition and performance, not excluding liturgical performance.[13] The conviction, prevalent in German-language scholarship, of the chronological primacy of prophecy over law and liturgical expressions, together with the tendency to date psalms late in the Second Temple period, even as late as the Maccabean period, also eased the birth of the hypothesis.[14] At any rate, the existence of cult prophecy as an important element in the temple liturgy, and of prophets as a distinct category of temple personnel, was accepted, sometimes with reservations, by several German-language scholars of note.[15] After the hypothesis was enthusiastically taken over by the Welsh scholar Aubrey Johnson, who also did his graduate studies in a German university, it entered the discussion and debate on Psalms and temple worship in English-language scholarship, at times with a more or less qualified assent.[16]

---

[12] Well-known examples, Alfred Haldar, *Associations of Cult Prophets among the Semites* (Uppsala: Almqvist & Wiksell, 1945); Arvid Kapelrud, successor to Mowinckel in the Old Testament Chair at the University of Oslo, *Joel Studies* (Uppsala: Lundquist, 1948); Johannes Pedersen, 'The Rôle played by Inspired Persons among the Israelites and the Arabs', in *Studies in Old Testament Prophecy. Presented to Professor Theodore H. Robinson*, ed. H. H. Rowley (Edinburgh: T. & T. Clark, 1950), 127–42.

[13] For early examples see H. Gunkel, 'Nahum 1', *ZAW* 13 (1893): 223–44 and 'Jesaja 33: Eine prophetische Liturgie', *ZAW* 42 (1924): 177–208, with his monograph *Die Psalmen übersetzt und erklärt* (HKAT; Göttingen: Vandenhoeck & Ruprecht, 1929). Gunkel's *Einleitung in die Psalmen* (Göttingen: Vandenhoeck & Ruprecht, 1933, 2nd edn, 1966) was completed by Joachim Begrich, another of his students. A good introduction to Gunkel's *Formgeschichte* is available in *The Psalms. A Form-Critical Introduction* (Philadelphia: Fortress, 1967), translated from Gunkel's 'Psalmen' in *RGG* IV 2nd edn, 1930, 1609–30.

[14] Both tendencies are exemplified in Bernhard Duhm, *Die Psalmen erklärt* (KHC 14; Freiburg: Mohr, 1899; 2nd edn: Tübingen: Mohr/Siebeck, 1922), 482–4 and *passim*.

[15] G. Von Rad, 'Die falschen Propheten', *ZAW* 51 (1933): 109–20; *Old Testament Theology. Volume II* (New York and Evanston: Harper & Row, 1965), 50–2, 190; H.-J. Kraus, *Gottesdienst in Israel* (Munich: Kaiser, 1954, 2nd edn, 1962), 122–33 = *Worship in Israel* (Oxford: Blackwell, 1966); W. Rudolph, *Chronikbücher* (HAT 21; Tübingen: Mohr [Siebeck], 1955), 170–1.

[16] Aubrey R. Johnson, *The Cultic Prophet and Israel's Psalmody* (Cardiff: University of Wales Press, 1979), following on his *The Cultic Prophet in Ancient Israel* (Cardiff; University of Wales Press, 1962). Space permits mention of only a few fairly

This hypothesis – that prophets not only were influenced by temple worship but formed a category of temple personnel – is an issue deserving a more thorough discussion than is possible here, but something must be said. We may begin by noting that five or six names of canonical prophets occur among the many names of temple singers in Chronicles and Ezra–Nehemiah: Isaiah (1 Chr 3.21; 25.3, 15; 26.25; Ezra 8.7, 19; Neh 11.7), Micah (1 Chr 23.20), Obadiah (1 Chr 9.16; 2 Chr 34.12), Joel (1 Chr 6.18, 21; 15.7, 11; 23.8; 2 Chr 29.12), Zephaniah (1 Chr 6.21), and perhaps Haggai (1 Chr 6.15). This is an interesting coincidence, but in no case is the father's name in Chronicles identical with the name in the prophetic books. Chronicles, for example, always refers to the Isaiah to whom the book is attributed as the son of Amoz, as in Isa 1.1; 2.1; 13.1,[17] perhaps to avoid confusion with other Isaiahs.[18] More to the point, the category of prophets is absent from lists of temple personnel in Chronicles and Ezra–Nehemiah, usually set out in the sequence: priests, Levites, musicians, gatekeepers.[19] Prophets would naturally frequent the temple from time to time and sometimes speak there, as Amos at

---

representative participants in the discussion on this subject vigorously if intermittently pursued in the decades from 1960 to 1990; rather less since then: H. H. Rowley, *Worship in Ancient Israel: Its Forms and Meaning* (London: SPCK, 1967), 144–75; E. Würthwein, 'Kultpolemik oder Kultbescheid? Beobachtungen zu dem Thema "Prophetie und Kult"', in *Tradition und Situation: Studien zur alttestamentlichen Prophetie. Artur Weiser zum 70. Geburtstag*, ed. E. Würthwein and O. Kaiser (Göttingen: Vandenhoeck & Ruprecht, 1963), 115–31; David L. Petersen, *Late Israelite Prophecy* (Missoula, Mont.: Scholars Press, 1977), 55–96; W. H. Bellinger, Jr., *Psalmody and Prophecy* (JSOTSup 27; Sheffield: JSOT Press, 1984).

[17] 2 Chr 26.22; 32.20, 32. This Amos (Hebrew: אמוץ) is not to be confused with the well-known prophet Amos (Hebrew: עמוס).

[18] There are five or perhaps six Isaiahs in Chronicles and Ezra–Nehemiah apart from the well-known prophet: one who came to Judah with Ezra's caravan (Ezra 8.7); a Levite recruited by Ezra from Casiphia in southern Mesopotamia (Ezra 8.19), perhaps identical with the one just named; a grandson of Zerubbabel and therefore a descendant of David (1 Chr 3.21); a Benjaminite (Neh 11.7); a temple treasury official (1 Chr 26.25); and a member of the Jeduthun temple musicians guild (1Chr 25.3, 15). Another Isaiah is named on a seal of uncertain origin, on which see N. Avigad, 'The Seal of Yesha "yahu"', *IEJ* 13 (1963): 324, and yet another of the same name is the father of Machseah, a witness to legal proceedings in the Aramaic texts from Elephantine AP 5.16, 8.33, 9.21; texts in A. Cowley, *Aramaic Papyri of the Fifth Century B.C.* (Osnabrück: Otto Zeller, 1967), 11, 23, 26.

[19] 1 Chr 5.17–6.48; 9.10–34; 15.11–24; 16.4–42; 23.2–32; 25.1–8; 2 Chr 5.11–14; 23.12–15; 29.25–30; 35.10–15; Ezra 2.36–42, 70; 3.10–13; 7.7; Neh 7.39–45; 10.28.

Bethel (Amos 7.10–17) and Jeremiah in Jerusalem (Jer 7.1–2),[20] but that is something quite different from having permanent employment as liturgical officiants.[21] This is an important difference between the Jerusalem temple and the hilltop shrines, probably dedicated to the worship of the local Baals, with which the ecstatics were in some way associated in the early period and no doubt even later. Unfortunately, we know too little about these interesting colonies of ecstatics. Saul meets a band of such enthusiasts *coming down* from the high place at Givʽat Elohim ('The Hill of God', 1 Sam 10.5, 10). Samuel, whom Saul later encounters presiding over a similar band in a state of extreme excitation (1 Sam 19.19–20), is elsewhere presented as peripatetic, not unlike Elijah and Elisha, those later 'men of God' who nevertheless also had their ties to local sanctuaries.

The hypothesis expounded by Sigmund Mowinckel and Aubrey Johnson has therefore not survived unscathed but, like other hypotheses in that condition, the proposal that there was a category of prophets in the service of the liturgy of the second Jerusalem temple, and perhaps the first, has opened up a wider range of reflection on and research into the issue of the relation between prophecy and psalmody. As a contribution to this ongoing attempt to broaden our understanding of this relation and how it may have come about, we will now undertake a re-reading of Isaiah, inevitably selective and preliminary, with a view to identifying psalms, whether whole, fragmentary, or embryonic, as well as themes, motifs, and epithets with parallels in psalms. I do this in the expectation, or at least the hope, that this intertextual exercise may deepen our appreciation for both of these texts, and perhaps even throw some light on an important phase of the religious history of ancient Israel.

---

[20]Amos uttered an oracle of political import in the principal sanctuary of the Kingdom of Samaria (7.13), but he was almost certainly Judaean, and was urged by the resident priest to go back there. Jeremiah is told to stand at one of the temple gates (Jer 7.1–2), or in the courtyard in front of the temple (26.1–2).

[21]Among those who have either rejected the hypothesis or expressed strong reservations about it we should mention G. Quell, 'Der Kultprophet', *ThLZ* 81 (1956): 401–4; R. de Vaux, *Ancient Israel. Its Life and Institutions* (London: Darton, Longman & Todd, 1961), 384–6; H. H. Rowley, 'The Prophets and the Cult', in *Worship in Ancient Israel: Its Forms and Meaning* (London: SPCK, 1967), 144–75; W. H. Bellinger, *Psalmody and Prophecy* (Sheffield: JSOT, 1984), 83–94; John Barton, 'The Prophets and the Cult', in *Temple and Worship in Biblical Israel*, ed. John Day (London: T. & T. Clark, 2005), 114–15, 118–19.

4

Psalmody in Isaiah 1–39

One of the clearest indications of a close relationship between Psalms and Isaiah is the presence of psalm material in Isaiah – psalms entire, embryonic, or fragmentary – manifesting terminology, themes, and religious orientation similar to the psalms collection, and doing so with much greater frequency than in other prophetic books. To demonstrate this as thoroughly as it deserves would require commenting on the entire range of material in Isaiah and would call for a substantial volume, which we leave to an Isaian scholar of the future. At this preliminary stage, we must be content with selecting examples for discussion from the three main sections of the book (chapters 1–39, 40–55, 56–66). We therefore begin by identifying psalmodic material of different kinds in Isa 1–39, taking each of the subsections of these chapters in turn.

Isaiah 1–12

Isaiah 6.1–13

These first twelve chapters are easily recognized as a distinct redactional unit put together with different kinds of material from different epochs. We shall see that the brief psalms at the conclusion of chapters 1–12 round out this first section by the repetition of the title 'the Holy One of Israel' (12.6; 1.4) and the threefold repetition of the word *yeshuʿah* (salvation), which brings to mind the prophet's name *yeshaʿyahu* at the beginning (12.2a, 2b, 3; 1.1). The vision report at 6.1–13, located at the centre of this first section of the book, is not of course a psalm, but it is convenient to discuss it at the start of our enquiry since it presents something like the *arrière-fond* of all the psalms. It consists in two parts. The first (6.1–7) presents a liturgy of praise in progress; the second part, 6.8–13 or, more probably, 6.8–11,[1] is an oracle of judgement communicated to the prophet, which the vision serves to authenticate. It may be compared with the vision of Micah ben Imlah (1 Kgs 22.19–23) and the great chariot throne vision of Ezekiel (Ezek 1–3), though neither features any liturgical action. The first part contains a residual psalm, much reduced in length, intoned not by the temple singers but by the seraphs, the fiery creatures in attendance on the Enthroned One:

Holy, holy, holy is the Lord of Hosts,
the whole earth is full of his glory.

The setting is often described as a throne room. There is a throne, certainly, but there is also an altar and a fire and the place is filled with smoke, presumably from incense, all unusual for a throne room the location of which would be the royal palace not the temple. The dubiety about the setting is caused by the close association between the ark and the throne of the Lord of Hosts in the inner sanctum of the Jerusalem temple. Psalm 80, assigned to the Asaph guild, offers prayer and petition to the Lord God of Hosts, the same title as in the vision, though in that psalm, as in Ps 99.1 and Isa 37.16, the Lord God is seated on the cherubim throne whereas here he is attended by seraphim.

The verse of a psalm chanted by the seraphim, the source for the Trisagion, the Sanctus, and the Qedushah, takes up the theme of the holiness of God prominent throughout the psalms collection. In Ps 22 God is holy, enthroned on the praises of Israel, and in Ps 99 the Enthroned One is proclaimed holy three times, as in the vision. The title 'Holy One of Israel' (*qĕdôš yiśrā'ēl*) occurs frequently in Isaiah (twenty-seven times) and somewhat less frequently in Psalms

---

[1]Several commentators have argued that all or part of vv. 12–13 is from the post-disaster period, among others Charles F. Whitley, 'The call and mission of Isaiah', *JNES* 18 (1959): 38–48; Marco Nobile, 'Jes 6 und Ez 1,1-3,15: Vergleich und Funktion im jeweiligen Redaktionellen Kontext', in *The Book of Isaiah/Le Livre d'Isaïe*, ed. Jacques Vermeylen (Leuven: University Press/Peeters, 1989), 209–16; Hans Wildberger, *Isaiah 1-12: A Commentary* (Minneapolis: Fortress, 1991 [1980]), 246–7; Bernard Gosse, 'Isaïe vi et la tradition isaïenne', *VT* 42 (1992): 340–9.

(Pss 71.20; 78.41; 89.19). The second line of this brief psalm of praise, 'the whole earth is full of his glory', transposes into third person what is addressed directly to God in Ps 57:

> God, be exalted above the heavens,
> let your glory be over all the earth. (vv. 6, 12)

Ps 72 ends in the same way:

> Blessed be his glorious name for ever;
> may his glory fill the whole earth. (v. 19)

In sum, Isa 6.1–7 is the kind of vision a devout and prophetically inspired member of one of the singers guilds might have composed, for example the prophet's namesake, a member of the Jeduthun guild listed according to 1 Chr 25.3, 15. The holiness of Yahweh is one of the great themes in Isaiah and Psalms.

Much of chapters 1–12 is taken up with a typically prophetic indictment of current mores including what sounds like a fairly definitive repudiation of the prescriptive daily sacrifices (1.10–17), which will claim our attention in a later chapter. These harsh criticisms directed at the civic and religious leaders, the court, and the court ladies ('daughters of Zion', 3.16–26) are, however, interspersed with projections and intimations of a different future – the redeemed city Zion inhabited by a purified people, later identified as the Servants of the Lord. The first of these (1.27–31), which replicates the more developed Zion theology in the last chapters of the book, begins as follows:

> Zion will be saved in the judgement,
> her penitents in the retribution,[2]
> but rebels and sinners will be destroyed together,
> those who forsake the Lord will cease to be. (1.27–28)

After the second title (2.1), there follows a more developed celebration of the same theme.

---

[2]Hebrew *šābîm*, from the verb *šûb* = 'return' or 'repent', 'do penance'/*tĕšûbāh*, permits the deliberate ambiguity of *šābîm* = 'those who return' or 'penitents'.

Isaiah 2.2–5 (=Micah 4.1–5)

> In days to come
> the mountain of the Lord's house
> will be set over all other mountains,
> raised high above the hills.
> All the nations will stream towards it,
> many peoples shall come and say,
> 'Let us go up to the mountain of the Lord,
> to the house of the God of Jacob,
> that he may teach us his ways
> that we may walk in his paths.'
> For instruction proceeds from Zion,
> and the word of the Lord from Jerusalem.
> He will judge between the nations
> and arbitrate among many peoples.
> They will beat their swords into mattocks
> and their spears into pruning-knives;
> nation will not wield sword against nation
> nor ever again be trained for war.
> House of Jacob,
> come, let us walk in the light of the Lord![3]

This prediction about the Zion of the end time looks at first sight more prophetic than psalmodic, but it owes a considerable debt to psalms which hymn the praises of Zion, especially those attributed to the Korahite and Asaphite guilds.[4] What strikes one at once is that the only title in this poem of the God whose dwelling is in Zion is 'the God of Jacob' of frequent occurrence in these psalms.[5] Other Zion motifs in this prophetic-eschatological passage reproduce mythic themes in psalms: Zion as the highest of the mountains, certainly not justified by Jerusalem's elevation but taken over from

---

[3]This last couplet, v. 5, belongs thematically to 2.1–4: it is addressed to 'the house of Jacob' whose God is 'the God of Jacob' (2.3), cf. Micah 4.5 which reads like an alternative conclusion to the passage.
[4]Korahite: Pss 46, 48, 84, 87; Asaphite: 76, 78.
[5]Pss 46.5, 8, 12; 76.7; 84.9; Note also 'the Strong One of Jacob' (*'ăbîr ya'ăqōb*) in Ps 132.2, 5. Both no doubt reflect the origins of the ark, and therefore the Zion traditions in the territory of the central and northern tribes.

Mount Zaphon of Canaanite-Jebusite mythology mentioned earlier (Pss 48.2-3, 78.54, 68; 87.1); Zion as the location of 'the house of the Lord' (Pss 46.5; 66.13; 76.3; 132.13) and as the site of arbitration between nations (Pss 9.20; 76.10; 87.5-6). Particularly interesting is the use of the rare verb *nāhar*, usually translated 'stream' or 'flow', with reference to the convergence of peoples from all nations on the future Zion in search of moral instruction (Isa 2.2b). Apart from the parallel Mic 4.1 and Jer 51.44, which predict that the nations will no longer 'stream' to Babylon, this verb occurs only here. It is a reasonable conjecture that at this point the author had in mind one of the Korahite psalms:

> There is a river (*nahar*) whose streams bring joy to the city of God,
> the holy dwelling of the Most High
> The Lord of hosts is with us
> the God of Jacob is our fortress. (Ps 46.5, 8)[6]

5.1-7

We must resist the temptation to put this passage in the category of psalm-like compositions. Usually called 'the Vineyard Song', it is a secular composition, whether classified as a love song or as something else.[7]

Isaiah 11.1-9

This prediction of a future spirit-endowed ruler in the line of David is not a psalm, but may be read in association with Pss 2 and 110, which anticipate the establishment of peace and justice among

---

[6] John T. Willis, 'Isaiah 2:2-5 and the Psalms of Zion', in *Writing and Reading the Scroll of Isaiah: Studies of an Interpretive Tradition. Volume One*, ed. C. C. Broyles and C. A. Evans (Leiden and New York: Brill, 1997), 295–316, concludes that 'if one set Isa 2:2-4 = Mic 4:1-3 apart from the two contexts in which it presently appears in the books of Isaiah and Micah, and placed it in the Psalter, it would pass for one of the Songs of Zion, or at least for a prophetic oracle which borrowed heavily from such a song'.

[7] For the options see Wildberger, *Isaiah 1-12*, 175–83.

nations in the future Zion through the instrumentality of a Davidic ruler. The final stanza of this messianic poem runs as follows:

> No longer will they hurt or destroy
> in all my holy mountain
> for the earth will be filled with the knowledge of the Lord
> as the waters cover the sea. (Isa 11.9)

It will at once bring to mind the Zion celebrated in several psalms. The expression 'my holy mountain' occurs frequently in psalms, as it does in the last section of Isaiah.[8] The Isaian authenticity of the poem, or at least of 11.9, also with minor variations in Isa 65.25 and Hab 2.14, is however often disputed.[9] The fate of the native dynasty remained at least sporadically of intense interest in the post-disaster period,[10] and the language in the opening verses is clearly of a late date.[11] However the date is decided, this splendid poem betrays no direct indication of dependence on psalms dealing with the dynastic theme, though both Isa 11.1–9 and Pss 2 and 110 fit the larger pattern of the 'once and future king', a theme broadly distributed, for example in the ancient Mesopotamian 'a ruler will arise' texts and Virgil's fourth eclogue which ushered in the Augustan age as a renewal of creation: *magnus ab integro saeclorum nascitur ordo*.[12]

Isaiah 12.1–6

Isaiah 12.1–6 concludes the first structurally identifiable section of the book with two psalm fragments, or mini-psalms, both introduced

---

[8]Pss 2.6; 3.5; 15.1; 43.3; 48.2; 99.9; Isa 56.7; 57.13; 65.11, 15; 66.20.
[9]For references see my *Isaiah 1-39*, pp. 263–5.
[10]Jer 23.5–6; 33.14–22; Ezek 37.24–28; Haggai and Zech 1–8.
[11]*hōṭer* ('branch') cf. Prov 14.3; *gēzaʿ* ('stock') cf. Isa 40.24; Job 14.8; *nēṣer* ('shoot') cf. Dan 11.7. Terms descriptive of the ruler's charisma – *hokmāh* ('wisdom'), *bînāh* ('understanding'), *ʿēṣāh* ('counsel'), *daʿat* ('knowledge') – are of frequent occurrence in Proverbs, Job and other didactic or sapiential texts.
[12]'The great line of the centuries begins anew'. See W. Clausen, *Virgil: Eclogues* (Clarendon: Oxford University Press, 1994). For the Mesopotamian texts see *ANET* 3rd edn, 606–7.

with the phrase 'You will say on that day', the first addressed to an individual (12: 1), the second to a plurality (12: 4):

> 1
> Lord, I thank you,
> for though you were angry with me
> your anger has abated and you have comforted me.
> God is my salvation,
> I will trust and feel no dread
> for the Lord is my strength and defence
> and has proved to be my salvation.
>
> 2
> Give thanks to the Lord, invoke him by name,
> make known his deeds among the peoples,
> proclaim that his name is exalted.
> Sing psalms to the Lord, for he has triumphed,
> let this be known over all the earth.
> Cry out, exult, you who dwell in Zion,
> for great in your midst is the Holy One of Israel.

The threefold repetition of the word *yeshu'ah* (salvation, redemption) in vv. 2–3 is surely intended to recall the name of the prophet, *yesha'yahu* (Isaiah), thereby closing out this first section of the book, which opens with his name in the first verse. The call to joyful participation in worship addressed to the inhabitants of Zion in the second fragment at once creates a link with the psalms in which Zion, as both reality and ideal, is the favourite theme of the singers guilds, in the first place the Korahite and Asaphite musicians and singers. Wherever Zion is mentioned, we can expect to hear the joyful sound of singing and instrumental music:

> Sing psalms of praise to the Lord who dwells in Zion,
> declare his deeds among the peoples (Ps 9.12)
> Let us shout for joy in praise of your victory! (Ps 20.6)

There are other psalms in the collection which encourage 'the children of Zion' to rejoice and to praise God with singing, dancing, and making melody with tambourine and lyre (Ps 149.2–3). Like so many of the canonical psalms, both pieces are thanksgiving psalms[13] in keeping with the instructions given to his temple musicians by David. Their task was to compose and perform psalms which offer God the homage of praise and thanksgiving, and that is what they do.[14]

Other clues to borrowings from psalms can be detected. First, in 12.1b the verb *'anap*, 'to be angry', is rare elsewhere with the exception of psalms (Pss 2.12; 60.3; 79.5; 85.6). All these texts refer to the divine anger; all occur in the context of prayer with the expectation that the anger will abate. Second, in Isa 12.2b the expression 'my strength and defence' (*ozzi wezimrati*) occurs also in Ps 118.14, and both appear to have borrowed the expression from 'the Song at the Papyrus Sea' (Exod 15.2). Third, the title 'the Holy One of Israel', frequent throughout Isaiah, occurs quite frequently in psalms (71.22; 78.41; 89.19; 106.16) and rarely elsewhere (only 2 Kgs 19.22; Jer 50.29; 51.5). Finally, the language about singing, making music, shouting for joy, and the like in 12.5–6 points unmistakeably to the temple musicians.

Isaiah 13–27

In terms of subject matter and theme Isa 13–27 divides into two parts. The first, chapters 13–23, is usually presented as 'Oracles against the nations' and the second as 'The Isaian Apocalypse'. Both titles call for explanation and disambiguation.

Isaiah 13–23

The first part opens with an oracle about the imminent fall of Babylon as presaging the final universal judgement (13.1–22). It is the first of ten such oracles directed against potential or actual enemies of Israel: Philistia (14.28–31), Moab (15.1–16.14), Syria (17.1–6), Egypt (19.1–15), Babylon again (21.1–10), Edom (21.11–12), other Arabs (21.16–17), the 'Valley of Vision',[15] and Tyre (23.1–18).

---

[13]Several psalms begin with thanksgiving or praise: Pss 9–10, 75, 105, 106, 111, 118, 136. 138.
[14]1 Chr 16.4, 41; 23.30; 25.3.
[15]Unidentified, but apparently understood by the scribe who added the comment in 22.8b–11 to refer to Judah and Jerusalem.

These may originally have formed a separate document of unknown authorship, but their unevenness in length, and especially the amount of editorial comment and extraneous material added to them, much of it apocalyptic in character, make it difficult to reconstruct the original form.[16] Here and there throughout these chapters, we hear echoes of language and theme suggestive of psalms and their authors: Zion as Mount Zaphon (14.12, as in the Korahite psalm 48), daughter Zion (16.1 cf. Ps 9.15), the people addressed as Jacob (14.1, cf. Pss 14.7, 79.7). Moreover, the God of Israel bears the title 'Lord of the Hosts' on numerous occasions in these chapters, but what is lacking is direct address to God in accents of praise, thanksgiving, petition, or lament. The absence of such indications renders the search for links with psalms unprofitable, and at the same time it raises serious questions about the place of these eleven chapters in the Isaian tradition, in spite of the prophet's name in the introductory title (13.1) and his part in the acted-out sign of judgement in chapter 20. As for psalms, the only music we hear or hear about in this section is the passage in which the commercial activities of Tyre are compared to the singing of an old, forgotten prostitute (23.26).

Isaiah 24–27

Beginning with the commentary of Bernhard Duhm, Isa 24–27 has been commonly referred to as 'the Isaian(ic) Apocalypse'.[17] Duhm identified the apocalyptic core of the section as Isa 24.1–23, 25.6–8, 26.20–27.1, 12–13, which he dated to the late second century B.C.E. during the Hasmonaean principate. He proposed that the author belonged to the *ḥāsîdîm* (*asidaioi*) mentioned in Daniel; in fact, he maintained that Isaiah could as well have written the book of Daniel as Isa 24–27. These extreme views are no longer in favour, not only on account of the epigraphic evidence of the Qumran Isaiah material. 'The Isaian Apocalypse' has nevertheless been widely accepted as a

---

[16]See, in addition to the commentaries, A. K. Jenkins, 'The Development of the Isaiah Tradition in Is 13-23', in *The Book of Isaiah/Le Livre d'Isaïe*, ed. Jacques Vermeylen (Leuven: University Press/Peeters, 1989), 237–51; Ulrich Berges, *Das Buch Jesaja. Kompositkion und Endgestalt* (Freiburg: Herder, 1998), 139–98.

[17]Bernhard Duhm, *Das Buch Jesaia* (4th edn, Göttingen: Vandenhoeck & Ruprecht, 1922), 172.

title for this section.[18] It contains such apocalyptic themes as the abolition of death (25.8), the resurrection of the dead (26.19), the darkening of the sun and moon (24.22), and the eschatological banquet (25.6–8), but lacks others including an explicit dualism, an apocalyptic view of history, heavenly journeys; and there is besides much here which has nothing to do with apocalyptic.

Isaiah 24.14–16

Of interest for the theme of our study is the alternation throughout the section of apocalyptic prophecy with psalms or psalm-like material. A clue to this feature can be found in 24.14–16 in which an anonymous speaker is reporting on a liturgy in which he himself is not a participant. A tentative translation of this difficult passage follows:

> They raise their voices in joyful singing,
> acclaiming from the west the majesty of the Lord,
> exulting in the east, they give glory to the Lord,
> to the name of the Lord, God of Israel, in the western islands.
> From the ends of the earth we hear songs of praise,
> 'Glory to the Conquering One!' (24.14–16a)[19]

This provokes the reflection:

> But meanwhile I thought: 'I have my secret! I have my secret![20]
> Woe to the faithless ones who deal without faith,
> who deal with an utter lack of faith!' (24.16b)

---

[18]E.g. J. Lindblom, *Die Jesaja-Apokalypse: Jes 24-27* (Lund: Gleerup, 1938); Georg Fohrer, 'Der Aufbau der Apokalypse des Jesajabuches', in *Studien zur alttestamentlichen Prophetie (1949-1965)* (Berlin: de Gruyter, 1967), 170–81. In recent years, however, it has become customary to speak more prudently of 'the so-called Isaian Apocalypse'.

[19]Taking *saddîq* in the same sense as the alternative meaning of *sĕdāqāh*, 'victory' or 'vindication' rather than 'righteousness', as in the later parts of Isaiah (59.9, 16–17, 21; 61.10–11).

[20]Rather than 'I pine away! I pine away!' (NRSV) or 'depravity! depravity!' (REB), or 'I am done for!' (Wildberger, *Isaiah 13-27*, 441 (English translation)), none of which makes sense in the context. A loan word from Persian into Aramaic and eventually Hebrew, *rāz* occurs elsewhere only in Daniel chapters 2 and 4, but that does not exclude its presence in Isa 24.16; compare *dērā'ôn* ('object of horror') only in Dan 12.2 and Isa 66.24.

This looks like a severe critique of current, official liturgical practice from the point of view of a sectarian or quasi-sectarian apocalyptically minded conventicle, using language familiar from the vocabulary of the temple musician guilds, as is in evidence throughout chapters 24–27.[21] We might compare this with the critique of the sacrificial system and the priests engaged in it in Isa 66.3–4, to be discussed in a later chapter.

Isaiah 25.1–5

While the arrangement of the diverse material in 24–27 is not always perspicuous, we detect something approaching alternation in 25.1–26.6: a psalm (25.1–5); a passage about the end time, including the menu at the eschatological banquet (25.6–8); a fragmentary psalm (25.9); comments about a future judgement on hostile forces (25.10–12); finally, another psalm (26.1–6). The first psalm (25.1–5) reads as follows:

> Lord, you are my God,
> I exalt you, I praise your name,
> for you have carried out your wonderful counsels,
> firm and sure, formed ages since.
> You have reduced the city to a heap of rubble,
> turned the fortified town into a ruin,
> the citadel of the insolent is destroyed
> never to be rebuilt;
> on this account cruel people will respect you,
> ruthless nations fear you.
> Truly, you have been a refuge to the poor,
> a refuge to the needy in their distress,
> shelter from the rainstorm, shade in the heat.
> You suppress the clamour of the insolent,
> the singing of the ruthless is silenced.[22]

---

[21]See the comments of Otto Plöger, *Theocracy and Eschatology* (Oxford: Blackwell, 1968), 57–8.
[22]See textual notes in my *Isaiah 1-39*, 361–2 for the translation, especially the omission of insertion in v. 5.

While not comparable in quality to the canonical psalms, it is recognizably a psalm of praise and thanksgiving on the theme, present throughout Isa 24–27, namely, the fate of the unnamed city, the opponent of Zion, City of God. It also has borrowed language and themes from the psalms collection.[23]

Isaiah 25.9

There follows a passage which presents some of the great themes of Jewish apocalyptic: the messianic banquet, the abolition of death, the drying of tears, the triumph of the righteous (25.6–8). All of this, in its turn, is followed by a small psalm fragment to be recited in the end time – 'on that day' – by those addressed, those, in other words, attentive to the prophetic message:

> Behold, this is our God,
> we have waited for him to save us.
> [This is the Lord, we have waited for him][24]
> Let us be glad and rejoice in his salvation.

Waiting for God (the title of Simone Weil's well-known reflections) is one of the more prominent themes in both Isaiah and Psalms.[25] Since this psalm fragment, unlike the longer one preceding it, is spoken by a plurality, the salvation hoped for is to be attained in the last days. It will be greeted with gladness and rejoicing, language associated pre-eminently with the singers guilds.[26]

---

[23]Examples: the combination of exalting and praising, cf. Ps 118.28; also Pss 30.2; 34.4; 99.5; 107.32; 145.1; the God who works wonders cf. Pss 77.15; 78; 12; 88.11; God as refuge for the poor and needy in distress, cf. Ps 37.39; the hostility of the insolent and ruthless, cf. Ps 86.14.

[24]This line is absent from LXX, probably an alternative version of the previous verse.

[25]The verb in question, *qwh*, occurs twice as often in Isaiah and Psalms as in all other biblical texts together.

[26]Here, too, the verbs used in this greatly abbreviated psalm, *gîl* and *sāmah* connoting rejoicing and celebration, are, together with the corresponding substantives, used more often in Psalms and Isaiah than in all other Hebrew Bible texts; eighty-seven times in Psalms, forty-four times in Isaiah.

Isaiah 26.1–6

The third psalm in the passage follows an unpleasant example of schadenfreude in which the author of 25.10b–12 contemplates with complacency the drowning of personified Moab in a cesspool. The event in real time to which this corresponds is unknown. Duhm proposed the conquest of Moab by the Hasmonaean Janneus in the early first century B.C.E., a date now ruled out by the presence of the passage in the Qumran Isaiah scroll. The psalm reads as follows:

> On that day this song will be sung in the land of Judah:
> A strong city is ours,
> established as a place of safety with walls and ramparts.
> Open the gates that a righteous people may enter,
> a people that keeps faith.
> Those of firm purpose you preserve in peace,
> in peace because in you they trust.
> Trust, then, in the Lord for ever, for the Lord is the rock of ages.
> He has brought low the dwellers on the height,
> he has thrown down the lofty city,
> levelled it to the ground, laid it in the dust.
> It is trodden under foot by the feet of the oppressed and the poor.[27]

The poem is introduced as a song (*šîr*), that is, a psalm,[28] but it is a poor example of a psalm which, we suspect, would not have been accepted for public use by the members of the Asaph or Korah guilds. It is nevertheless modelled on the canonical psalms and reproduces themes prominent in them: Zion well defended against hostile assaults (Pss 48, 76, 84, 87, 102, 147); opening the gates, but the gates of the city rather than the temple, for the righteous qualified to live in it (Pss 24.3–4; 118.19–20); finally, the Lord God as the Rock of Ages, a theme taken over in one of the great old hymns (Deut 32.4; Ps 62.8).

---

[27] For textual issues see my *Isaiah 1-39*, 361–2.
[28] Compare 'the songs of Zion' of Ps 137.3 which the exiled Judaeans were asked to sing to entertain their captors.

Isaiah 26.7–21

The passage following the psalm in 26.1–6 is difficult to characterize and define. It has been described, inter alia, as a communal lament,[29] a psalm of the wisdom type,[30] a reflective meditation, a contribution to a kind of prayer book for eschatological sectarians.[31] It begins with expressions of an intense desire to seek for God (vv. 8–9) but passes on to an equally intense prayer to God not to spare the wicked, followed by a prediction of their post-mortem fate (v. 14). There follows a lament about the punishments God has inflicted on his chosen people in the past, and the futility of the people's own efforts to make a difference in the world expressed in rather laboured gynaecological metaphors (vv. 16–18). The affirmation of the resurrection of the dead in v. 19 was probably added to mark the contrast between the post-mortem destiny of the righteous and that of the unrighteous stated in v. 14:

> Your dead will live,
> their corpses will rise from the dead;
> you that lie in the dust, awake and sing for joy!
> Your dew is a radiant dew,
> and earth will bring forth the shades of the dead. (v. 19)

The final admonition to the faithful to take cover during the period of divine anger and judgement associated with the end time is taken from, or at least associated with, Isa 2.6–22 (vv. 10, 19, 21) and is only residually related to what precedes it. In sum, 26.7–21 has borrowed some elements from both psalms and earlier Isaian texts but is too lacking in coherence to be a psalm as the genre is defined on the basis of the canonical psalms.

Isaiah 28–35

This section can be further divided into three subsections: chapters 28–31, 32–33, and 34–35. The first section consists in a series

---

[29] Hans Wildberger, *Isaiah 13-27*, 459.
[30] Ulrich Berges, *Das Buch Jesaja. Komposition und Endgestalt*, 191.
[31] Otto Plöger, *Theocracy and Eschatology*, 54, 66.

of pronouncements of woe on various individuals[32] alternating with oracular utterances including a kind of parable (28.23–29) and an oracle (30.6–7). The second begins and ends with poems dealing with the ideal ruler to come (32.1–8; 33.17–22), a theme addressed in the biblical didactic writings (Prov 20.8, 26, 28) and familiar throughout the ancient Near East.[33] The third subsection, chapters 34 and 35, serves to recapitulate the message of the book in eschatological terms by contrasting the ultimate destiny of Zion with that of Edom, now successor to Babylon as the evil empire par excellence.[34] Since this section ends with the theme of the pilgrim highway, the *via sacra*, with which Isa 40–55 begins, there is also the issue of the transition from First Isaiah to Second Isaiah.[35]

Themes recurring throughout Psalms can be found in these chapters: the foundation of Zion, its inviolability and immovability, 'the city of our appointed festivals' (28.16–17; 33.17–24). We also come upon a list of moral attributes which will ensure survival of the final fiery judgement, a kind of eschatologized moral catechism comparable to Pss 15, 24 and, more succinctly, Ps 118.19–20. These psalms are interpreted as stating moral qualifications for participation in the temple liturgy. They may be compared with the so-called Negative Confessions in the Egyptian Books of the Dead reciting which secured freedom from condemnation after death.[36]

---

[32] Isa 28.1–4; 29.1–8, 15–16; 30.1–5; 31.1–3.
[33] Hans Wildberger, *Jesaja 3: Jesaja 28-39* (BKAT; Neukirchen-Vluyn: Neukirchener Verlag, 1982), 1255–6; Hugh G. M. Williamson, 'The Messianic Texts in Isaiah 1-39', in *King and Messiah in Israel and the Ancient Near East*, ed. John Day (Sheffield: JSOT, 1998), 264–70.
[34] Edom is also code for Rome in the Targum. The Targumic rendering of Isa 34.9 reads: 'The streams of Rome shall be turned into pitch and her soil into brimstone; her land shall become burning pitch'. Bruce D. Chilton, *The Isaiah Targum* (Collegeville, Minn.: Liturgical Press, 1987), 68.
[35] Raised in an acute form by Charles C. Torrey, *The Second Isaiah: A New Interpretation* (Edinburgh: T. & T. Clark, 1928), 121–6, 295–6, who argued that these two chapters originally belonged to Deutero-Isaiah but were separated from it by the insertion of chapters 36-39.
[36] Miriam Lichtheim, *Ancient Egyptian Literature. Volume II: The New Kingdom* (Berkeley and Los Angeles: University of California: 1974), 124–9.

Isaiah 33.2–6

The only passage in these chapters which looks like a psalm, one in which the Lord God is addressed in praise, thanksgiving, and petition, is 33.2–6. Many years ago Gunkel, in an exegetical *tour de force*, tied together all the disparate elements in chapter 33 to create a prophetic liturgy of which 33.2–6 would be a part.[37] Given the complexity of the elements in the chapter, however, it seems better to focus on this one passage which is recognizable as liturgical. It has more than its fair share of textual problems,[38] but a tentative translation may be attempted:

> Lord, show us your favour,
> on you we wait;
> be our support every morning,
> our salvation in time of trouble.
> At the sound of a tumult people take to flight,
> when you rise up in majesty nations are scattered.
> Then spoil is gathered as the locusts gather spoil,
> like swarming locusts they settle upon it.
> The Lord is exalted, he dwells on high,
> he has filled Zion with justice and righteousness,
> he will be her stable support throughout her existence,
> wisdom and knowledge are riches that lead to salvation;
> her treasure is the fear of the Lord.

This poem, with ideas and images strung together haphazardly is, on the literary and aesthetic level, no improvement on the essays in psalmody in Isa 25.1–5 and 26.1–6. Like them, it has drawn freely on the canonical psalms of petition and praise. Several of these open with a prayer for mercy and favour,[39] and speak of waiting for God as an expression of trust and hope, as if waiting *with* God.[40]

---

[37] Hermann Gunkel, 'Jesaja 33, eine prophetische Liturgie', ZAW 42 (1924): 177–208. For a critical review of the debate about this chapter from Gunkel to the time of writing see Hugh G. M. Williamson, *The Book Called Isaiah. Deutero-Isaiah's Role in Composition and Redaction* (Oxford: Clarendon Press, 1994), 221–39.
[38] For textual notes and emendations see my *Isaiah 1-39*, 437.
[39] Pss 4.2; 6.3; 51.3; 56.2; 57.2; 67.2. Cf. Isa 8.17; 25.9.
[40] For example, Pss 25.5, 21; 27.14; 37.34.

In these psalms, the morning is the good time of the day, the time divine assistance can be expected, perhaps after participating in a nocturnal temple service or performing an incubation ritual.[41] As in several psalms, petition is addressed to God in time of trouble.[42] The final verse may be taken to illustrate the dependence of the authors and editors of this section of the book on the didactic and aphoristic collections.

Isaiah 36–39

There has been, and continues to be, much discussion on these four chapters, and some commentators have assigned primary importance to them in the formation and structure of the book as a whole.[43] My claim on their behalf will be quite modest. I conclude that they form a narrative appendix to the first major section of the book, while at the same time serving as structural parallel to the account of the reign of Ahaz, an earlier king of Judah, in a Jerusalem also under threat from hostile forces. Both Hezekiah and Ahaz will be urged not to be afraid (Isa 7.4–9; 37.6–7), both will receive a sign reassuring them of survival (Isa 7.10–17; 38.7–8), but in both cases there is the more distant prospect of exile – for Samaria in Isa 8.1–4 and for Jerusalem in Isa 39.5–8. Both episodes, finally, are reported with significant variations in both the official history and the book of Isaiah. This narrative appendix deals with three episodes: The unsuccessful attempt of the Assyrian king Sennacherib to take Jerusalem (36–37), the illness of Hezekiah cured by Isaiah (38), and the visit of Babylonian envoys to Hezekiah after his recovery,

---

[41]Pss 5.4; 30.6; 46.4; 59.17; 143.8. The rare plural *bôqĕrîm* occurs only here (Isa 33.2) and at Pss 73.14; 101.8; Job 7.18; Lam 3.23.
[42]*bĕ‘et sārāh*, as in Ps 37.39. Similarly *bĕyôm sārāh*, Pss 20.2; 50.15.
[43]Among treatments of Isaiah 36-39 in the context of the book and its formation are those of Peter R. Ackroyd, 'Isaiah 36-39: Structure and Function', *Studies in the Religious Tradition of the Old Testament* (London: SCM, 1987), 105–20; Hugh G. M. Williamson, *The Book Called Isaiah: Deutero-Isaiah's Role in Composition and Redaction* (Oxford: Clarendon, 1994), 189–239; Ulrich Berges, *Das Buch Jesaja. Komposition und Endgestalt* (Freiburg: Herder, 1998), with bibliography to the time of writing.

a visit the outcome of which was the prediction by Isaiah of exile in Babylon.

It is somewhat paradoxical that while several prosaic-sounding passages in Isaiah are set out in verse in modern translations, the first of Hezekiah's two prayers in the temple (37.14–20) is set out in prose, though it approximates a psalm in form and vocabulary at least at the beginning and end. The point can be made by presenting the text as a psalm, with the prose part in italics:

> Lord of hosts, God of Israel, enthroned on the cherubim,
> you alone are the God of all the kingdoms of the earth.
> You made the heavens and the earth.
> Incline your ear, Lord, and hear,
> Open your eyes, Lord, and see,
> *Hear all the words of Sennacherib insulting the living God. It is true, Lord, that the kings of Assyria have devastated every land and have consigned the gods of those lands to the flames, since they are not gods at all but objects made of wood and stone, of human manufacture, and so they could be destroyed.*
> So now, Lord our God, rescue us from his grasp,
> so that all the kingdoms of the world may know
> that you alone, Lord, are God.

The language of psalmody is in evidence: the Lord of Hosts enthroned on the cherubim (Pss 80.2; 99.1), ruler of all the kingdoms of the world (cf. Ps 99.2), Maker of heaven and earth (Pss 115.15; 121.2; 124.8; 146.6). Petitioning the Lord to hear, see, listen is also of frequent occurrence in psalms.

The same prosodic issue does not affect Hezekiah's second prayer offered with fear and trembling during his sickness (38.9–20) and, as its concluding verse suggests, offered in the temple, 'the house of the Lord' (38.20). It is undoubtedly a psalm, combining the features of personal lament and the assurance of an answer to prayer, as often in the canonical psalms. Most commentators assume that this psalm was inserted into the narrative of Hezekiah's reign in keeping with a common practice in the historical and prophetic books, for example the Song at the Papyrus Sea (Exod 15.1–18); David's psalm on being rescued from Saul (2 Sam 22) and Jonah's on being spewed out of the whale's belly (Jon 2).

The prayer itself is introduced as a written text, an inscription (*miktab*), like the letter from Sennacherib's messengers which Hezekiah took with him on an earlier visit to the temple (37.14). It is quite common to emend *miktab* to *miktām*, and the emendation should probably be accepted. The term occurs in the initial rubrics of six psalms (Pss 16, 56–60), four of which (16, 56, 57, 59) are psalms of *individual* thanksgiving, as is Hezekiah's psalm.[44] In addition, one or other of the six celebrates deliverance from death, from the Underworld, and the Pit, and concludes with joyful singing and making melody in thanksgiving to God for being alive. This provokes reflection: One of the most disconcerting ideas for the contemporary Jewish or Christian believer is that for the dead there is a loss of contact with God to whom it is no longer possible to offer praise and thanksgiving:

> Sheol cannot thank you,
> death cannot praise you,
> those who go down to the Pit
> cannot hope for your faithfulness (Isa 38.18)

Compare:

> In death there is no remembrance of you,
> in Sheol who can give you praise? (Ps 6.6)

It is this image of death as oblivion which gives an edge to the psalmists' vitality and joy in the presence of God in the temple, an almost ecstatic joy expressed in adoration, praise, and thanksgiving:

> You show me the path of life.
> In your presence there is fullness of joy,
> in your right hand are pleasures for evermore. (Ps 16.11)

> You have rescued me from death,
> my feet from stumbling,
> so I may walk in the presence of God
> in the light of life. (Ps 56.14)

---

[44] The meaning of the term *miktām* is uncertain. LXX has *proseuchē* or *stēlographia*, Vulgate *oratio*. See the references in Köhler-Baumgartner.

> I will sing and make melody.
> Awake, my soul!
> Awake, harp and lyre!
> I will waken the dawn! (Ps 57.8)
>
> I shall sing of your strength
> and acclaim your love when morning breaks
> I shall sing a psalm to you, my strength,
> for God is my strong tower,
> my gracious God. (Ps 59.17–18)
>
> The Lord is at hand to save me,
> so let the music of our praises resound
> all our life long in the house of the Lord. (Isa 38.20)

We do not know whose hand inserted this psalm of Hezekiah into the record of the pious king's vicissitudes, but it is difficult to set aside the suspicion that it belonged to a member of one of the singers' guilds.

5

Prophecy and Psalmody in Isaiah 40–55

The architecture of Isaiah 40–55

Chapter 40 marks the beginning of a new section in the book of Isaiah, one noticeably different from chapters 1–39 in language, theme, and historical setting, though still under the attribution in the original title to the book. If we leave aside the narrative in chapters 36–39, inserted into the book from 2 Kgs 18.13–20.19, the original link between Deutero-Isaiah and Proto-Isaiah is the theme of the highway, the *via sacra* leading to Zion in Isa 35.8–10, a theme taken up in 40.3–5 with reference to the anticipated return from exile, the ultimate destination of which is also Zion. It is therefore insinuated from the beginning that the principal theme of this mid-section of the book will be repatriation and citizenship in Zion. But with the addition of the narrative in chapters 36–39 a new link is created. After the visit of the Babylonian delegation to Hezekiah, newly recovered from illness, the prophet predicts exile in Babylon (Isa 39.5–8), a prediction which prepares the reader for the return from exile and repatriation in Isa 40.

The credit for first recognizing the distinctive character of Isa 40–66 vis-à-vis 1–39 is usually given to Johann Christoph Döderlein at the University of Altdorf writing in the 1770s and 1780s, and his discovery received broad but not unanimous acceptance after its appearance in the Isaiah commentary of

Wilhelm Gesenius published in 1821. The further step of identifying a third distinctive section – Third or Trito-Isaiah – was taken by Bernhard Duhm in his commentary of 1892, famous in the annals of biblical scholarship.[1] Duhm identified Isa 55.12–13, a celebration of the joyful departure from exile, as the conclusion of Deutero-Isaiah, corresponding to 40.3–11 at its beginning:

> You will go out with joy,
> you will be led out in peace.
> Before you mountains and hills will break out in shouts
>   of joy,
> all the trees in the countryside will clap their hands.
> In place of the thornbush cypresses will grow.
> All this will be a monument for the Lord,
> a perpetual sign that will not be cut off.

The place of this passage in the book as a whole is more clearly revealed by the affirmation of the power and efficacy of the word of God which immediately precedes it:

> So it is with my word which issues from me;
> It does not return to me empty.
> It accomplishes what I purpose,
> it achieves what I send it to do. (55.10–11)

This statement recalls the affirmation at the beginning of Deutero-Isaiah that 'the word of our God endures for ever' (40.8), which, in the context of Deutero-Isaiah as a whole, means the word communicated through the prophet. In fact, the entire chapter 55 may be read as a summary of chapters 40–54, and may have been added precisely to serve that purpose. In that case, the preceding chapter 54 would have

---

[1] Bernhard Duhm, *Das Buch Jesaja übersetz und erklärt* (HKAT 3/1; Göttingen: Vandenhoeck & Ruprecht, 1892; 4th edn, 1922). Duhm's contribution to our understanding of Isaiah as a tripartite text is discussed by Christopher R. Seitz, *Zion's Final Destiny: The Development of the Book of Isaiah* (Minneapolis: Fortress, 1991), 1–35.

marked the *original* conclusion to Deutero-Isaiah. The chapter ends as follows:

> This, then, is the destiny of the Servants of the Lord God,
> their vindication from me: a word of the Lord God. (54.17b)

This statement serves to link the Servant of the Lord in 40–54, and in particular the Servant of Isa 52.13–53.12, with the Servants of the Lord who receive honourable mention in Psalms and the last two chapters of Isaiah. They will claim our attention in a later chapter.

A further point about structure which needs to be made is that Deutero-Isaiah comprises two sections, chapters 40–48 and 49–55, which are as different from one another in theme as Deutero-Isaiah from Trito-Isaiah. In 49–55, we hear no more about Cyrus and the expectations raised by his conquests, the principal theme of 40–48, and no more about Babylon. There is no more satire directed against the manufacture and use of idols as in Isa 44.9–20; and whereas in 40–48 'Jacob', often combined with 'Israel', is the preferred designation for the prophet's Judaean contemporaries, in 49–55 Zion, the city rather than the people, is the focus. Reference to the key term 'servant' is also quite different. In 40–48, the 'Servant of the Lord' is for the most part a collective with reference to Jacob/Israel, the people as a whole, with the sole exception of 42.1–4, the first of Duhm's *Ebedlieder*, together with the comment appended to it in 42.5–9. The comment begins as follows:

> I, the Lord, have summoned you in righteousness,
> I have grasped you by the hand;
> I preserve you, and present you
> as a covenant for the people,
> a light for the nations

The summons and the grasping of the hand correspond to elements of official protocol in the ceremony of installation in office of a Mesopotamian ruler, and these are applied explicitly to Cyrus in Isa 45.1–7, the central discourse in Isa 40–48. In this address, Cyrus is the anointed of the Lord; the Lord grasps him by the right hand, summons him by name, and confers a title of honour on him.

The language reflects the propagandistic Cyrus Cylinder in which Marduk, the principal Babylonian deity, calls Cyrus by name. Another inscription from the Abu-Habba collection in the British Museum refers to Cyrus as the servant of Marduk who rouses him to conquer the Medes, a commission which in the course of time he fulfils.[2] The task confided to this servant, to establish an international order based on law, justice, and consideration for the powerless is clearly a task for a ruler not a prophet.

Isaiah 40–48 therefore moves on the axis of servanthood: the Lord Yahweh's servant Israel-Jacob and Cyrus, the servant anointed to bring about a new world order which will be to the benefit of the servant people of God. Isaiah 49–55, on the other hand, is dominated by the figure of an individual prophetic Servant of the Lord, and it is around this figure that the remaining psalm passages are grouped, as we shall see. In Trito-Isaiah, on the other hand, especially the last two chapters, the emphasis will be on 'the Servants of the Lord' whom we take to be the disciples of the Servant of the Lord in Isa 49.16, 50.4–11, and especially 52.13–53.12. More will be said about these Servants of the Lord later.

The distinction between chapters 40–48 and 49–55 is fundamental, but other significant structural features have been noted. Attention has been drawn to the urgent call to leave Babylon at the conclusion of the first section in 48.20–21, which is repeated in 52.11–12 in somewhat different language. Both are followed immediately by passages about the Servant of the Lord, respectively the second and fourth of Duhm's *Ebedlieder* (49.1–6 and 52.13–53.12).[3] I can offer no plausible explanation of this complex situation except to remind myself and the reader of how much can happen to a text over a period of about five centuries. It is not surprising if, in its present form, the book betrays the existence of several superimposed divisions and structures, somewhat analogous

---

[2]For the texts, see *ANET*, 315–16; Paul-Alain Beaulieu, *The Reign of Nabonidus King of Babylon 556-539 B.C.* (New Haven and London: Yale University Press, 108).
[3]These superimposed structural features will remind us that the book of Isaiah has been subject to a cumulative and incremental restructuring throughout its long history. On Isa 48.20–21 and 52.11–12, see Odil H. Steck, 'Gottesknecht und Zion', in *Gesammelte Aufsätze zu Deuterojesaja* (Tübingen: Mohr Siebeck, 1992), 149–72; Reinhard G. Kratz, *Prophetenstudien* (FAT 74; Tübingen: Mohr Siebeck, 2011), 200–9.

to the plan of an excavated archaeological site displaying successive strata with superimposed transparencies.

Who wrote Deutero-Isaiah?

Isaiah 40–55 is anonymous. Anonymity is not unusual in the Hebrew Bible and ancient texts in general; in fact, the prophetic books are the only texts in the Hebrew Bible which carry the names of putative authors, which names cannot, however, be taken for granted. The name *Malachi*, for example, is adapted from the reference to 'my messenger' (*mal'aki*) in Mal 3.1. It is clearly a pseudonym, and it may not be the only one. Once attached to Isa 1–39, however, the anonymous Isa 40–55 came under the authorship of the Isaiah whose name appears in the first verse of the book. It has long been obvious, notwithstanding, that the Isaiah of Isa 1.1, 2.1, 13.1, last mentioned as active under Hezekiah (ca. 715–687 B.C.E.), cannot also have been active during the reign of the Persian Cyrus II (559–530 B.C.E.), who plays a central role in Isa 40–48. Perhaps this will help to explain the curious circumstance that on the history of events between these two reigns, including the decisive event of the fall of Jerusalem, the destruction of the temple, and the deportation and exile of a significant part of the population, the book is silent.[4]

If, given this situation, we wish to pursue the question of authorship, we must be content with identifying the environment and the circles within which the different sections of the book were composed, redacted, and attached to each other. This will be no easy task. In the absence of direct attribution, we must rely on a study of key texts, major themes, idiom, literary types – including the brief hymns spaced throughout the work – and language in general, without aspiring to reach beyond a reasonable probability. We can

---

[4]Ulrich Berges, *Jesaja. Der Prophet und das Buch* (Leipzig: Evangelische Verlagsanstalt, 2010), 91, holds that the omission was deliberate. He claims that an account of the fall and sack of Jerusalem in 586 B.C.E. would be incompatible with the central theme of the inviolability of Zion illustrated by the failure of Sennacherib to take the city in 701 B.C.E. (Isa 36–38). Fair enough, but one wonders whether the redactor would have thought it proper to simply expunge the fall of Jerusalem, the destruction of the temple, and the deportations from the historical record rather than providing a theological explanation of how it happened.

begin by taking a brief look at some of the structurally critical points in Deutero-Isaiah discussed in the previous section, in the hope of finding clues to origins, milieu, and collective authorship.

The prologue (40.1–8) is the obvious place to begin. It consists in three imperatives: a summons to comfort and reassure the people and Jerusalem, but especially Jerusalem, addressed to a plurality (vv. 1–2); a command addressed to the same plurality to prepare the way for the return of God to his city (vv. 3–5); a voice, presumably that of the Lord, addressed to an individual who is told to proclaim the impermanence of everything human in contrast to the word of God, which endures for ever. This last is, in effect, a cautionary comment on what is said about humanity ('all flesh') in the previous verse. Who then form the plurality addressed in vv. 1–2 and 3–5 and who is the one addressed in vv. 6–8? We can begin by setting aside the view that Isa 40.1–8 is a transcript of a session in the divine council with Yahweh presiding, an opinion often encountered in English-language scholarship. The problem here is that Isa 40.1–8 has nothing in common with the available examples of such a scenario, namely, the vision of Isaiah (Isa 6.1–13), that of the prophet Micaiah ben Imlah (1 Kgs 22.19–23), and Job 1–2, all of which describe a *deliberative* session rather than a simple issuing of orders.[5] The Old Greek version identifies those addressed as priests, but the Targum identifies them as prophets, which seems to be correct since the affirmations of divine speech in each of the three brief discourses – 'says your God' (v. 1), 'the Lord himself has spoken' (v. 5), and especially 'the word of our God endures forever' (v. 8) – are typical prophetic formulations.

The second section of Deutero-Isaiah (chapters 49–55) also opens with prophetic speech (49.1–6). This is the second of the four *Ebedlieder*, and the message of comfort and hope for the future in

---

[5] In Isaiah's vision, the prophet pre-empts discussion by offering his services. See my *Isaiah 40-55*, 179–80. On the divine council hypothesis, see Frank Moore Cross, *Canaanite Myth and Hebrew Epic* (Cambridge, Mass.: Harvard University Press, 1973), 186–90; Roy F. Melugin, *The Formation of Isaiah 40-55* BZAW 141; Berlin: de Gruyter, 1976), 82–4; Christopher R. Seitz, 'The Divine Council: Temporal Transition and New Prophecy in the Book of Isaiah', *JBL* 109 (1990): 229–47; Hugh G. M. Williamson, *The Book Called Isaiah*. Deutero-Isaiah's Role in Composition and Redaction (Oxford: Clarendon, 1994), 37–8.

Isa 52.7–10, another structurally significant juncture, points in the same direction:

> How welcome on the mountains are the footsteps of the herald
> announcing well-being, bringing good tidings, announcing victory,
> declaring to Zion: 'Your God reigns as king!'
> Listen! Your watchmen raise their voices,
> with one accord they shout out for joy,
> for with their own eyes they are witnessing
> the return of the Lord to Zion. (52.7–8)

The herald is a kind of messenger (*mal'ak*), a term well attested as a synonym for 'prophet'.[6] The watchman can also refer to a type of prophet, a kind of antenna or early warning system for the community to which the watchman belongs. The duties attached to this function are set out comprehensively in Ezekiel.[7] In general, the first of the two sections of Deutero-Isaiah, dealing with the message about a new political order to be inaugurated by Cyrus (40–48), is full of oracular discourse, that is, first-person discourse of deity, and exhibits a pressing need to provide confirmation of the truth of the prophetic message, with an abundance of rhetorical questions. An essential feature of this persuasive discourse is the insistence that the new actor on the international scene and the new events taking place represent the fulfilment of prophecy, which would certainly suggest an origin in prophetic circles.

The second section, which contains the three Servant passages with attached comments,[8] is also dominated by prophetic discourse, but the question of authorship is complicated by the apostrophes to Zion and the prevalence of the Zion theme throughout the section. Mention of Zion and the Zion theme in Isaiah and its only slightly less frequent appearance in Psalms obliges us to ask whether the temple liturgy had a part to play in the formation of Deutero-Isaiah and the book of Isaiah as a whole. During the time when the cultic prophet was still a lively issue the answer would have been in the

---

[6] 2 Chr 36.15; Isa 44.26; Hag 1.13.
[7] Ezek 3.17; 33.1–9; see also Jer 6.17 and, probably, Isa 56.10.
[8] Isa 49.1–12; 50.4–11; 52.13–53.12.

affirmative. Sigmund Mowinckel attributed Deutero-Isaiah to a single author, a member of the circle of Isaiah's disciples referred to in Isa 8.16. He says nothing here about temple cult, but in the context of his work as a whole its influence on these chapters would have been taken for granted.[9] Others, writing in the middle decades of the last century, alluded to the influence of temple worship on chapters 40–55.[10] Since then, the influence of the temple cult is occasionally mentioned, generally without pursuing the proposal in detail. In his commentary on Isa 40–66, Claus Westermann contented himself with remarking that Deutero-Isaiah was in some way connected with the temple singers since in Israel psalms were at the centre of life. Unfortunately, however, he does not elaborate.[11]

In some respects, these attempts to establish a connection between Deutero-Isaiah and the temple liturgy and its practitioners go against the grain of more recent Isaian studies with their tendency to concentrate on the composition and redaction of the book, its diversity, unity, final form, and the connections between its several parts.[12] In an article under the title 'The Destiny of the Nations in the Book of Isaiah,' Graham Davies reminded those who seek for unity in Isaiah along these lines that 'the primary focus of unity is the tradition which underlies it (i.e. the book of Isaiah), and that means above all the Jerusalem cult tradition with its cosmic and universal perspective'.[13] The point of the remark may

---

[9]*Prophecy and Tradition* (Oslo: Jacob Dybwad, 1946), 68–9. See also his *Psalmenstudien III* and *The Psalms in Israel's Worship* (New York and Nashville: Abingdon, 1962), II 53–73.

[10]D. R. Jones, 'The Tradition of the Oracles of Isaiah', ZAW 67 (1955): 226–46; John H. Eaton, 'The Origin of the Book of Isaiah', VT 9 (1959): 138–57; idem, *Festal Drama in Deutero-Isaiah* (London: SPCK, 1979); J. M. Vincent, *Studien zur literarischen Eigenart und zur geistigen Heimat von Jesaja, Kap. 40-55* (Frankfurt am Main: Peter Lang, 1977).

[11]Claus Westermann, *Isaiah 40-66. A Commentary* (London: SCM Press, 1969), 8 (E.T. of *Das Buch Jesaia 40-66* (Göttingen: Vandenhoeck & Ruprecht 1966).

[12]One example of relevance to our theme would be Hugh G. M. Williamson, *The Book Called Isaiah. Deutero-Isaiah's Role in Composition and Redaction* (Oxford: Clarendon, 1994) in which the internal connections between Deutero-Isaian and Isa 2-12, 13-27, and 28-39 are explored.

[13]Graham I. Davies, 'The Destiny of the Nations in the Book of Isaiah', in *The Book of Isaiah/Le Livre d'Isaïe*, ed. Jacques Vermeylen (Leuven: University Press, 1989), 119-20.

be accepted without underestimating the significance of studying the redactional history of the different sections in the book and the interconnections between them, and it will be borne in mind as we proceed with our enquiry.

In the last few years, Professor Ulrich Berges has advanced a quite specific theory on the authorship of Deutero-Isaiah. Impressed by the psalm material in Isa 40–55, to be considered shortly, he proposed that the temple singers deported to Babylon together with other temple personnel after the fall and sack of Jerusalem put together while in exile the core of Deutero-Isaiah as their 'oratorio of hope'. This presumably written composition served as a response and counter to *Lamentations* composed by their professional colleagues in Jerusalem who had escaped deportation. No sooner repatriated – according to Berges under Darius I rather than Cyrus II.[14] – the exiled singers proclaimed their joyful message to Jerusalem/Zion that the bad times were over, that the Lord God would return to Zion in royal splendour, and that the city would be rebuilt, repopulated, and renewed as the centre not only for Israel but for all peoples. In written form, this message of hope and renewal would presumably be Deutero-Isaiah, or at any rate its core content.[15]

---

[14]It seems a little hasty to reject the possibility of a first *aliya* during the reign of Cyrus II. The biblical texts themselves suggest some of the reasons for the delay in beginning work on rebuilding the temple in accord with the decree of Cyrus. All three versions of the decree (2 Chr 36.22–23; Ezra 1.1–4; 6.3–5) have the rebuilding of the temple as the main reason for the repatriation. What I suggest happened is that successive returns were conflated and backdated to 'the first year of King Cyrus of Persia' (2 Chr 36.22; Ezra 1.1). This first repatriation, within a year of the fall of Babylon (539–538), assimilates to itself several later returns: in connection with the conquest of Egypt by Cambyses which necessitated passage through Palestine (525); another during or after the first dynastic revolt in Babylon, that of Nidintu-bel alias Nebuchadnezzar III (December 522); then during or shortly after the second Babylonian revolt, that of Arakha alias Nebuchadnezzar IV (late summer 521). Centuries later, leaders of the Damascus sect likewise backdated the origins of their own group to the *ri'šōnîm*, the first to return from exile, the pioneers (CD iv–v). For this timetable in the early Achaemenid period, see Muhammad A. Dandamaev, *Persien unter den ersten Achämeniden (6. Jahrhunderd v.Chr.)* (Wiesbaden: Dr. Ludwig Reichert Verlag, 1976), 255–6.

[15]Ulrich Berges, *Das Buch Jesaja. Komposition und* Endgestalt (Frieburg: Herder, 1998), 322–413; *Jesaja. Der Prophet und das Buch*, 36–46.

The hypothesis is stimulating and worthy of close consideration. That temple singers were deported with other temple personnel is a reasonable deduction from the biblical record, and their repatriation is in fact explicitly attested.[16] Moreover, it was fortunate that for purposes of political and fiscal control Babylonians permitted, probably even mandated, the displaced Judaeans to form their own distinct assembly (*hatru*) like other ethnic and national displaced groups, a situation confirmed by our knowledge of Babylonian imperial policy and reflected in correspondence between Judah and the deportees reported in Jeremiah.[17] These epistolary exchanges also testify to the presence and activity of prophets among the deported, some of whom, in rejecting Jeremiah's advice to seek the welfare of the city in which their God had exiled them (Jer 29.7), were predicting a return to a greater city, the holy city Zion, doing so at the risk of a horrible death, as indeed was the lot of the prophets (and martyrs?) Ahab ben Kolaiah and Zedekiah ben Maaseiah, both condemned nevertheless by Jeremiah (Jer 29.21–23).[18]

There were therefore prophets among the deported Judaeans in Babylon, but there were also temple singers. Those who wept by the rivers of Babylon and declined a request from their Babylonian 'hosts' to put on a performance of Zion psalms (Ps 137) must have been professional temple singers. We learn, in fact, that 148 Asaphite singers, twice as many as Levites, were among the first to be repatriated (Neh 7.43–45). The expatriate communities would have found ways to worship in common, and there are indications that they did so. Before setting off on the long journey to Jerusalem, Ezra discovered that Levites were absent from his caravan. He therefore sent a delegation to a location referred to as 'Casiphia the place' somewhere in southern Mesopotamia, under the direction of

---

[16]The deportations in 2 Kgs 24.14, 16; 25.11–12; Jer 52.15–16, 28–30; the repatriations in Ezra 2.41; Neh 7.44; 1 Esd 5.27.

[17]Jer 29.8, 15, 21–23; see also Ezek 3.15; 8.1; 14.1; 33.30–31. On the situation in the Babylonian diaspora, see my essay 'The Age of the Exile', in *The Biblical World: Volume One*, ed. John Barton (London and New York: Routledge, 2002), 427.

[18]Jeremiah denounces the 'dreams' of their prophets as deceptive immediately after advising them to build houses, settle down and start families (29.4–9). The dreams were therefore probably about a return to Jerusalem-Zion in the not too distant future, in defiance of Jeremiah's advice – ironically reminiscent of Ps 126.1, 'When the Lord restored the fortunes of Zion we were like people in a dream'.

a certain Iddo, a priestly name. Their mission was to recruit Levites and other temple personnel for eventual service in the temple to be rebuilt in Jerusalem (Ezra 8.15–20). The repetition of the word *māqôm* ('place') in this brief passage, shorthand for 'place of worship', together with the presence there of different categories of cult personnel, indicates that Casiphia was a diaspora substitute for the temple in Jerusalem, and it would be unthinkable that music, and therefore musicians, were absent from worship there.

Professor Berges' theory therefore traces the original core of Isa 40–48 to an 'oratorio of hope' composed by temple singers exiled in Babylon, brought back with them on their repatriation, eventually expanded by the addition of Isa 49–55, then eventually linked with Isa 1–39, hence placed under the authoritative name of the great eighth-century prophet. The theory is imaginative; it broadens the base of discussion on the book of Isaiah and its relations with temple singers and temple worship in general, but questions remain to be answered, as is generally the case, especially since there is much in Isa 40–48, and indeed in all Deutero-Isaiah, which cannot easily be traced to this source. The polemical and disputatious tone throughout is foreign to temple psalmody – there are eight rhetorical questions in chapter 40 alone – and the combined themes of Babylon and the commissioning of Cyrus by the God of Israel are the subject matter of prophetic rather than liturgical concern. At this point, however, a survey of the distinctive psalm material in Deutero-Isaiah may provide further clarification.[19]

Psalm elements in Isaiah 40–55

The criteria for identifying psalms, either whole or fragmentary, in Isaiah or any other prophetic text, are inevitably somewhat

---

[19] In addition to Ulrich Berges, *Jesaja. Der Prophet und das Buch*, see his treatment of Deutero-Isaiah in *Das Buch Jesaja. Komposition und Endgestalt* (Freiburg: Herder, 1998), 322–413, in which he attributes 40–48 to disciples of Isaiah who gathered his sayings together and expanded them into the composition as we have it (411). At this writing, his most recent writing on the subject is 'Singt dem Herrn ein neues Lied'. Zu den Trägerkreisen von Jesajabuch und Psalter. in J. Bremer, F. - L. Hossfeld and T. M. Steiner (eds), *Trägerkreise in den Psalmen* (Göttingen: Vandenhoeck & Ruprecht, 2016), 11–33.

subjective. In order, therefore, to avoid over-identifying, I propose to limit the selection according to a combination of the following criteria listed in order of importance: (1) direct address to God in praise and thanksgiving; (2) the presence of language and themes prominent in psalms; (3) context; (4) prosody. The application of these criteria leaves us with three passages in Isa 40.40–48 and four in Isa 49–55.[20]

Isaiah 40–48

(1) 42.10–12

Sing a new song to the Lord,
his praise from one end of the earth to the other,
let the sea roar, and all creatures in it,[21]
coastlands, islands, and all that live there.
Let the wilderness and its settlements raise their voices in praise,
with the encampments which Kedar inhabits.
Let the dwellers in Sela shout for joy,
crying out from the mountaintops.
Let the coastlands and islands give glory to the Lord,
proclaiming his praise.

There has been much discussion about the extent of the psalm and its relation to Isa 42.1–9.[22] I exclude v. 13 since it introduces a different subject, the fury of Yahweh the warrior-God and what

---

[20]Claus Westermann, *Das Buch Jesaia 40-66* (ATD 19; Göttingen: Vandenhoeck & Ruprecht, 1966), ET *Isaiah 40-66. A Commentary* (Philadelphia: Westminster, 1969), 19–20, has the same selection of what he calls 'eschatological hymns of praise'. Ulrich Berges, *Das Buch Jesaja. Komposition und Endgestalt* (Freiburg: Herder, 1998), 327–30, adds 48.20–21 and 54.1–3 and omits 51.9–11. Space forbids a thorough interpretation of the relevant psalms for which consultation of the commentaries will be required.

[21]Following Pss 96.11 and 98.7, I read *yir'am hayyām ûmĕlo'ô*, for MT *yôrĕdê hayyām ûmĕlo'ô*.

[22]For a thorough review up to the time of writing, see W. S. Prinsloo, 'Isaiah 42, 10-12 "Sing to the Lord a New Song"', in *Studies in the Book of Isaiah. FS Willem A. M. Beuken*, ed. J. Van Ruiten and M. Vervenne (Leuven: Leuven University Press/ Peeters, 1997), 289–301.

will come of it (42.13–16), and because this first psalm begins and ends with the keyword *tehillah* (praise). Praise and thanksgiving are the most prominent themes in the liturgical psalms. In addition, it seems to me that, as a 'new song', it refers to what precedes rather than what follows, serving as an appropriate conclusion to the 'new things' announced in the verse immediately preceding, namely the sponsorship of the conquests of Cyrus II by Yahweh God of Israel. This theme also appears in Isa 42.1–4, the designation of Cyrus as Yahweh's agent, with its attached comment in 42.5–9.[23] The prophetic author, seeking for a way to celebrate this event, decidedly a new event when a foreign power acts on behalf of rather than against Israel, would have been drawn to those liturgical hymns designated as 'new songs', namely, Pss 33, 40, 96, 98, and 149. Among these, his attention would have been drawn especially to Pss 96 and 98, both psalms of praise inviting the whole world, from one end of the earth to the other, to join in the rapturous praise of God. This first Deutero-Isaianic psalm has much in common with these two canonical psalms.

(2) 44.23

Exult, you heavens, for it is the Lord's doing;
shout aloud, you depths of the earth!
Break into song, you mountains,
forests with all your trees;
for the Lord has redeemed Jacob,
in Israel his glory is manifest.

This brief hymn of praise rounds out the equally brief admonition to remember, which immediately precedes it and which also celebrates the redemption of Jacob/Israel (44.21–22). The call to break out in song and loud cries of joy set the tone for the announcement immediately following of the mission of Cyrus, acting as agent of the God of Israel, to create a new world order which would also be to the advantage of the author's fellow-Judaeans (44.24–45.7).

---

[23]For a defence of this interpretation of Isa 42.1–4 see my *Isaiah 40-55. A New Translation with Introduction and Commentary* (AB 19A; New Haven and London: Yale University Press, 2002), 208–12.

The positioning of the hymn would further suggest that it was composed specifically for this context, and its dependence on the canonical psalms is apparent from language typical of the temple singers' guilds, for example in Pss 96, 98 and 149.[24]

(3) 45.8

> Rain righteousness, you heavens,
> Let the skies above pour it down
> Let the earth open that salvation may bloom,
> and that righteousness may likewise spring forth.

The positioning of these three psalms is clearly deliberate. Isaiah 42.10-12 celebrates the new event of the commissioning of Cyrus as the servant of Yahweh, announced in the passage immediately preceding (Isa 42.1-9). This theme is highlighted by the arrangement of Isa 44.23 and 45.8, as follows:

44.23	psalm
44.24–45.7	Cyrus and his mission
45.8	psalm

The choice of psalm material was also deliberate. Appeal to the heavens and the earth (44.23) is appropriate in view of the international, we might say, global implications of the mission of Cyrus. It is also a familiar trope in the canonical psalms, no doubt due in good part to the diasporic experience. Both 44.23 and 45.8 belong, as distant relatives, to those psalms which express the reassurance of divine power at work in the world, manifested in both the sky above and the earth beneath. One example, the Korahite psalm 85, may suffice:

> Faithfulness springs up from the earth,
> righteousness looks down from the sky (v. 12)

---

[24] Terms typical of the singers guilds in the hymn are *rānnû* ('exult'; cf. Pss 96.12; 98.4, 8; 149.5, etc), *hārî'û* ('shout aloud'; Ps 98.4, 6, etc), *pishû rinnāh* ('break into song'; Ps 98.4, etc).

Here, too, therefore, Deutero-Isaiah has appropriated themes and language from the canonical psalms, in whatever form they were available to him at the time of composition. The psalms were inserted to add the note of celebration, joy, and uplift to the oracular statements either preceding or following them.

Isaiah 49–55

(1) 49.13

> Heavens, shout for joy, earth, rejoice!
> Mountains, break out into joyful song!
> The Lord has comforted his people,
> he has pitied them in their distress.

The announcement that the Lord has redeemed his people, and that they should therefore embark on the exodus from Babylon as their ancestors departed from Egypt (48.20–21), marks the conclusion to the first section of Deutero-Isaiah, and this critical juncture in Deutero-Isaiah is further emphasized by the following verse: 'There can be no well-being for the wicked'. The second section opens with another commissioning of a servant of the Lord God, no longer Cyrus as in Isa 42.1–4 but the prophet himself representing the people (49.1–6). This second of the Duhmian *Ebedlieder*, like the first, has a comment attached to it (49.7–12) followed by the psalm fragment (49.13). The theme which binds the comment with the psalm is the compassion of the Lord God for his afflicted people.[25]

(2) 51.3

> The Lord comforts Zion,
> he brings comfort to all her ruins;
> he will turn her wilderness into Eden,

---

[25] With *niham* (comfort) 13b cf. *nahămû, nahămû 'ammî* (40.1), *rahămîm* (compassion) is another keyword in Deutero- and Trito-Isaiah (49.10, 13, 15; 54.8, 10; 55.7; 60.10).

> her deserted places into the garden of the Lord.
> Joy and gladness will be found in her,
> thanksgiving and the sound of music.

This message of comfort to Zion, the present, historical city devastated by the Babylonians and still awaiting rebuilding and restoration, is incorporated into an address to those seeking righteousness (51.1–8) and therefore is not presented as a psalm, though in other respects that is what it is. Several psalms contain prayers for the restoration of Zion, calling on the Lord to keep in mind the city in which he had chosen to dwell. The Asaphite Ps 74.2–3, for example, prays that God may remember Mount Zion where he came to dwell, and that he would take note of the 'perpetual ruins'.[26] In both psalm and Deutero-Isaiah, this plea is made in the expectation that the ecstatic joy evoked by Zion would once again be experienced and expressed in music and song.

(3) 51.9–11

> Awake, awake! Arm of the Lord, put on strength;
> awake as in days of old, in ages long since.
> Was it not you that hacked Rahab in pieces,
> that ran the Dragon through?
> Was it not you that dried up the Sea,
> the waters of the Great Deep?
> Was it not you made the depths of the sea
> a way for the redeemed to traverse?
> Those ransomed by the Lord will return,
> entering Zion with shouts of joy,
> crowned with joy everlasting.
> Gladness and joy will be theirs,
> sorrow and sighing will depart.

The structuring of the individual units is not so clear in this second section of Deutero-Isaiah, but there is continuity of thought and language between 51.4–8, preceding this passage, and 51.12–16,

---

[26]See also Pss 51.20; 69.36; 79.2; 102.17.

following it. There is emphasis on the removal of fear (vv. 7, 12–13), on reassurance and reliance on the Creator God (vv. 6, 13, 16), and on the arm of the Lord (v. 5), which suggests that the intervening psalm was inserted as an appeal for the Lord Yahweh to show his arm, recalling the 'mighty hand and outstretched arm' of the Exodus tradition (e.g. Deut 4.34). This quasi-psalm also reflects the joyful return to Zion in the previous psalm-like text (51.3). The call to the Lord to awaken, to become active ('*ûrî*, '*ûrî*, 51.9), is heard in several psalms (44.24; 59.5; 80.3), and the victorious combat with monstrous creatures, embodiments of physical and moral chaos (Rahab, Tannin, Yam, Leviathan), is occasionally a theme for the authors of psalms. The author of Isa 51.9–11 may in fact have modelled his composition on Ps 74, which laments the destruction of Jerusalem, begs God to remember Mount Zion chosen as his residence, and reminds him of earlier victories won:

> You divided the sea by your might,
> you broke the heads of the dragons in the waters,
> you crushed the heads of Leviathan,
> giving him as food for the creatures of the wilderness. (Ps 74.13–15)

(4) 52.7–10

> How welcome on the mountains are the footsteps of the herald announcing well-being, bringing good tidings, announcing victory, declaring to Zion: 'Your God has begun his reign!'
> Listen! Your watchmen raise their voices,
> with one accord they shout for joy,
> for with their own eyes they are witnessing
> the return of the Lord to Zion.
> With one accord break out in joyful shouts,
> you ruins of Jerusalem!
> The Lord has comforted his people,
> he has redeemed Jerusalem.
> The Lord has bared his holy arm
> in the sight of all the nations.
> All the ends of the earth shall see
> the victory of our God.

While this joyful announcement of a new age inaugurated by the resumption of divine rule in Zion is not formally a psalm as defined by our criteria, it has many linguistic and thematic features in common with psalms, especially those expressive of joy at the prospect of redemption available to all humanity ('the ends of the earth'). Its most prominent link with psalms is the proclamation 'Your God has begun his reign!' This is the message announced by the lookouts on the city wall who are the first to witness the return of the Lord Yahweh to Zion, which of course implies the return of those coercively expatriated since there can be no king without a people. The message *YHWH malak* (v. 7) reproduces the signature statement of the 'Kingship Psalms' (Pss 93.1; 96.10; 97.1; 99.1), especially Ps 99, a hymn of praise to Yahweh God enthroned on the cherubim in Zion, whose rule extends to all the peoples of the world.[27] On this high note, the clearly identifiable borrowings from psalms and adaptations of psalmodic themes and language in Deutero-Isaiah come to an end.

---

[27] On the hypothesis, proposed by Sigmund Mowinckel, of a liturgical setting for the kingship psalms in an autumn festival celebrating the enthronement of Yahweh, see Mowinckel, *He That Cometh* (Oxford: Blackwell, 1959), 125–86 especially 140–3; idem, *The Psalms in Israel's Worship* (New York and Nashville: Abingdon, 1967), 106–92. The theory is discussed by – inter alios – Hans-Joachim Kraus, *Die Königsherrschaft Gottes im Alten Testament* (Tübingen: J. C. B. Mohr, 1951), 102–5; idem, *Gottesdienst in Israel* (Munich: Kaiser, 1962), 266 = *Worship in Israel* (Oxford: Blackwell, 1966), 231; Ben C. Ollenburger, *Zion The City of the Great King* (JSOTSup 41; Sheffield: Sheffield Academic Press, 1987), 23–52.

6

Prophecy and Psalmody in Isaiah 56–66

The identity and structure of Isaiah 56–66

The proposal, first presented by Bernhardt Duhm in 1892, that chapters 56–66 of Isaiah form a section of the book distinct in language and theme from the preceding sixteen chapters known as Deutero-Isaiah, is by now for the most part taken for granted. Deutero-Isaiah is neatly rounded off by its final verses (55.12–13) which return to the theme of repatriation and restoration announced at the beginning (40.1–5). Isaiah 55.10–11, the verses immediately preceding, reaffirm confidence in the word of God communicated by the prophet in the opening verses (40.8). Then, on the probable assumption that chapter 55 was added to provide a final summary of the message of Deutero-Isaiah, as many commentators hold, the concluding verse of the previous chapter would have been the original finale of Deutero-Isaiah:

> This, then, is the lot of the servants of the Lord,
> their vindication from me: a word of the Lord. (54.17b)

This statement serves as a link between the individual Servant of the Lord in 40–55, especially the 'Suffering Servant' in 52.13–53.12, and the Servants of the Lord in Trito-Isaiah, disciples of the Servant, who constitute the core of the renewed community of the future – one of the great themes of Trito-Isaiah. These Servants of the Lord will claim our attention in a later chapter.

The integrity of Isa 56–66 as the third major section of the book is confirmed by its impressive structure. Its central panel, consisting in chapters 60–62, celebrates the Zion of the future age of salvation, a favourite theme of the psalmists, which will be taken up in the following chapter of our study. Chapters 60–62 contrast starkly with the four preceding chapters (56–59) and the four following (63–66), which denounce corrupt religious leaders and condemn practitioners of syncretic and necromantic cults. In other words, they deal with the often intractable affairs of life in the real, contemporary world. At the centre of chapters 60–62, the precise centre, stands the self-presentation of the prophetic author, his autograph, and signature (61.1–3), with forty-four stichometric lines before and after it announcing and celebrating a future very different from the unsatisfactory present, a restored Zion and its people (60.1–22; 61.3b–62.12).[1] Finally, there are parallels between the sections which precede and follow this central panel: The intervention of Yahweh as a warrior (59.15b–20; 63.1–6), laments for a condition of spiritual disorientation and godforsakeness (59.1–15a; 63.7–64.11), condemnation of syncretic cults (57.3–13; 59.9–15a; 65.1–7), and an inclusive reference at the beginning and end of Trito-Isaiah to the final ingathering of people from all lands (56.1–8; 66.18–21).[2]

The date of the production of the different materials in Isa 56–66 has occasioned a long and inconclusive debate which cannot

---

[1] We may be hearing the voice of the same prophetic author at the conclusion of the first passage in Trito-Isaiah: "This is the word of the sovereign Lord God who gathers the dispersed of Israel: I shall add yet more to those already gathered" (56.8) and at the conclusion of the first of the three sections: "This is my covenant with them, declares the Lord God: My spirit that rests upon you and my words that I have put in your mouth will not fail you from generation to generation of your descendants, from this time forward and for ever more" (59.21).

[2] Another structural feature caught the eye of Bernhard Duhm, that is, the repetition of the catchphrase 'There can be no well-being for the wicked' in Isa 48.22 and 57.21. Taken together with the final verse of Trito-Isaiah and therefore of the book, which serves as vivid illustration of this assertion (66.24), Duhm took Isa 48.22, 57.21 and 66.24 as marking out chapters 49–66, the second part of the book, into three equal scrolls (megillot) of nine chapters each. See his *Das Buch Jesaia übersetzt und erklärt* (4th edn, Göttingen: Vandenhoeck & Ruprecht, 1922), 367, 435. Duhm's proposal may find some confirmation in 1QIsaᵃ in which a space is left at lines 48.22 and 57.21.

be adequately addressed here.[3] The situation described is evidently post-disaster, but how long after 586 B.C.E. remains uncertain. The texts speak of 'the ancient ruins' of Jerusalem (58.12; 61.4), the ruined cities of Judah (61.4; 64.9), the walls and gates of the city still awaiting rebuilding (60.10), and the temple not yet rebuilt (63.18; 64.10). The return of deported Judaeans is still anticipated (Isa 56.8; 60.4; 66.20–21), which simply confirms what seems to be evident, that repatriation was in progress over a considerable period of time rather than taking place all at once, as the first two chapters of Ezra might suggest. These statements would be difficult to explain if made after the completion of work on the city wall and gates by Nehemiah in the twentieth or twenty-first year of Artaxerxes I (445–444 B.C.E.), or even after the rebuilding of the temple in the sixth year of Darius I (516–515 B.C.E.). This is not to deny that there is still much in Trito-Isaiah that could come from a considerably later time.

Isaiah 56–59; 63–66

If only for convenience of study, we can divide the eleven chapters of Trito-Isaiah into three sections: 56–59, 60–62 the central panel, and 63–66, with a view to identifying psalms, or psalm-like material, or indications of interactivity and intertexuality with the canonical psalms. The prevalence of traditional formulae for introducing prophetic speech in the first of the three sections is not encouraging, though prophetic oracles do have a place in psalms, especially laments.[4] The opening discourse, 56.1–8, offers the prospect for the most marginal elements in society – those of foreign origin and eunuchs – of citizenship in the Zion of the future ('within my walls') and membership, even active participation, in the temple community and its worship ('in my house') – this in defiance of the law in Deuteronomy (23.2–4). A note is therefore

---

[3] As a stop-gap, I may refer to my *Isaiah 56-66: A New Translation with Introduction and Commentary* (Anchor Bible19B; New York and London: Doubleday, 2003), 42–54 and the bibliography, 95–126.
[4] For example, in Isa 56.1, 4, 8; 57.14, 15, 19, 21; 58.14b; 59.20, 21.

struck at the beginning which resonates throughout Isaiah,[5] and the way in which the vision of the future city and temple is presented, even when, as here, Zion is not named, reproduces one of the great themes of the canonical psalms, often in identical language.[6]

Two prophetic judgements (56.9–12; 57.3–13a)

There follow two prophetic judgements. The first (56.9–12) condemns corrupt religious leaders referred to as shepherds of the flock. They include prophets represented as irresponsible guards and as dogs too lazy or fearful to bark at the approach of dangerous animals.[7] The second (57.3–13a) is a denunciation of a dysfunctional and corrupt family – a sinful brood of children, an adulterous father, and a mother of loose morals, a sorceress addicted to cults of a sexual nature. This highly figurative way of representing cultic practices at odds with traditional Yahwistic religion owes a debt to Hosea's marriage with Gomer and the couple's three children (Hos 1–3), perhaps also to Ezekiel's condemnation of Jerusalem as Yahweh's faithless and dissolute bride (Ezek 16; 23). Wedged between these two judgement sayings is a lament for the death of a righteous one (*saddîq*) who has entered into peace and for devout individuals (*'anšê-hesed* = *hāsîdîm*), probably disciples of the *saddiq*, who have been removed, probably also dead, unnoticed and unmourned (57.1–2). We shall return to this mysterious text at a later point.

The denunciation of the sorceress and her children, which has nothing in common with psalms, is followed by a word of assurance:

> The one who takes refuge in me will inherit the land,
> and possess my holy mountain. (57.13b)

---

[5]Isa 2.2–5; 49.6; 51.4; 60.3; 66.18–21.
[6]'My holy mountain' Pss 2.6; 3.5; 15.1; 43.3; 48.2; 99.9; 'My walls' Ps 122; 'My house' Pss 5.8; 36.8–10; 42.5; 52.10; 69.10; 84.5, 11. The expression *bêt tĕpillātî* 'my house of prayer', 56.7, however, occurs only here.
[7]The term *sōpeh*, 'sentinel' 'lookout', is a well-attested synonym for prophet as embodying a kind of early warning system; see Ezek 3.16–21, 14.12–20, 33.1–9.

In several of the psalms, the place of refuge and safety is in the temple, beneath the outstretched wings of the cherubim who protect the sacred ark, the focus of temple worship. We hear this prayer for security often in psalms:

> How precious is your steadfast love, O God!
> All may seek refuge in the shadow of your wings. (Ps 36.7)

> Guard me as the apple of your eye,
> hide me in the shadow of your wings. (Ps 17.7)[8]

There is something strange but somehow consoling in this image. It is followed by the promise of inheriting the land and possessing the holy mountain, a central theme in Isaiah and Psalms. It is spelled out more fully in the conclusion to Ps 69:

> God will save Zion and rebuild the cities of Judah,
> his servants shall live there and possess it,
> the descendants of his servants shall inherit it,
> those who love his name shall live there. (Ps 69.36–37)

Two Laments (59.9–20; 63.7–64.11)

Lament features prominently in Trito-Isaiah, in both the first and last of the three major sections. Dwelling on the catastrophe of 586 B.C.E. – the ancient ruins (58.12; 61.4), the destroyed walls and gates of the city (60.10–11), the temple burnt to the ground (63.18) – is itself a kind of lament or mourning, an embryonic version of the more formal laments of the guild of Asaph which add the slaughter of God's servants and devotees and the desecration of their bodies (Pss 74 and 79). Before taking a closer look at the laments, we should be aware that there is no authoritative definition of a lament psalm and only partial agreement on its essential constituent parts. At a minimum, however, it would be agreed that a lament will contain a description of the cause of the lament, and that since lamenting is a form of prayer it will be addressed to God. There

---

[8] Also Pss 31.2, 20; 57.2; 91.4.

will also more often than not be a reply, or at least an expression of assurance of divine assistance.[9]

Isaiah 59.9–20

This sorrowful confession of sin and religious disorientation on the part of the community to which the speaker belongs (59.9–15a) is strongly introspective but is also directed to God and therefore unquestionably a lament:

> Our transgressions against you are many,
> our sins bear witness against us. (59.12)

In its present context, this communal confession of sin is part of a larger unit. It is followed by a prophetic oracle which provides the answer to the lament, and therefore serves as assurance of a response (59.15b–20). Such oracular statements can also be found in canonical lament psalms.[10] The confession is preceded by a commination – rather like a brief sermon – which purports to explain why God has hitherto remained unresponsive and inactive (59.1–8). This too belongs to the same unit, as is evident from the '*al-kēn* ('therefore') at the beginning of the lament (59.9), but it is not formally part of the lament. It seems as if the entire chapter, exclusive of the prophetic signature at its conclusion (59.21), was in fact designed as one text put together with different materials, one of which was the lament similar in its general lines to the canonical psalms and the book of Lamentations (Threnoi). In fact, Charles Cutler Torrey made out a good case for reading the entire chapter 59 inclusive of the lament as a single composition. He summarized it as follows:

> This great poem *de profundis* stands alone in the collection as a picture of sin and misery. The prevailing impression, through most of its extent, is of *darkness*. Sin has separated the people

---

[9]Based on these criteria, I identify ten psalms as belonging to the communal lament type: Pss 12 (David), 44 (Korah), 59 (David), 60 (David), 74 (Asaph), 79 (Asaph), 83 (Asaph), 85 (Korah), 89 (Ethan), 106 (Hallelujah Psalm).
[10]For example, Ps 89, a lament for the loss of the Davidic dynasty which paraphrases the oracle of Nathan (2 Sam 7.4–17) in vv. 4–5 and 20–38 and in which the actual lament begins only in v. 39.

from their God (verse 2), his face is hidden from them. Thus the light is gone; they have become as blind men, staggering in the dark, groping for support, stumbling at noon as in twilight.[11]

Isaiah 63.7–64.11

I propose to read this passage in a straightforward way rather than as a composite of strata assembled over a considerable period of time,[12] also as a purely literary work indebted to the canonical psalms rather than itself liturgical in origin.[13] It falls naturally into five sections. The first speaks of YHWH's benevolent deeds (*hasdê YHWH*), his love and compassion on behalf of Israel as recorded in its early history (63.7–9). The recital continues with Israel's failure to reciprocate in spite of divine assistance at the Papyrus Sea and in the wilderness (63.10–14). The third section is a complaint, now addressed to God as father, that he remains distant, has hardened their hearts, and has allowed their enemies to destroy the temple, their most precious possession (63.15–19a). The lament continues in the fourth section (63.19b–64.6), concluding with a prayer of petition – we are your people, and we are in distress (64.7–10). The entire passage ends with questions: 'In view of all this, will you stand aloof? Will you keep silent and afflict us beyond measure?' (24.11).

---

[11]Charles Cutler Torrey, *The Second Isaiah: A New Interpretation* (New York: Scribner, 1928), 439.
[12]As, for example, K. Pauritsch, *Die neue Gemeinde. Gott sammelt Ausgestossene und Arme (Jesaja 56-66). Die Botschaft des Tritojesaja* (Rome: Pontifical Biblical Institute, 1971), 144–71; S. Sekine, *Die Tritojesajanische Sammlung (Jes 56-66) redaktionsgeschichtliche untersucht* (BZAW 175; Berlin: de Gruyter, 1989), 148–64; Odil Hannes Steck, 'Autor und/oder Redaktor in Jesaja 56-66', in *Writing and Reading the Scroll of Isaiah: Studies of an Interpretive (sic) Tradition. Vol.1*, ed. C. C. Broyles and C. A. Evans (Leiden: Brill, 1997), 219–59. The most thorough study of the passage in recent years known to me is Johannes Goldenstein, *Das Gebet der Gottesknechte.Jesaja 63,7-64,11 von Jesajabuch* (Neukirchen-Vluyn: Neukirchener Verlag, 2001).
[13]As, for example, Hugh G. M. Williamson, 'Isaiah 63,7-64,11: Exilic Lament or Postexilic Protest?' *ZAW* 102 (1990): 48–58; idem, 'Laments at the Destroyed Temple', *BRev* 6/4 (1990): 12–17.

The debt of this lament to psalms, and especially to psalms of communal lamentation, will be obvious. This is especially so with those psalms in which historical reminiscence and the rehearsal of a history of moral failure, a refusal to response to the benevolent acts of their God, play a prominent part (Pss 78, 89, 107).[14] The relation of God to Israel during those early years is encapsulated in the term *hesed*, difficult to define but connoting benevolence and fidelity, a keyword which occurs more often in psalms than in all other biblical texts together. The plural, *hasdê YHWH*, which appears twice at the beginning of the Isaian lament with the meaning 'benevolent deeds' is often used in psalms in similar situations.[15] The misfortunes which are the lot of Israel in the lament reach their climax – or nadir – in the loss of the temple (Isa 63.18–19; 64.10), which brings to mind those canonical psalms in which the failure of their God to protect the Jerusalem temple, his own house, is a source of pain and bewilderment (Pss 74.3–8; 79.1). These are the major points of contact with and dependence on the canonical psalms; a detailed verse-by-verse reading would no doubt bring to light others, but for this the reader must turn to the commentaries.

In one respect the Isaian lament differs from the standard form of the communal lament in Psalms: It ends with questions addressed to God rather than an assurance of a hearing and reply, as we find, for example, in Pss 69.31–37 and 79.13. The last verse of the lament (Isa 64.11) reads as follows:

In view of all this will you stand aloof?
Will you keep silent and afflict us beyond measure?

The situation here seems to be similar to what we have seen with the corresponding lament in 59.9–20. Psalmody is one of several sources, certainly a principal source, for the final author or redactor, and this obliges us to take account of the literary context in which it is embedded and to which it is adapted. The community lament in Isa 63.7–64.11 has no obvious connection with the preceding

---

[14]To these we should add Neh 9.6–37, a psalm of lament attributed to Ezra.
[15]Pss 17.7; 25.6; 89.2, 50; 106.7, 45; 107.43; 119.41.

passage about a bloodbath in Edom (63.1–6), but it is possible to read the passage following, that is 65.1–7, as a substitute for the expected 'assurance of a hearing' or, rather, as an explanation for the absence of such an assuring conclusion:

> I was ready to be sought out, but they did not ask for me;
> I was ready to be found, but they did not seek me.
> I said, 'Here I am, here I am'
> to a people that did not invoke my name.

The passage continues by denouncing a variety of syncretic cult practices which their Judaean ancestors practised and which they themselves continue to practise. This, I suggest, marks an important turning point. Beginning here, the principal issue in Trito-Isaiah will be the decision about who is and who is not a member of God's people. In the passage immediately following, those designated 'Servants of the Lord' are compared to the few good grapes in a bunch that has gone bad, another way of stating the old prophetic theme of the remnant (Isa 65.8–12). The Targumist made the same point by referring to the few who found salvation with Noah in the great deluge. From now on, emphasis will be on a renewed people for whom the future Zion will be prepared in a renewed world: new heaven, new earth, new city, new people (Isa 65–66).

Isaiah 60–62

This central panel of Trito-Isaiah begins with the announcement of good news for those who mourn over Jerusalem/Zion. It is presented as an apostrophe addressed to Zion, mother of the new people which will inhabit the city. It is close to the comforting words about Zion and her new family, and the apostrophe addressed to her, in Deutero-Isaiah (Isa 49.14–23; 54.1–17). In order to get the signature of the prophetic author in 61.1–3, precisely in the centre of chapters 60–62, the last strophe of the apostrophe is separated from the rest and located after that passage (61.3b–7). An affirmation of the truth of the prophet's prediction follows (61.8–9), then a brief psalm of praise and thanksgiving, similar to the fragmentary psalms we identified in Deutero-Isaiah. This brief psalm (61.10) concludes this first part of the central section.[16]

> I will rejoice in the Lord with all my heart,
> my whole being will exult in my God,
> for he has clothed me in the garments of salvation,
> he has covered me with the robe of victory;
> like a bridegroom with his festal garment,
> like a bride decked out in her jewels.

The language of rejoicing is characteristic of the hymns or psalms of praise and thanksgiving. These psalms also refer to the salvation and victory of God as a cause for rejoicing (e.g. Pss 24.5; 51.16). We meet the bridegroom and the bride again in the following passage about the New Jerusalem, still presented as a woman, the spouse of the Lord, now united or reunited with her children (62.1–5).[17] The brief address which follows draws attention to the watchmen or guards on the city walls (62.6–7). One would think that their task was keeping an eye on those approaching the city and, where necessary, defending it against the approach of enemies, but we are told that what they actually do is to constantly invoke the name of the Lord or, more literally, activate God's memory, keeping the Lord in remembrance of his promise to establish Jerusalem solid and firm and spread her renown throughout the world. This function is more in line with the temple singers who, we might say with some poetic licence, were never silent, functioning in the temple by day and night, and invoking the Lord God with music and singing. Perhaps, then, the author has conflated two distinct functions or used this unusual way to emphasize the importance of the temple cult and the role of the Levitical singers for the safety and well-being of the city.

---

[16]Isa 61.11 should be attached to 61.8–9 with which it is compatible. Its horticultural metaphor makes a poor match fit with the bride decked out in her finery in the previous verse.
[17]This passage will come up for discussion in the context of the Zion theme in the following chapter.

The core section of Trito-Isaiah concludes with a passage which stands by itself:[18]

> Pass through the gates, go out,
> Clear a road for my people;
> build a highway, build it up,
> remove the boulders;
> hoist a signal for the peoples.
> This is the Lord's proclamation
> to earth's farthest bounds:
> Tell the daughter of Zion,
> 'See, your deliverance comes.
> His reward is with him,
> his recompense before him.'
> They will be called the Holy People,
> the Redeemed of the Lord;
> and you will be called Sought After,
> City No Longer Forsaken
> raise a signal over the peoples. (62.1–12)

Five imperatives are addressed to a plurality, probably the prophet of 61.1–3 and his disciples; they are to prepare the processional route to the temple in the centre of Zion. A further command is given to announce to Zion that her salvation is at hand. God is near and his reward is with him; his recompense for what she has suffered goes before him. The light which was to come at the beginning of this mid-section is now identified with salvation. Beyond that, the imperatives will bring to mind the commands at the beginning of Deutero-Isaiah to prepare a way (40.1–5), but where the route was then for the repatriation of exiled Judaeans in real time, here it is a projection into the future, but a future which can change reality in the present.[19]

---

[18] The most important of the Qumran Isaian scrolls (1QIsa^a) has a significant gap between 62.9 and 62.10 and an empty half line between Isa 62.12 and 63.1. The translation is from the Revised English Bible.

[19] There is also a connection with Isa 40.9–10; Isa 62.11b repeats verbatim 40.10b ('His reward is with him/his recompense before him'). See also the cluster of imperatives at Isa 48.20 and 52.11–12.

7

Zion as reality and symbol in Psalms and Isaiah

Origins of the Zion traditions

The name Zion, of uncertain derivation, is certainly ancient since we first hear of it with reference to the pre-Israelite, Jebusite fortress in Jerusalem occupied by David and his band and thereafter known as the City of David.[1] In the course of time, the name came to be applied to Jerusalem, to the Jerusalem temple, and occasionally to the inhabitants of the city. Information on pre-Israelite Jerusalem is not abundant, limited as it is to what can be learned from reports on excavations in and around the city, often subject to revision, the Egyptian execration texts in which it is mentioned (nineteenth to eighteenth century B.C.E.) and, four centuries later during the Amarna period, the correspondence between the Pharaonic court and the Hurrian prince Abdi-Heba, vassal ruler under the Pharaoh of the city then called Urusalim (fourteenth century B.C.E.).[2] The mythology of pre-Israelite Jerusalem seems to have contributed to Zion's prestige as a holy place. The city took on some of the mythic features of the sacred Mount Zaphon, seat of the Syrian god Baal

---

[1] 2 Sam 5.7; 1 Kgs 8.1; 1 Chr 11.5.
[2] Texts in *ANET*, 328–9, 483–90; William L. Moran, *The Amarna Letters* (Baltimore and London: Johns Hopkins University Press, 1992); see the index under Jerusalem/ Urusalim.

and the assembly of lesser deities, identified with *Jebel 'el-Aqra'* near the estuary of the Orontes in north Syria. The myths associated with this site, familiar from the texts discovered at Ras Shamra-Ugarit on the Syrian Mediterranean coast, seem to have served as a model for Zion as a sacred site:

> Great is the Lord and most worthy of praise
> in the city of our God.
> His holy mountain is fair and lofty,
> the joy of all the earth.
> The mountain of Zion, the far recesses of the north
> is the city of the great King.
> God in her palaces
> is revealed as a tower of strength. (Ps 48.2–3 (E.T. 1–2))

The same motif appears in the boast of the king of Babylon in Isa 14.12–13:

> How have you fallen from the sky,
> Star of the dawning day!
> You thought in your heart:
> 'I will ascend to the sky,
> I will set up my throne
> higher than the highest stars,
> I will take my seat on the Mount of Assembly,
> in the furthest reaches of the north'.

Mount Zaphon (the word means 'north') is also a place of celebration and joyful festivity, like the Garden of Eden (Isa 51.3; Ezek 36.35). Zion likewise is 'the joy of all the earth' and through it flows a river, emblem of fertility and healing:

> There is a river whose streams bring joy to the city of God,
> the holy dwelling of the Most High (Ps 46.4)

> There (in Zion) the glorious name of the Lord will be ours,
> it will be a place of broad rivers and streams (Isa 33.21).

The mythology of pre-Israelite Jerusalem therefore contributed depth to Israelite Zion and gave it a more universal appeal.³ The sanctity of Zion was nevertheless due to the presence in it of the holy ark, the sacred emblem of the deity known as Lord of Hosts (*YHWH sĕbā'ôt*).

The history of the ark can be traced back to the sanctuary of Shiloh in the Central Highlands, territory of the tribe of Ephraim (1 Sam 3.3, 11), leaving open the possibility that the deity worshipped at Shiloh was only subsequently identified as Yahweh. Carried into battle as a war palladium, it was captured by the victorious Philistines, eventually returned by way of Beth-shemesh to Kiriath-jearim in Judah where it remained for twenty years (1 Sam 4.1–7.2), and from there transported in solemn procession by David to the City of David (2 Sam 6.1–19). It came to its final rest in the temple built by Solomon in Jerusalem (1 Kgs 8.1 = 2 Chr 5.2), according to the author of Chronicles on the site of the threshing floor of the Jebusite Araunah (in 1 Chronicles: Ornan) purchased by David (2 Sam 24.18–25).⁴ As the name, 'Lord of armies', suggests, this deity's earliest associations were with warfare, the many small-scale wars waged by its devotees and the need for protection in battle.

---

³On this mythic background to Zion, see Gerhard von Rad, 'Die Stadt auf dem Berge', in *Gesammelte Studien zum Alten Testament* (Munich: Kaiser, 1958), 214–24; Hans-Joachim Kraus, *Gottesdienst in Israel* (Munich: Kaiser, 1962), 213–20, 234–9 = *Worship in Israel. A Cultic History of the Old Testament* (Oxford: Blackwell, 1966), 181–3, 201–5; K. Rupprecht, *Der Tempel von Jerusalem. Gründung Salomos oder Jebusitisches Erbe?* (BZAW 144; Berlin and New York: de Gruyter, 1977); Ronald E. Clements, *Isaiah and the Deliverance of Jerusalem* (JSOT Sup 13; Sheffield: JSOT, 1984), 72–89; idem, 'Zion as Symbol and Political Reality: A Central Isaianic Quest,' in *Studies in the Book of Isaiah. FS. Willem A. M. Beuken*, ed. J. Van Ruiten and M. Vervenne (Leuven: Leuven University Press, 1997), 3–17; Hector Avalos, 'Zaphon, Mount (Place)', *ABD* VI. 1040–1; W. H. Mare, 'Zion (Place)', *ABD* VI 1096-97.

⁴1 Chr 21.28–22:1; 2 Chr 3.1. On the origins of the Zion tradition, see J. Jeremias, 'Lade und Zion. Zur Entstehung der Ziontradition', in *Probleme biblischer Theologie. Gerhard von Rad zum 70. Geburtstag*, ed. H. W. Wolff (Munich: Kaiser, 1971), 192–6; J. J. Roberts, 'The Davidic Origins of the Zion tradition', *JBL* 92 (1973), 329–44; B. Ollenburger, *Zion: the City of the Great King* (JSOTSup 41; Sheffield: JSOT, 1987); Jon D. Levenson, 'Zion Traditions', *ABD* VI: 1098–1102. On the early history of the ark see my *Gibeon and Israel. The Role of Gibeon and the Gibeonites in the Political and Religious History of Early Israel* (Cambridge: Cambridge University Press, 1972), especially pp. 65–83.

The hosts (armies) were, however, transferred from the earthly to the heavenly realm quite early, to judge by the appearance of the commander of the heavenly host to Joshua (Josh 5.13–14). There is also the vision of the prophet Micaiah ben Imlah during the reign of Ahab in the kingdom of Israel in which he saw the Lord enthroned and surrounded by the host of heaven (1 Kgs 22.19–23).

Several psalms preserve traces of the origins of temple worship outlined above, together with the sacred emblem of the object of worship which irradiated such great power. The pilgrim Ps 132 recalls the procession from Kiriath-jearim to Jerusalem. In recollecting the ancestral traditions, the Asaphite Ps 78 retells how their God abandoned his dwelling in Shiloh, chose the tribe of Judah over that of Ephraim, and established his new abode on Mount Zion like the high heaven (Ps 78.60–72). Psalm 68 records the effect on nature of the power emanating from the ark as the Israelites carried it with them in their journey through the wilderness, and Ps 24 concludes with what looks like the final stage in the ark's itinerary from Kiriath-jearim:

> Life up your heads, you gates,
> lift them up, you everlasting doors
> that the King of Glory may come in.
> Who is he, this King of Glory?
> The Lord of Hosts, he is the King of Glory.[5]

The title 'King of Glory', a title which occurs only here, has a particular significance. 'Glory' (*kābôd*) is an evocative term practically

---

[5] A similar 'entrance liturgy' is assumed for Pss 15.1–5, 100.4–5 and 118.19–20. In their discussion of Ps 118, Frank L.Hossfeld and Eric Zenger, *Psalms 3. A Commentary on Psalms 101-150* (Eng. Tr. Linda M. Maloney; Minneapolis: Fortress, 2011), 240–1, explain these passages as reflecting an official process of admission to participation in temple worship. Psalm 24.3–6 may qualify as such, for Ps 24.5–10 is about the entrance into the temple of 'the King of Glory', with allusion to the destination of the ark. Psalm 100 seems to refer to the temple musicians who did not need permission since they were participants in the liturgy. This may be deduced from the language associated with the *měšōrěrîm* ('singers') in v. 1 referring to exaltation, joyful singing, thanksgiving and praise. Psalm 118 is simply a request by a member of the public who wishes to enter to make a *tôdāh* (thanksgiving offering). Isaiah 33.14–15 seems to be modelled on the catechetical list in Ps 15 but not as qualifying for entry into the temple, not explicitly at any rate.

synonymous with the holy ark. It was there at the beginning of the recorded history of the ark as a component of the name Ichabod given the child born to the priest Eli's daughter-in-law after she heard that the ark had been taken by the Philistines.[6] It was still there at its final destination in Solomon's newly built temple, for we are told that the Glory filled the temple, though concealed by the numinous cloud of incense (1 Kgs 8.11). Wherever mention is made in psalms of God's glory and power ('*ōz*), we may suspect an allusion to the holy ark. Psalm 29.1 and Ps 96.7 urge the worshippers to 'ascribe to the Lord glory and power' and in Ps 63.3 the psalmist says to the Lord, 'I have looked on you in the sanctuary, beholding your power and glory'. When referring to the Philistine victory and capture of this sacred palladium, the author of Ps 78.61 confesses that Yahweh had 'delivered his power into captivity, his glory into the hands of the enemy'. But even more in evidence in Psalms and Isaiah than 'King of Glory' is the title 'Lord of the (heavenly) Hosts' which also originated in Ephraimite Shiloh (1 Sam 1.3, 11; 4.4). We shall return to these titles at a later point in the discussion.

Zion in Psalms: The pilgrim psalms

We begin with the 'Psalms of Ascent' or 'Pilgrim Psalms' (Pss 120–134), since the destination of the pilgrimage, which includes the return from exile, is Zion. *Zion* is named thirty-eight times in Psalms and forty-seven times in Isaiah, more than in all other books in the Hebrew Bible together. In Psalms, it is named most frequently in the fifth book (Pss 107–150, fourteen times), which includes the fifteen pilgrim psalms to be sung when 'going up' to Zion. They replicate the original transfer of the ark from Shiloh by way of Kiriath-jearim while also commemorating the return to Zion from the land of exile in Babylon – whatever their original purpose may have been.[7] Ps 126 celebrates the reversal of fortune, the return from exile, in the

---

[6] 1 Sam 4.21–22. The meaning of this name of ill omen (*'i-kābôd*) is uncertain: either 'where is the Glory?' or 'alas, the Glory', or 'the Glory is no more'.
[7] According to m. Sukkah 5.4 'countless Levites played on harps, lyres, cymbals, trumpets and (other) instruments of music on the fifteen steps leading down from the Court of the Israelites to the Court of the Women, corresponding to the fifteen Songs of Ascent in the Psalms'. Much the same in m. Middot 2.5.

physical language of the temple singers – laughter, shouting for joy, loud singing, all like a dream come true.[8] We recall that the temple singers were deported with other temple personnel who survived the sack of the city, the murder and the mayhem, in 586 B.C.E. and, according to one account (Neh 7.43–44), 148 singers of the guild of Asaph, twice as many as Levites, were eventually repatriated. Psalm 132 recalls the primal 'ascent', the transfer of the ark to Jerusalem by David and the establishment of the liturgy in Solomon's temple by the priests in their splendid vestments and the Levitical singers with their loud, joyful acclamations.[9] Ps 133, in which brotherly love is celebrated with the odd metaphor of the precious oil on Aaron's beard, has given rise to a great deal of mostly inconclusive discussion, with one commentator suggesting that Aaron has been dragged into it by the beard.[10] Leaving aside the beard for the moment, I venture to add one more hypothesis to those available. Mention of Aaron in connection with the blessings of friendship and good relations may be read as an implicit rebuke directed by the dominant Aaronite–Zadokite priesthood at the Levitical claim to greater autonomy and control in the temple economy and the conduct of the services, this at a time when the temple singers were already co-opted into the ranks of the Levites. This claim, with the tension within the temple personnel to which it led, is an important aspect of second temple studies first put on the agenda, to the best of my knowledge, by Hermann Vogelstein in 1889.[11] We shall return to it in a later chapter.

---

[8]REB 'like people renewed in health' derives MT כחלמים (v. 1) from חלם, 'to become strong', 'to regain strength' rather than 'to dream', but חלם, with the meaning accepted by REB, occurs only once, at Job 39.4, and in any case MT seems more appropriate in the context.

[9]That the *ḥāsîdîm* ('devout') mentioned together with the priests are in fact *měšōrěrîm* ('singers') seems to be suggested by their loud acclamations (*rinnāh*), language closely associated with the temple singers (132.9, 16). In much the same way, the *'ăbādîm* ('servants of the Lord)' of Ps 134.1 who take up their position (literally 'stand') by night in the house of the Lord may also refer to the temple singers. Reference to a night service of praise and thanksgiving is hinted at here and there in psalms (42.9; 88.2–3; 92.3; 119.55, 62) and is stated explicitly in 1 Chr 9.33.

[10]For a review of the range of opinion on these three verses, see most recently Hossfeld and Zenger, *Psalms 3*, 469–83.

[11]Hermann Vogelstein, *Der Kampf zwischen Priestern und Leviten seit den Tagen Ezechiels: Eine Historisch-Kritische Untersuchung* (Stettin: Verlag von Friedrich Nagel

Psalms of the Korahite guild

The psalms in which Zion is most clearly thematic are those assigned to the Korahite and Asaphite guilds. Rubrics attached to most of the psalms assign twelve each to these two guilds.[12] We saw earlier that Korah is listed as one of Esau's sons, therefore Edomite or south Judaean, to whom the author of Chronicles has assigned a Levitical pedigree as descendant of the patriarch Levi (1 Chr 6.1–8, 22–23, cf. Gen 36.14). Korah is said to have died in the earthquake which brought the Levitical rebellion in the wilderness to an abrupt conclusion, but his sons survived, according to Num. 26.11, a notice which acknowledges the presence and activity of the Korahite guild ('the sons of Korah', as in the psalm rubrics) in the temple service at the time of writing. Nothing in the psalms of Korah alludes to the Edomite origins of the Korahites. They have been thoroughly indigenized in Judah and several of them evince a strong attachment to Jerusalem-Zion. The Korahite author of Ps 42–43 prays passionately that he may return soon to 'the holy mountain', to God's dwelling in order to praise God (Ps 43.3–4).[13] Ps 46.5 mentions a river which brings joy to the city of God, an evidently mythic embellishment since rivers are not found on mountains, perhaps, therefore, suggested by antithesis to the quaking

---

(Paul Niekammer, 1889). See also R. Meyer, 'Levitische Emanzipationsbestrebungen in nachexilischer Zeit', *Orientalische Literaturzeitung* 41 (1938): 721–8.

[12]Asaphite psalms: 50, 73–83. Korahite psalms: 42–49, 84–85, 87–88. Psalms 42 and 43 are listed as distinct but structurally make up one psalm only, as is clear from the refrain at Ps 42.6, 42.12 and Ps 43.5. On the Korahite psalms, see Günther Wanke, *Die Ziontheologie der Korachiten in ihrem tradttionsgeschichtlichen Zusammenhang* (BZAW 97; Berlin: de Gruyter, 1966); Erich Zenger, 'Zur redaktionsgeschichtlichen Bedeutung der Korachpsalmen', in *Neue Wege der Psalmenforschung*, ed. K. Seybold and E. Zenger (Freiburg: Herder, 1994), 175–98.

[13]The author of Ps 42 recalls the temple and its liturgies with longing while resident in 'the land of Jordan, Hermon and Mount Mizar', this last generally taken to be one of the peaks of Mt. Hermon (v. 6b). We are given no hint why he was languishing in that region near the sources of the Jordan. Perhaps an earlier version read Hebron (וחברו) for Hermon (חרמון) and Yizhar (יצהר) for Mizar (מצער), both names associated with the southern Judaean origins of Korah (1 Chr 2.43; Exod 6.18). Psalm 84.7 refers to 'the valley of Baca' meaning either 'the waterless valley' (as REB) or 'the valley of weeping' following LXX (*en tē koiladi tou klauthmōnos*) and Vulg.(*in valle fletus*). See Frank-Lothar Hossfeld and Erich Zenger, *Psalms 2* (Minneapolis: Fortress, 2005), 349, 355.

mountains and foaming waters immediately preceding. The same psalm has a refrain, 'the Lord of Hosts is with us, the God of Jacob is our fortress' (vv. 8, 12), which inevitably brings Zion to mind. We should note in passing that the frequent allusion in these psalms of Korah to 'the people of Jacob' (Pss 44.5; 85.2), 'the pride of Jacob' (Ps 47.5), and 'the God of Jacob' (46.8, 12; 84.9), this last parallel with the quintessential Zion title 'Lord of Hosts', does not imply a northern Israelite provenance for the Korahite singers. 'Jacob' occurs frequently in Deutero-Isaiah in apposition to Israel and with reference to the prophet's Judaean contemporaries. In Isa 2.2–5, 'the God of Jacob' is another name for the God resident in Zion.

The Korahite psalm 48 begins by offering praise 'in the city of our God':

> Great is the Lord and most worthy of praise
> in the city of our God.
> His holy mountain is fair and lofty,
> the joy of the whole earth.
> The mountain of Zion, the far recesses of the north,
> is the city of the great King. (Ps 48.2–3)

The psalm ends with an invitation to the reader to visit Zion, count its towers and consider well its ramparts, a conclusion reminiscent of Gilgamesh's invitation to Urshanabi on his return to Uruk to inspect the ramparts, foundations, and brickwork of his great city which, if so, would demonstrate that the singers were readers as well as singers.[14] Here and throughout these psalms we hear this note of intense attachment to Zion, its temple, and the God whose dwelling it is. In Ps 84, the author declares those fortunate who, like himself, live in God's house.[15] A day in the temple is worth a thousand anywhere else, and he asserts that he would rather find himself at the threshold of the temple without being able to enter it than dwell in the tents of the wicked.[16] The same enthusiasm for

---

[14] *ANET* 2nd edn, 97.
[15] The temple singers and instrumentalists were on call day and night, as the psalms themselves attest (Pss 42.9; 88.2; 92.2–3; 134.1), and therefore had quarters in the temple precincts as stated in 1 Chr 9.33.
[16] Ps 84.11b. The NRSV translation 'I would rather be a doorkeeper in the house of my God than live in the tents of wickedness' is misleading. There is no doorkeeper

city and temple informs Ps 87. This Korahite psalm is introduced with praise of Zion, beloved of God:

> The city the Lord founded stands on the holy hills.
> He loves the gates of Zion
> more than all the dwellings of Jacob.
> Glorious things are spoken about you, city of God.

There is a range of opinion on the five foreign peoples named in the following verses as to whether they are foreigners, proselytes, or diaspora Jews, and whether what is described is conceived as happening in real time or in an imagined future.[17] What at least is clear is that they are being registered as citizens of Zion. The lands of origin of these foreigners represent the four cardinal points as seen from Zion, the centre of the world, the *axis mundi*: Rahab (i.e. Egypt, as Isa 30.7; 51.9) to the south; Babel (i.e. Babylon) to the east; Philistia to the west; and Tyre to the north. Kush, usually translated 'Ethiopia' or 'Nubia', seems to have been added as an afterthought, perhaps because it is so often linked with Egypt (Isa 20.3–5; 43.3; 45.14), or on account of the Jewish settlement on the island of Elephantine (Jeb) at the first cataract of the Nile. At all events, the basic theme is repatriation, a process which will be completed at an indeterminate date in the future, or perhaps only in the last days, as an Isaianic saying with the customary eschatological incipit 'on that day' attests:

> On that day the Lord will extend his hand yet a second time to recover the remnant that is left of his people, from Assyria, Egypt, Patros, Ethiopia (Kush), from Elam, Shinar, Hamath and the coastlands of the sea. (Isa 11.11)

The list is more complete than the list of those registered by the Lord in Ps 87, but all five named in Ps 87 are also among those repatriated

---

(*šōʻēr*) in this verse, and the verb used (*hištopēp*, hapax) means to stand (JPS) or linger (REB) at the threshold (*sap*) without entering.

[17] See, among many others, C. A. Briggs and E. G. Briggs, *A Critical and Exegetical Commentary on Isaiah*. Vol.II (Edinburgh: T. & T. Clark, n.d.), 239–42; Günther Wanke, *Die Zionstheologie der Korachiten* (Berlin: Töpelmann, 1966), 21–2, 31–40; Artur Weiser, *The Psalms. A Commentary* (Philadelphia: Westminster, 1962), 579–84; Hossfeld and Zenger, *Psalms 2*, 377–88.

in Isa 11.11. Assyria can stand for Mesopotamia, Patros is 'the south land' of Egypt, and 'the coastlands of the sea' correspond to Philistia and Tyre. The citizens of the future Zion include repatriated Jews certainly but, in keeping with a dominant Isaianic theme, Zion will be open to all people who seek righteousness. *It will be the religious capital of the world*.[18]

The message of this Ps 87 is a source of joy and a cause for celebration. Unfortunately, however, the final verse (Ps 87.7) is textually defective and its translation somewhat speculative, as we see from recent English-language versions:

> Singers and dancers alike say, 'All my springs are in you.' (NRSV)
>
> Singers and dancers alike say, 'The source of all good is in you.' (REB)
>
> Singers and dancers alike [will say]: 'All my roots are in you'. (JPS)

Perhaps what the poet was trying to say is that the rejoicing at this ceremony of accreditation of new citizens of Zion took the form of a party with dancing to the tune of a love song for the city, here as in Isaiah addressed as a woman;[19] a song perhaps composed for the occasion with the title *kol-maʿyānay bāk* which could with a little license be translated to 'In you are all my springs of life-giving water'.

Psalms of the Asaphite guild

By the time of Ezra in the mid-fifth century B.C.E., this guild of temple singers was pre-eminent and not yet incorporated into the ranks of the Levites. The list of the first of the deported to be repatriated under Cyrus II includes 128 Asaphite singers according to Ezra 2.41 or 148 according to Neh 7.44, twice the number of Levites (74). During the governorship of Nehemiah, a member of the guild was even overseer of the Levites (Neh 11.22). These Asaphite singers performed their service as musical specialists,

---

[18]Isa 2.2–5; 11.11; 19.24–25; 60.1–3; 66.18–23.
[19]Isa 52.1–2; 54.1–17; 60.1–22; 62.1–5; 66.7–11.

we are told, according to the prescriptions of David and Solomon since 'in the days of David and Asaph long ago there was a leader of the singers, and there were hymns of praise and thanksgiving to God' (Neh 12.46). The author of Chronicles fills in the details. Asaph, eponymous founder of the guild, was appointed, together with Heman and Ethan, by David to minister before the ark with singing and musical accompaniment.[20] He and his associates performed the same task at the dedication of Solomon's temple (2 Chr 5.12), and from then on, as long as the temple stood.

The Asaph collection consists in Pss 50 and 73–83. Psalm 50 presents a scene in which the Lord God indicts his people from his throne in Zion, 'the perfection of beauty', in the presence of all creation, the heavens and the earth. Zion is therefore represented as the centre and axis of the world built, as another Asaph psalm puts it, 'like the high heavens, like the earth he has founded for ever' (Ps 78.69). Psalm 78, the longest in the Asaph group, presents a résumé of the prehistory which emphasizes the failure of the central and northern tribes referred to as Ephraim or Joseph to be faithful to their God, the last phase of which begins with the delivery of the ark (the divine glory and power) into the hands of the enemy and the abandonment of the Shiloh sanctuary ('the tent of Joseph', 78.67), concluding with the election of Judah and the establishment of Zion:

> He chose the tribe of Judah,
> Mount Zion which he loved,
> He built his sanctuary like the high heavens,
> founded like the earth to last for ever. (vv. 68–69)

This psalm will remind us that in both Psalms and Isaiah Zion is not just the focus of shared desires and aspirations for the future; it is a present political and religious reality, chosen as the location for David and his successors through whom the divine power would be brought to bear in the political realm (Pss 2, 110, 20). It involves a real history. The rejoicing in the Asaphite Ps 76 when the God of Zion 'broke the flashing arrows, the shield, the sword, and the weapons of war' may, for example, reflect the euphoria following the failure of Sennacherib's Assyrians to take Jerusalem in 701 B.C.E.,

---

[20] 1 Chr 6.24; 15.17–19; 16.5,7,37; 25.1–2, 6, 9.

as recorded in Isa 36–37. Psalm 74 describes the sack of Jerusalem and the burning of the temple, calling on God to remember Mount Zion and take note of the 'perpetual ruins' (74.2). The author of Ps 51 prays that God might 'do good to Zion, rebuild the wall of Jerusalem' (51.20), while another psalm petitions that he might 'save Zion and rebuild the cities of Judah' (69.36). Yet another psalmist hopes that God will build up Zion and appear in his glory (102.17). Psalm 137, which all lovers of the Hebrew language will know by heart, testifies to the sadness of temple singers in the Babylonian diaspora who are asked by their Babylonian neighbours to sing 'the songs of Zion', that is, the psalms composed by them for the temple liturgy, but feel obliged to decline. Then, finally, there is Ps 126, in which the psalmist and his fellow musicians, perhaps members of the same singers guild as in Ps 137,[21] either anticipate a proximate return from exile or have actually returned.

The most striking aspect, however, and the one with the greatest emotional charge, is the presentation of Zion as the object of desire and longing on the part of those far distant from it or deprived of access to it. This should not surprise us since what has come to be called Zionism, whether ancient or modern, is essentially a diasporic phenomenon. So the psalmist prays:

> If only deliverance for Israel might come from Zion!
> When the Lord restores his people's fortune;[22]
> let Jacob rejoice, let Israel be glad. (Ps 14.7 = Ps 53.7)

Zion in Isaiah

In the book of Isaiah, there is the same duality about Zion as in Psalms: on the one hand, the actual city Jerusalem with its many problems, its often incompetent and corrupt leaders both secular and religious, and its precarious position in relation to the current

---

[21]Suggested by the allusion to 'singing aloud for joy' (*rinnāh*, vv. 2 and 6), a term often associated with the singers.

[22]The meaning of the expression *šûb šĕbût* refers either to reversal of fortune in a general sense or to return from exile, depending on the context. The expression is most common in Jeremiah where the exilic context is almost always explicit (Jer 29.14; 30.3, 18; 31.23; 32.44; 33.7, 11, 26).

imperial power; on the other hand, an eschatological symbol of light in the surrounding darkness, the original *cité lumière*, a place of security and salvation for the righteous and of judgement for sinners.[23] So, for example, Isa 1.8 speaks with some exaggeration about 'daughter Zion' besieged and left looking like a hut in a plot of cucumbers, probably with reference to the actual siege of Jerusalem by the Assyrian army in 701 B.C.E. In Isa 3.16–26, 'daughters of Zion', namely, Jerusalemite women, probably at the court, are berated for going around with necks thrust out, ogling eyes, and walking with mincing gate, though in truth none of these seems to be serious infractions of the social order. Throughout the entire first major section of the book, there is much political commentary, condemnation of neighbouring and therefore hostile peoples, especially in Isa 13–23, and assurances addressed to the inhabitants of Jerusalem-Zion, especially in Isa 28–35.

The contemporaneity of Zion is therefore fully in evidence in Isaiah, as it is in Psalms, but Zion is also, and frequently, a focal point in the distant future or in the end time. This is apparent in Isa 1.27–31, the final addition to the first chapter of the book:

Zion will be redeemed by justice,
her penitents by righteousness,
but rebels and sinners will be destroyed together,
and those who forsake Yahweh will be consumed. (1.27–28)

What is said here is compatible with what is said about Zion in Third Isaiah, in keeping with other links between the first and the two last chapters of the book: the radical distinction between penitents[24] and those who rebel against God (59.20; 66.24), the prospect of salvation for the renewed community in Zion and judgement on the reprobates

---

[23]In chapters 36–39, we find only a reference to 'the virgin daughter Zion' (37.22) and to 'Mount Zion' (37.22); the former in an oracular statement of the prophet (37.22-29), the latter in a sign given to reassure Hezekiah. The absence of any allusion to Zion in chapters 38 and 39 creates a problem for the interesting thesis of the centrality of these chapters in the book as argued by Ulrich Berges, 'Die Ziontheologie des Buches Jesaja', *Estudios Biblicos* 58 (2000): 167-98.

[24]Hebrew *šābîm*, which can also be translated 'those who return' (>verb *šûb*), namely, from exile.

(66.12–16), and the image of the inextinguishable fire of judgement (66.15, 24 cf. 1.31).[25] The second title in Isa 2.1 is followed by a statement of what will happen 'at the end of the days' when the mountain of the Lord's house will be set over all other mountains (Isa 2.2–5). The temple in Zion will be the spiritual centre of the world. People from all nations will come there in pilgrimage to find enlightenment and moral instruction. The oracle goes on to predict that arbitration will take the place of conflict, warfare will be abolished, and a restored and purified community will live in security on its own land. This eschatological vision, which has lost none of its resonance, together with a similar statement about the core community of the last days in Isa 4.2–6 introduced with the formula 'on that day', the most common eschatological indicator in prophetic texts, serves to bracket the denunciations of different examples of moral disorder in contemporaneous society (Isa 2.6–4.1). An oracular passage later in the book addressed to 'my people who dwell in Zion' (Isa 10.20–23) predicts exile from which only a remnant will return: 'A remnant will return, the residue of Jacob to God their strength ... destruction is decreed, retribution comes like a flood, for the Sovereign Lord of the hosts will bring about the destruction that is decreed in the midst of the earth' (Isa 10.20–23). In the following paragraph, the inhabitants of Zion are told to put aside fear; the oppressor's burden will be removed from their shoulders and his yoke destroyed (10.24–27):

> My people who dwell in Zion, do not be afraid of the Assyrians when they beat you with a rod and wield their stick over you as the Egyptians did. In a short while the time of wrath will be over, and my anger will be directed at their destruction.[26]

In reading such passages, we bear in mind that the story of Israel is a story, often repeated throughout history to the present, of small

---

[25] Also reproduced, Isa 1.29–30 is the condemnation of idolatrous cults associated with sacred trees and gardens (Isa 57.5; 65.3–5; 66.17).

[26] Verbal parallels in Isa 10.22–27 with the book of Daniel suggest a date late in the Hellenistic period for these verses; see Dan 11.36 which predicts that the tyrant (Antiochus IV) will prevail *'ad-kālāh zaʻam kî nehĕrāsāh neʻĕsātāh*, 'until wrath is spent, when what is decreed is accomplished'. Cf. *kālāh zaʻam* in Isa 10.25, which suggests that the Assyrians stand for the Seleucids, the dynasty to which Antiochus belonged, in the same way that elsewhere in Isaiah 'Egyptians' can stand for the Ptolemies, for example, in Isa 19.24–25.

countries faced with the ambitions and resources of great empires and superpowers. The inhabitants of Zion are also addressed in 30.19-22. They are told to weep no more, for even though they will suffer affliction, their teacher will no longer remain hidden but will continue to guide them, if not in person then as they remember him and put into practice his teaching. In both 10.20-27 and 30.19-20, the inhabitants of Zion are the 'remnant', the core of a new community which will be described more fully in the last major section of the book as 'the servants of the LORD' and 'those who tremble at his word'.[27]

In several other texts in Isa 1-35 in which Zion appears, sometimes against the grain of the surrounding text, Zion stands for a future of security for the afflicted, poor, and destitute (14.28-32), a place where justice and righteousness can flourish (28.14-22; 33.2-5), and a space which the oppressive power of empires – Assyrians, Babylonians, or whichever – cannot penetrate (31.10; 33.17-24).[28]

A provisional conclusion: We saw earlier that the ark tradition was transmitted along both cultic and prophetic channels, but if we are to speak of interdependence of some kind, it appears more likely that the authors and editors of the book of Isaiah, more especially

---

[27] Isa 65.8-10, 13-16; 66.5. On the identity of the unnamed and mysterious teacher, see my essay 'Who is the Teacher in Isa 30:20 who will no Longer Remain Hidden?', in *Recognizing the Margins: Developments in Biblical & Theological Studies. Essays in Honour of Seán Freyne*, ed. Werner G. Jeanrond and Andrew D. H. Mayes (Dublin: Columba Press, 2006), 9-23.

[28] On Zion in Psalms and Isaiah, there is a formidable bibliography. See Jon D. Levenson, 'Zion Traditions', *ABD* VI 1098-1102; Hans Wildberger, 'Die Völker Wallfahrt zum Zion: Jes II 1-5', *VT* 7 (1957): 62-81; John H. Hayes, 'The Traditions of Zion's Inviolability', *JBL* 82 (1963): 419-26; G. Wanke, *Die Ziontheologie der Korachiten in ihrem traditionsgeschichtlichen Zusammenhang* (BZAW 97; Berlin: de Gruyter, 1966); Ronald E. Clements, *Isaiah and the Deliverance of Jerusalem* (Sheffield: JSOTSup 13, 1980); idem, 'Zion as Symbol and Political Reality: A Central Isaianic Quest', in *Studies in the Book of Isaiah. FS. For Willem A. M. Beuken*, ed. J. Van Ruiten and M. Vervenne (Leuven: Leuven University Press, 1997), 3-17; Ben Ollenburger, 'Zion, the City of the Great King', *JSOT* 41 (1987); Christopher Seitz, *Zion's Final Destiny: The Development of the Book of Isaiah. A Reassessment of Isaiah 36-39* (Minnesota: Fortress, 1991); Ulrich Berges, 'Die Ziontheologie des Buches Jesaja', *Est. Bibl.* 58 (2000): 167-98; Coriana Körting, *Zion in den Psalmen* (FAT 48; Tübingen: Mohr Siebeck, 2006); Tomas Willi, 'Zion und der Sitz im Leben der "Aufstiegslieder" Psalm 120-134', in idem (ed.), *Israel und die Völker: Studien zur Literatur und Geschichte Israels in Perserzeit* (SBA 55; Stuttgart, 2012), 71-81.

with respect to the first major section of the book, were drawing on these ancient traditions of Zion passed on and perpetuated in the temple liturgy. This would be the case especially with regard to the Zion of the end times. The Zion of the book of Isaiah is primarily and most strikingly an eschatological symbol, a focus of aspirations for a future quite different from the unsatisfactory present, and a future for all peoples everywhere. This aspect is not absent in Psalms, but the greater emphasis is on the actual city which, after the destruction of 586 B.C.E. and the deportations, was the destination greatly desired, and by some attained, among expatriate Judaeans including members of the temple musician guilds.[29] However, in the present state of our knowledge, or rather ignorance, the wiser course may be to think in terms of an ongoing, rich interactivity, the authors of both compilations drawing on the same themes and sharing similar language. It is tempting to think of an actual encounter of temple singers and composers awaiting repatriation, or actually repatriated, with the learned and pious scribes who, then or later, were poring over and annotating the words of the great prophet of the eighth century B.C.E., long dead, but on such a 'meeting of minds' the texts are silent.[30]

Titulature of the God of Zion

The Lord of Hosts enthroned upon the cherubim

The title most intimately associated with the holy ark, temple worship, and Zion, 'The Lord of Hosts enthroned upon the cherubim', may have belonged to a local Syrian-Palestinian deity in the pre-Israelite

---

[29]The list of those returning under Cyrus II in Ezra 2 includes 128 Asaphite singers (Ezra 2.41).
[30]On the respective *Trägerkreise* of these Isaianic and Psalmodic compositions, their putative authors and their interactions, see most recently Ulrich Berges, *Jesaja. Der Prophet und das Buch* (Leipzig: Evangelische Verlagsanstalt, 2010), 11–46; idem, '"Singt dem Herrn ein neues Lied" Zu den Trägerkreisen von Jesajabuch und Psalter', in *Trägerkreise in den Psalmen*, ed. J. Bremer, F.-L. Hossfeld and T. M. Steiner (Göttingen: Vandenhoeck & Ruprecht, 2016), 11–33.

period.³¹ Given the constant struggle for territory and endemic tribal warfare of the period of the Israelite settlement, the deity, now Yahweh God of Israel, was expected to provide assistance and protection in battle, and the failure to do so in a hostile encounter with the Philistines was the occasion for great consternation only mitigated by the trouble which the ark, captured in battle, brought on the victors (1 Samuel 4–6). The ark dedicated to 'the Lord of Hosts' became the central object of worship in the Jerusalem temple liturgy, though what shape it assumed, whether representative of an empty throne, or a footstool to the throne (suggested by Ps 99.5 and 1 Chr 28.2), or some other form, remains unclear. The title itself occurs with great frequency in Isaiah (fifty-five times), rather less so in Psalms (fifteen times). Its essentially liturgical character is most clearly in evidence in the vision of Isa 6.1–13 in which the seraphim engage in a liturgy of praise to the thrice-holy Lord of Hosts and in which the prophet has a glimpse of the same Lord enthroned in glory:³²

The Holy One of Israel

Closely related to *YHWH sĕbā'ôt* is 'the Holy One of Israel' (*qĕdôš yiśrā'ēl*), of frequent occurrence in Isa 1–55 (twenty-six times) but only twice in Third Isaiah, in an apostrophe to Zion, the city destined to shed light upon a dark world (Isa 60.9, 14). It is fairly frequent in Psalms (71.22; 78.41; 89.19), but in no other biblical text, with the sole exception of Jer 50.29 and 51.5.³³ I take this distribution

---

³¹As pointed out by von Rad, 'The Tent and the Ark', in *The Problem of the Hexateuch and Other Essays* (Edinburgh and London: Oliver & Boyd, 1965), 114–16. The ark is referred to in 1–2 Samuel as 'the ark of God' almost as often as 'the ark of YHWH'.
³²For the full form of the title, see Pss 80.2 and 99.1, also 1 Sam 4.4, 2 Sam 6.2, 2 Kgs 19.15 = Isa 37.16, 1 Chr 13.6. The reference is to a throne the armrests of which are in the form of protective deities or sphinxes, generally part-leonine or bovine, part-aquiline and part-human (German: *Mischwesen*).
³³The long section comprising Jer 50–51 is dated by several scholars close to Deutero-Isaiah in the mid-sixth century B.C.E. and its parallels with Deutero-Isaiah's anti-Babylonian polemic are not difficult to detect. See the commentaries of Volz, Rudolph, Weiser, Bright ad locum and, more recently, William McKane, *Jeremiah Volume II* (Edinburgh: T. & T. Clark, 1996), 1249–1359. Zion is mentioned frequently in these two chapters.

of the term to be one more indication that these two compilations – Isaiah and Psalms – constitute a distinctive modality of religious expression arising out of shared traditions and a shared liturgical experience. Where in Isaiah 'the Holy One of Israel' is addressed or speaks, more often than not reproach and condemnation in the present alternates with the prospect of a chastened and enlightened people in the end time. This prospective note is sounded in the psalm which rounds off Isa 1–12, as was noted earlier.

The Strong One of Jacob

Another title closely associated with 'the Lord of Hosts' is 'the Strong One of Jacob' (*'ăbîr ya'ăqôb*), which, apart from Jacob's deathbed oracle on his son Joseph, father of Ephraim and Manasseh (Gen 49.24), appears only once in Ps 132 and three times in Isaiah, once in each of the three major sections (Isa 1.24; 49.26; 60.16). Psalm 132 celebrates the finding and transfer of the ark by stages from Shiloh. According to the opening verses of the psalm, this came about as a consequence of a vow of David to find a permanent abode for the Strong One of Jacob, another title of the Lord Yahweh, as the same psalm makes apparent (Ps 132.1–5). This title appears to have originated in the Kingdom of Samaria, as also the similar 'Strong One of Israel' (*'ăbîr yiśrā'ēl*), both perhaps as demythologized forms of the deity worshipped at Bethel under the figure of a bull (*'abbîr*), as Bernhardt Duhm suggested many years ago.[34] The similar title 'the God of Jacob' occurs only once in Isaiah, in an eschatological saying about the future Zion in which the resident deity is 'the "God of Jacob" and Zion's inhabitants are described as "the house of Jacob"' (Isa 2.2–5, cf. Mic 4.1–4). This eschatological passage is also in debt to those psalms which offer praise and thanksgiving to the God of Jacob, including three Asaphite psalms (Pss 75, 76, 81) and two from the Korahite guild (46, 84).[35] Together with other

---

[34] Bernhardt Duhm, *Das Buch Jesaja* (Göttingen: Vandenhoeck & Ruprecht, 1892), 34. He wondered whether Isaiah would have been as strict as the Masoretes in the spelling of the word.

[35] The other references to the God of Jacob are in Pss 20.2; 94.7; 114.7; 146.5. Also relevant is the mention in Ps 80 of the Lord God of hosts enthroned in the presence of Joseph, Benjamin, Ephraim, and Manasseh.

indications, these titles indicate that the Jerusalem cult owed a debt to traditions from the region of the northern and central tribes. This conclusion would not be surprising in view of the origins of Levites, and therefore Levitical singers, in the former kingdom of Israel. This came about following on the exclusion by Jeroboam of descendants of Levi from service in cult centres in that kingdom (1 Kgs 12.31-32), their subsequent transfer to Judah, and, after surviving many vicissitudes, their service in the rebuilt temple of Jerusalem (2 Kgs 23.9). In short, it seems that the Isaian scribes were able to draw on a rich source of liturgical usage, which finds one of its clearest expressions in Ps 132.

8

The two ways in Psalms and Isaiah

The two ways

In the present chapter, we will discuss language and terminology in Psalms and Isaiah indicative of stages in the formation of self-segregating religious groups and, eventually, sects. The title of this chapter, which will bring to mind the first sentence in the *Didache* ('The Teaching of the Twelve Apostles'), perhaps also the teaching on the Two Spirits in the Qumran Community Rule,[1] locates the discussion within the broader framework of basic moral teaching in both Judaism and Christianity. A feature common to both Psalms and Isaiah is the display of religious and moral character in terms of contrasting categories as, for example, the righteous, the devout, the poor, the servants of the Lord over against the wicked, the sinners, the scoffers, the godless. These dichotomies are not of course confined to Psalms and Isaiah but they are most clearly in evidence there. The use of such terminology and language achieves social visibility when those in the first set are able to maintain their moral integrity and their identity only by a degree of withdrawal and separation within the society, at which point self-segregation takes the form of conventicles, the ecclesiolae in the

---

[1] *Didache* 1.1: 'There are two ways, one of life and one of death, and there is a great difference between these two ways'; 1QS 3.17: 'God created humanity to rule the world and placed within them two spirits for them to deal with until his appointed time'.

ecclesia mentioned earlier, and eventually, in some instances, sects. We have a good example of this tendency in the first psalm, which sets up a sharp contrast between the righteous (*saddîqîm*) and the unrighteous (*rěšāʿîm*) with reference to the moral character of their lives and their ultimate fate. A close reading of Ps 1 will provide an introduction to the moral characterization by type common to both Psalms and Isaiah and, at the same time, to an important aspect of social and religious life in Jewish communities during the Persian and Hellenistic periods, namely, the emergence of self-segregating or coercively segregated groups or conventicles, which will contribute eventually to the well-known sects (*haireseis*) of the Graeco-Roman period, those noticed by Josephus – Pharisees, Sadducees, and Essenes[2] – and those which escaped his attention, for example the *nazōraioi* (Nazarenes) of Acts 24.5.

The righteous (*saddîqîm*)

A basic term for moral approval in Psalms and Isaiah is *sedāqāh*, usually translated 'righteousness', the quality possessed by the righteous person (*saddîq*). In biblical usage, this term, whether as substantive or adjective, has a wide range of meanings. It can mean simply being right as opposed to being wrong (e.g. Isa 41.26); it can connote legitimacy, for example with respect to a claimant to Davidic descent (e.g. Jer 23.5), or innocence established by judicial process (e.g. Exod 23.7–8; Isa 5.23; 29.21). Less commonly, it can mean success in warfare viewed as vindication of one's cause as righteous, for example where the future saviour king of Zech 9.9 is described as 'triumphant and victorious' (*saddîq wěnôšāʿ*).[3] The most common meaning, however, is righteousness or moral probity which occurs often in Psalms, most frequently in Books 1 and 5, beginning with Ps 1. While this meaning entails concern for and observance of the rules of good behaviour in society, the moral

---

[2] *Ant.* 13.171; 18.11–22; *War* 2.119–166.
[3] 180 The translation is from NRSV; compare REB 'his cause won, his victory gained'. In later usage, the corresponding substantive *sědāqāh*, usually translated 'righteousness', has the extended meaning of vindication or salvation, following on a judicial decision either human or divine (e.g. Isa 1.27; 59.9; 61.10–11).

order is always associated with good relations with God, with being acceptable to God. This is the meaning which continues to be in evidence in the use of the corresponding Greek term *dikaios* in early Christian writings. A special instance is the use of the epithet to characterize certain individuals in terms of uniquely exemplary life and closeness to God. In this sense, Noah was *saddîq* (Gen 6.9; 7.1) and the same is predicated of Abraham, friend of God, in equivalent terms (Gen 15.6). For the Qumran sectarians, this title is attached to the Teacher of Righteousness (or perhaps, 'the Legitimate Teacher'), and its antonym *rāšā'* ('wicked') characterizes his priestly opponent.[4] In the New Testament, *dikaios*, 'the Righteous One', is a title of Jesus (Acts 7.52; 1 Jn 2.1; James 5.6), probably one aspect of the presentation of Jesus as the Servant of the Lord of Isaiah 53.[5] Finally, *saddîq* is predicated in the first place of God as the origin and source of the moral life, especially in the context of prayer.[6]

As far as we can tell, *saddîq* in the plural never became a title or label for a specific subgroup in Second Temple Judaism, one of the same type as, for example, the Asidaeans (*hāsîdîm*, 'devout') active at the time of the Maccabean revolt.[7] Close attention to the incidence of the term in Psalms and Latter Prophets, especially Isaiah, will nevertheless bring to the surface some aspects of the process which, in the late Persian and early Hellenistic period, led to the emergence of identifiably distinct sub-groups. One of the most striking features

---

[4]1QpHab I 13; IX 9–10; XI 4–5; 4QpPs[a] IV 3–10.8. The antithetic word pair *saddîq-rāšā'* is of frequent occurrence in the Qumran sectarian texts as one would expect; for example, CD I 19; IV 7; XX 20; 1QpHab I 12; 1QH[a] XV 12.

[5]In Isa 53.11b, the adjective *saddîq* has been added inappropriately before the substantive '*abdî* ('my servant'), perhaps attracted by the related verb *yasdîq* ('vindicate') in the same line (11b), but perhaps by design. For other early Christian usage, see Frederick W. Danker, *A Greek-English Lexicon of the New Testament and Other Early Christian Literature* (3rd edn, Chicago and London: University of Chicago Press, 2000), 246–47 and for more on the root sense and range of meanings of the lexeme *sdq*, see Klaus Koch in *TLOT* 2:1046–62.

[6]Deut 32.4; Ezra 9.15; Neh 9.8, 33; Isa 24.16; 45.21; Jer 12.1; Zeph 3.5.

[7]Christoph Levin, 'Das Gebetbuch der Gerechten: Literargeschichtliche Beobachtungen am Psalter', *ZTK* 90 (1993): 355–81, argued that the *saddîqîm* of Psalms refer to the circle or circles of authors and editors of psalms and the *rĕšā'îm* to their enemies, and that therefore Psalms should be considered the prayer book of the righteous rather than the hymn book of the Second Temple. A problem with this hypothesis is the lack of evidence for a cohesive group called *saddîqîm* comparable to the *asidaioi* who could claim descent from the *hāsîdîm* of Psalms.

of the canonical psalms is the binary contrast between the righteous and those the righteous considered impious and wicked. In some psalms – for example, Pss 34 and 37 where it is the dominant theme, but it is in evidence throughout the collection, often in the final verses of a psalm which serve as summation of the preceding prayer and reflection.[8] There are also instances where language characteristic of sectarian – or quasi-sectarian or pre-sectarian – ideology occurs, as if the righteous now formed a conventicle or assembly segregated from the rest of the community to which they belong. Something of this can be found in Ps 1, generally considered as the keynote to the collection as a whole. As such, it deserves a closer look.

Psalm 1

The psalm begins as follows (my translation):

> Happy are those who do not walk in the way of the wicked,
> or take their place[9] in the conclave of sinners,[10]
> or their seat in the company of scoffers.[11]
> But their delight is in the law of the Lord,
> and on his law they meditate day and night.

---

[8]Pss 1, 5, 34, 75, 97, 112, 140, 142, 146.
[9]Literally 'stand'.
[10]Reversing *ba'ăsat* (1a) and *bĕderek* (1b), with the Syriac version and BHS, to bring *derek* together with *hālak* which gives better sense. In late classical Hebrew, *'ēsāh* can mean 'council' in addition to 'counsel', 'advice', for example, Ps 14.5–6 where *'ăsat 'ānî* ('the assembly of the Poor') is associated with *dôr saddîq* ('the company of the righteous'); similar expressions can be found in the Qumran Community Rule: *'ăsat haqqôdeš*, *'ăsat harābbîm* ('the holy assembly', 'the assembly of the Many'), 1Q II 25; III 2; VI 16; VIII 11. See *HALOT* 2.866; Roland Bergmeier, 'Zum Ausdruck עצת רשעים in Ps I 1, Hi 10 8, 21 16 und 22,18', *ZAW* 79 (1967): 229–32; J. Alberto Soggin, 'Zum ersten Psalm', *ThZ* 23 (1967): 84.
[11]*môšāb*, usually with the meanings 'dwelling', 'settlement' or 'seat', 'place at table' can also be translated 'assembly', 'company' as here. See Ps 107.32 where *biqĕhal-'ām* ('in the congregation of the people') is parallel with *bĕmôšab zĕqēnîm* ('in the assembly of the elders').The same usage is attested in the Qumran *yahad* and the Damascus Document (1QS VI 8; VII 10–11; 1QSa II 11; CD XII 19) where *môšab ha-rābbîm* translates 'the assembly of the Many', that is, the community of the sectarians in plenary session.

This brief declarative statement at the beginning of the psalm is paralleled at the end with a statement about the condition of the wicked (*rěšā'îm*, vv. 5–6):

> Therefore the wicked shall not stand firm in the judgement,
> nor shall sinners find a place in the assembly of the righteous.
> For Yahweh watches over the way of the righteous,
> but the way of the wicked will perish.

Only here, at the end, are those spoken of at the beginning identified as *saddîqîm* (5–6), whereas the non-righteous are sinners (*hattā'îm*, 1b,5), scoffers (*lēsîm*, 1b), and wicked (*rěšā'îm*, 1a, 4, 5, 6). Hence, *'adat saddîqîm* ('the assembly of the righteous') at the end parallels *'asat hattā'îm* ('the conclave of sinners') at the beginning. In between, the description of the beatitude of the righteous is contrasted with the misery awaiting the non-righteous, each description introduced with the connecting particle *kî 'im* ('but rather', vv. 2, 4b) in keeping with the careful structuring of the psalm. The beatitude of the righteous, encapsulated in the verb *hāgah* ('murmur', 'meditate'), consists in prayer and praise, as elsewhere in psalms,[12] but also in studying and meditating on the divine law day and night. In keeping with the information provided in 1 Chr 9.33–34, according to which the temple musicians had lodgings in the temple precincts and were on call day and night, other psalms allude to round-the-clock prayer and study.[13] The practice of nocturnal prayer and meditation anticipates both Christian monasticism and the Qumran sect whose members meditated and prayed at night with the help of the mysterious 'Book of Meditation'.[14] The deep satisfaction and joy of the temple singers and instrumentalists in the performance of their duties, whether by day or by night, will be obvious to anyone reading the psalms with feeling and sympathy.

These linguistic data point to the probable origin of Ps 1 in the guilds of temple singers and instrumentalists who had rooms in the temple and were on call both day and night. The same impression is

---

[12]Pss 35.28; 37.30; 71.24. In antiquity in general, reading and praying mentally, without articulating, at least in an audible murmur, was the exception not the rule.
[13]In Ps 42.9, the psalmist tells us that at night 'His (God's) song is on my lips, a prayer to the God of my life'. See also Pss 88.2; 92.3; 119.55, 62; 134.1.
[14]*sēper hāgî*, 1QSa 1.7; CD X 6; XIII 2; XIV 8; 4q418. 43–45. On these night liturgies, see also 1QS VI 6–7; 1QM XIV 13014.

given in the following v. 3 in which the good fortune of the righteous is described in a striking metaphor:

> They are like trees
> planted beside channels of water
> which yield their fruit in due season,
> and their foliage never fades.
> [They prosper in all that they do][15]

The formulation is reminiscent of statements in other psalms in which the tree located in the temple is an image of human flourishing. One psalmist rejoices that he is like a green olive tree in the house of God (Ps 52:10). Another is certain that the righteous flourish like a palm tree or a cedar of Lebanon 'planted in the house of God, flourishing in the courtyards of our God' (Ps 92.13–14). Taking this kind of language together with that of those psalms which evince a strong attachment to the temple and a strong sense of close encounter with the God whose dwelling it is[16] confirms the hand of the liturgical poets and singers in the production of these and similar psalms in the collection. As professional temple musicians, one of their principal tasks would in any case have been the composition and rendition of psalms.[17]

Terms for self-segregating conventicles

As used in Psalms, the term '*ēdāh* (LXX *sunagōgē*) can refer to a plurality in very general terms, including a band of troublemakers (Pss 22.17; 86.14) or even a herd of bulls (Ps 68.31). It can also be

---

[15] I follow BHS in taking v. 3c as a gloss dependent on Josh 1.8, intended as a comment on the metaphor preceding.
[16] See Pss 43, 84, 116, 132, 149.
[17] Further on Ps 1: W. Vogels, "'A Structural Analysis of Psalm I'" (Bibl 60 (1979): 410–15; N. H. Snaith, "'Psalm i l and Isaiah xl 31'", *VT* 29 (1979): 363–4; Reinhard G. Kratz, "Die Tora Davids. Psalm 1 und die doxologische Fünfteilung des Psalters'", *ZTK* 93 (1996): 1–34; M. Lee Roy, "'Delighting in the Torah: The Affective Dimension of Psalm 1'", *OTE* 23 (2010),: 708–23; Susan Gillingham, "'Entering and Leaving the Psalter: Psalms 1 and 150 and the Two Polarities of Faith'", in Ian Provan and M. J. Boda (eds.), *Let Us Go Up to Zion. Essays in Honour of Hugh G. M. Williamson n the Occasion of his Sixty-Fifth Birthday*, ed. Ian Provan and M. J. Boda (VTSup 153; Leiden: Brill, 2012), 383–93.

used of Israel in plenary assembly in texts dealing with the founding events (Ps 74.2). With a similar connotation, it occurs in the Aramaic texts from the Jewish colony on the island of Elephantine with reference to that community in plenary session.[18] A case of particular interest is the *'edāh* of Dathan and Abiram in revolt against the authority of Moses in the wilderness, where the term manifestly designates a faction, a subgroup within the body politic (Ps 106.17-18). And, finally, the same term serves to identify the assembly of the divine beings in session:

God takes his place in the divine council (*'ădat-'ēl*),
in the midst of the gods he pronounces judgement. (Ps 82.1)

This is the Israelite version of the Mesopotamian *puhur ilāni*, 'the council of the gods', and the Ugaritic *'dt ilm*, with the same meaning, an image familiar from the prophet Micaiah's vision in 1 Kgs 22.19-23, the prologue to the dialogue in Job 1.6-12, and the throne room in Isaiah's vision in the year of Uzziah's death where the Lord Yahweh solicits the opinion of those assembled, and one said one thing and another another (Isa 6.1-13).

The assembly of the righteous in Ps 1 is consistent with frequent allusions elsewhere in Psalms to such conclaves or conventicles, using a range of more or less equivalent terms. One psalmist states with confidence that 'God is in the company of the righteous' (*bĕdôr saddîq*, Ps 14.5), another proposes to praise God 'in the company of the upright, in the assembly' (*besôd yĕšārîm wĕ'ēdāh*, Ps 11.1), and elsewhere there is reference to a 'council of the holy ones' (Ps 89.8) and an 'assembly of the upright' (Ps 112.2).[19] These terms do not in themselves necessarily presuppose a sect or even a socially visible group, the determination of which will depend on the context. But the use of such terms may be regarded as anticipating the self-designation of the Qumran sectarians as a 'community of holiness' (*'ădat qôdēš*, !QS V 20). The same designation, minus the holiness, was attached to those sectarians whom the Qumran *yahad* and the Damascus sect regarded as enemies.[20]

---

[18]Cowley: AP 15.22, 26, a marriage contract.
[19]For *dôr* and *sôd* as roughly synonymous with *'ēdāh*, see *TDOT* Volume III (1978): 169-81 and Volume X (1986): 171-8.
[20]1QM 15.9; 1QH 2.22; 6.5; 7.34; 1QS 5.1. On the different meanings of *'ēdāh* in the Hebrew Bible and Qumran, see *TDOT* Volume X (1999): 468-81.

The devout (*ḥāsîdîm*)

This designation must be included even though it appears in Isaiah only in the alternative form *'anšê-ḥesed* in Isa 57.1–2. Apart from Psalms, where it appears twenty-five times, this term occurs in biblical texts only seven times, three of which are either identical with or an alternative form of canonical psalms.[21] In psalms it is paired with designations of a morally and religiously positive nature: with the righteous, 31.18–19, 37.28–40; the poor, 12.6, 86.2; the Servants of the Lord 79.2, 10; 86.2, 4, 16; the blameless, 15.2; 18.14, 26; the 'faithful', 12.2; 31.24; and the holy, 16.3; 31.24.[22] It can be assigned to individuals, pre-eminently Levi (Deut 33.8; 4Q175.14 = 4Q *Testimonia*) and David (Ps 89.20–21), to the people as a whole (Pss 50.5; 148.14), and pre-eminently to God (Pss 18.26; 145.17). The term *ḥāsîd* is of special interest on account of its close affinity with the title 'Servants of the Lord', of great importance in the book of Isaiah in general and Third Isaiah in particular, somewhat less explicitly with the temple singers and their compositions (Pss 132.9; 149.5). It also merits consideration as the only one of the terms under consideration which became the title of an acknowledged sect from the Hasmonaean and Roman periods, namely, the Asidaeans, perhaps also, indirectly, the Essenes.[23]

Psalms are not generous in providing clues to their origin, much less their authorship, but there are psalms in which we hear the

---

[21] 2 Sam 22.26 (David's psalm) = Ps 18.26; Mic 7.2 = Ps 12.2; 2 Chr 6.41–42 = Ps 132.9. Levi is a *ḥāsîd* in Deut 33.8 (Moses' Blessings on the Tribes) and we are told in 1 Sam 2.9 (Hannah's psalm at Shiloh) that God will guard the footsteps of his *ḥāsîdîm*. This leaves Prov 2.8 in which this is repeated, and in Jer 3.12, Yahweh affirms that God is *ḥāsîd*, meaning unfailing in his love.

[22] The Hebrew terms are, in the same order, *saddîqîm*, *'ăniyyîm*, *'ăbādîm*, *tāmîm*, *'ĕmunîm*, *qĕdôšîm*.

[23] On the derivation of the name 'Essene' from the Aramaic equivalent of the Hebrew *ḥāsîd*, see Emil Schürer, *The History of the Jewish people in the age of Jesus Christ*. Vol. II (revised and edited by Geza Vermes et al. (Edinburgh: T. & T. Clark, 1979), 558–9 and Martin Hengel, *Judaism and Hellenism. Volume One* (Philadelphia: Fortress, 1964), 175. The opinion, which goes back to St. Jerome, that the name Sadducee derives from *saddîq* is contested; see Gary G. Porton, 'Sadducees', in *ABD* 5.892.

voice of a *hāsîd* (a devout one) speaking in the first person with language characteristic of the temple musicians and sharing the mood of intense joy and uplift of these guild members. In Ps 16, the psalmist confesses:

> my heart is glad, my soul rejoices,
> my body also rests without fear.
> You have not delivered me over to Sheol,
> nor let your devout one (*hasid*) see the Pit

and concludes:

> You show me the path of life.
> In your presence there is fullness of joy,
> at your right hand are pleasures for evermore.

In Ps 30, the *hāsîdîm* are urged to sing a song of praise to the Lord and of thanksgiving to his holy name – the two principal themes of the temple musicians. They do so, and conclude in language typical of the singers guilds:

> You have turned my laments into dancing,
> you have removed my sackcloth and clothed me with joy,
> that I may praise you without ceasing.
> Lord, my God, I shall praise you forever.

Psalm 52 concludes along the same lines:

> I am like a verdant olive tree in God's house
> for I trust in God's faithful love for ever and ever.
> I will thank you for ever for what you have done,
> and glorify your name among the devout.

One of the pilgrim psalms which commemorates the *translatio* of the holy ark from Kiriath-jearim to Jerusalem expresses a wish in somewhat unusual terms:

> Let your priests be clothed with righteousness,
> your *hăsîdîm* shout for joy! (Ps 132.9)

The response comes later in the psalm:

> I shall clothe her (Zion's) priests with salvation,
> her *hăsîdîm* with shouts of joy. (v. 16)

We would expect priests and Levites to be mentioned in tandem, as in the same author's account of the event in which priests and Levites, the latter commissioned to bear the ark and provide liturgical music, played the dominant role (1 Chr 15.1–28). The loud exultation of the devout is also characteristic of the singers, as in Ps 149, which opens with a reference to singing the praises of God 'in the assembly of the devout' (Ps 149.1), and in which these same people are urged to praise God with exultation and loud shouts of joy (v. 5).[24] The assembly of the devout of Ps 149 may be taken to represent a transitional stage in the process of group formation leading to the Asidaeans (*asidaioi*) of the Maccabean period. These *asidaioi* are described as warriors and zealous for the Torah (1 Macc 2.42), like the devout and the singers of Ps 149 who praise God sword-in-hand and execute vengeance on their enemies.[25] To commemorate the occasion when sixty Asidaeans were treacherously seized and put to death by Alkimos, who had bought the high priesthood from Demetrios I Soter (1 Macc 7.12–18), the author of 1 Maccabees cites from Ps 79, perhaps from memory:

> They have given the bodies of your servants
> to the birds of the air for food,
> the flesh of those devoted to you
> to the wild beasts of the earth. (Ps 79.2)

---

[24] The verb *yĕrannēnû* (> *r n n*, 'shout for joy') is one of the more frequent in describing the activity of the temple singers.

[25] I find unpersuasive Tournai's reading of Ps 149.6 as 'Let the high praises of God be on their lips like a two-edged sword in their hand' (waw adaequationis); even more so Hossfeld-Zenger's recourse to a *waw explicativum* reading 'Let the praises of God be in their throats, and let that be a two-edged sword in their hand'. See R. J. Tournai, 'Le psaume 149 et la "vengeance" des Pauvres de YHWH', *Rbib* 92 (1985): 149; Hossfeld/Zenger, *Psalms 3*, 651. These seem to me to be desperate and contrived attempts to make the *hăsîdîm* less bellicose and the psalm more reader-friendly.

It fitted the occasion, but the citation cannot by itself be taken as support for the hypothesis of a Maccabean date for Ps 79 or for Ps 116, which declares the death of the *ḥāsîdîm* to be precious in the sight of God. It demonstrates, nevertheless, a sense of continuity, connection and affinity between this Asidaean assembly and the *ḥāsîdîm* of the biblical texts.

saddîq and *ḥāsîd* in Isaiah

The designation *saddîq* occurs in all three sections of the book of Isaiah, as it does in most of the prophetic collections, and with the same range of usage and application as in Psalms – right as opposed to wrong (Isa 41.26), innocent (Isa 3.10; 5.23; 29.21), a righteous individual (Isa 26.7), the people as a whole (Isa 26.2; 57.1; 60.21), and the righteous God (24.16; 45.21). One text which claims our attention and which creates a close connection between the two designations under discussion is the brief lament for a dead and unnamed righteous person and those associated with him in Isa 57.1–2. The passage reads as follows (my translation):

57.1
The Righteous One has perished, and no one takes it to heart,
the devout[26] are taken away,[27] and no one gives it a thought.
It was on account of evildoing that the Righteous One was taken away.

57.2
He enters into peace.
They repose in their last resting places.[28]
He was upright in his conduct.[29]

---

[26]*'anšê-ḥesed* is a variant of *ḥāsîdîm*, a designation of the same type as *saddîqîm* and of frequent occurrence in Psalms. The *ḥāsîdîm* (the devout) are the precursors of the Asidaeans (*asidaioi*) of the Hasmonean period mentioned in the books of Maccabees (1 Macc 2.42; 7.12–13; 2 Macc 14.6).
[27]*ne'esāpîm*, literally 'gathered', an abbreviation of 'gathered to the ancestors' (Gen 25.8, 17; 35.29).
[28]The term *miškāb*, more commonly 'bed' or 'couch' (cf. Isa 57.7–8), also connotes the bier on which the body is placed (2 Chr 16.14) or the grave (Ezek 32.25).
[29]*hōlēk* (*hālak*?) *nĕkohô*, literally 'he walked uprightly'.

This brief, relatively isolated and, in v. 2, disjointed saying has given rise to a great deal of ingenuity among the interpreters ancient and modern in their attempts to render a consecutive sense. It may be described provisionally as a lament for the death of a leader, probably a prophet, and a group associated with him. It will bring to mind the beginning of Ps 12: 'Save us, O Lord, for the devout (*hāsîdîm*) are no more' (12.2), or Ps 116: 'Precious in the sight of the Lord is the death of his devoted ones' (*hāsîdîm*, 116.15), or Mic 7.2: 'The devout (*hāsîd*) has perished from the earth, there is no upright person (*yāšār*) to be found.' In the case of the *saddîq* of Isa 57.1–2, a death by violence is intimated, but with the *'anšê-hesed* it is left open; we are simply told that they were gathered to their ancestors.

Since the second verse does not render consecutive sense, an alternative reading may be suggested. The repetition of the a-b-a pattern of the first verse (the righteous one – the devout – the righteous one) permits in the second verse the proposal that we read it as a series of three brief glosses following the same sequence as in the first verse. The first encapsulates the post-mortem destiny of the *saddîq* in the term *šālôm*, peace, well-being in the fullest sense of the word; the second hints at the same outcome for the devout followers of the *saddîq* since they too will have rest and satisfaction in full measure; the third returns to the *saddiq*, reaffirming that his death was in no sense the outcome of his own moral failings.

If we go on to enquire about the identity and destiny of this Righteous One, we will sooner or later have to consider the claim on behalf of the Servant of the Lord whose painful life and death are recorded in Isa 52.13–53.12. The idea that the Righteous One of Isa 57.1–2 is to be identified with this also unnamed sufferer has been mooted occasionally but, to my knowledge, never seriously argued.[30] The main points of resemblance are as follows.

---

[30] James D. Smart, *History and Theology in Second Isaiah* (Philadelphia: Westminster, 1965), 240–1, notes the connection but takes *hassaddîq* and *anšê hesed* as parallel terms referring to a plurality. The same conclusion is reached by Paul D. Hanson, *The Dawn of Apocalyptic* (Philadelphia: Fortress, 1975), 197, for whom the *saddîq* stands for Hanson's 'oppressed prophetic group'. See also Wolfgang Lau, *Schriftgelehrte Prophetie in Jes. 56-66* (Berlin: de Gruyter, 1994), 235–6, for whom the expression *'anšê hesed* implies a collective interpretation of the Suffering Servant in Isaiah 53. For a more complete exposition of my view outlined above, see *Isaiah 56-66. A New*

In Isa 53.11b, towards the end of the threnody pronounced by a disciple of the Servant, we read that 'my righteous servant will vindicate the many' (*yasdîq saddîq 'abdî lārabbîm*). It seems that *saddîq* has been added to this statement since it precedes rather than follows the noun and it also overburdens the verse. The addition was either an error, by attraction to the preceding verb *yasdîq* or, as I prefer to argue, a deliberate insertion with a view to identifying the Servant with the Righteous One of Isa 57.1–2. As the death of the Righteous One was due in some way to evildoing, so the Servant of the Lord was 'taken away' (*luqqah*), that is, taken to his death, 'by oppressive acts of judgement', that is, by a deliberate miscarriage of justice (53.8a). Furthermore, for both the *'ebed YHWH* and the *saddîq*, the death went unregarded ('Who gives a thought to his fate?', 53.8a). In neither case, however, was death the last word since it is promised that after his painful life the Servant will see light and be satisfied (53.11a),[31] and in the same way the Righteous One enters into peace. Not least important, both have a plurality associated with them, for the one a group of *hāsîdîm* ('devout'), for the other the Servants of the Lord (*'ăbādîm*) of Trito-Isaiah introduced towards the end of Deutero-Isaiah (Isa 54.17), no doubt in order to associate them with the Servant who suffers and dies in Deutero-Isaiah (Isa 52.13–53.12). At this point, a closer examination of the key term *'ebed YHWH* ('Servant of the Lord') is indicated and will be taken up in the following chapter.

Translation with Introduction and Commentary (AB 19B; New York: Doubleday/ New Haven: Yale University Press, 2003), 148–52 and 'Who is the *Saddiq* of Isaiah 57:1-2?' in *Studies in the Hebrew Bible, Qumran, and the Septuagint: Presented to Eugene Ulrich*, ed. Peter W. Flint, Emanuel Tov and James C. Vanderkam (Leiden and Boston: Brill, 2006), 109–20.

[31] *'ôr*, 'light' is added after *yir'eh* with LXX, 1QIsa^a and 1QIsa^b. The verb *śābā'*, 'satisfy' occurs in Psalms with the meaning of spiritual satisfaction, satiety of joy in the presence of God, the beatific vision (Pss 17.15; 63.6; 65.5).

9

The Servants of the Lord in Psalms and Isaiah

Servants of the Lord and related titles in Psalms

The designation 'servant' (Hebrew: *'ebed*) is one of several which encapsulate different aspects of a personal or group relationship to God in the Hebrew Bible, with particular frequency and force in Psalms and Isaiah. The term can have several meanings in Psalms. It can refer in a purely secular way to slaves as, for example, Joseph in Egypt (Ps 105.17), likewise to dependents (Pss 123.2; 133.9) and state officials (Pss 22.20; 36.9; 37.5, 24). It can also serve as a deferential way of referring to oneself in the presence of a superior, and therefore in prayer of supplication to God (e.g. Pss 19.12; 27.9; 69.18). As a title of honour, 'Servant of God/the Lord' is applied to the great figures in the tradition: Abraham (Ps 105.6, 42), Israel-Jacob (136.22), Moses (Ps 105.26), and, most frequently, to David, founder of the guilds of temple musicians.[1] Used in the plural with a religious connotation – which is our special concern in this discussion – it occurs thirteen times in Psalms: once in Book I (Ps 34.23), once in Book II (Ps 69.37), twice in the same psalm in Book III (Ps 79.2, 10), five times in three psalms in Book IV (Pss 90.13, 16; 102.15, 29; 105.25), and four times in three psalms in Book V (Pss 113.1; 134.1; 135.1, 14). Where it stands for the

---

[1] Pss 18.1; 36.1; 78.70; 89.4; 132.10; 144.10.

religiously faithful members of the community in general it is often synonymous with such designations as the righteous (*saddîqîm*), the devout (*ḥāsîdîm*), those who seek the Lord God (*dōrěšê YHWH*), and the poor (*'ănāwîm*).

In our discussion of the Zion theme in Psalms, we saw that Zion is more often than not a present reality, the actual city of Jerusalem either before or after its destruction and depopulation at the hands of the Babylonians, more often after than before. In Psalms, more often than not, the Servants of the Lord and associated terms refer to the inhabitants of Jerusalem-Zion, either the faithful in the actual city or those destined to inhabit the visionary Zion of the future.[2] The Asaphite Ps 79 laments the destruction of Jerusalem, the violent deaths of God's servants (*'ăbādîm*) and his devoted ones (*ḥāsîdîm*), and the desecration of their bodies. It has proved difficult to decide whether this psalm is referring to the event of 586 B.C.E., to a catastrophe during the disturbances in the early Hellenistic period, or to the desecration of the temple during the numerous wars and disturbances in the early Hellenistic period.[3] At any rate,

---

[2]Ulrich Berges, 'Die Knechte im Psalter, Ein Beitrag zu seiner Kompositionsgeschichte', *Bib* 81 (2000): 153-78, refers to a constellation of motifs consisting in Zion, the Poor (*'ănāwîm*) and the Servants of the Lord. Examples can be found in Pss 9, 37 and 149. Note, however, that the precise meaning of the term *'ănāwim* can vary with different contexts; witness the six terms used by NRSV to translate *'ănāwîm* in Psalms: afflicted (9.13), oppressed (10.12; 76.12), meek (10.17; 37.10), poor (22.27), humble (25.9, 34.3, 149.4) and needy (69.33). See also Berges, 'Die Armen im Buche Jesaja. Ein Beitrag zur Literaturgeschichte des AT', *Bib* 80 (1999): 153-77.
[3]For a defence of the view that Ps 79 refers to the sack of Jerusalem in 586 by the Babylonians, see Hossfeld and Zenger, *Psalms 2*, 304-5. Several commentators have followed Gunkel, *Einleitung in de Psalmen*, 349-50 (cited in Hossfeld and Zenger, 304) who drew attention to the fact that the temple is here said to have been defiled not destroyed as in Ps 74. However, the same psalm adds that the enemy laid Jerusalem in ruins which would surely have included the temple which provided religious legitimacy for the revolt. A third possibility is that an original reference to the disaster of 586 has been editorially updated during the persecution of Antiochus IV, as suggested by Briggs and Briggs, *A Critical and Exegetical Commentary on the Book of Psalms. Vol. 2*, 197. Psalm 79.2 is cited in 1 Macc 7.17 in connection with the murder of sixty Asidaeans (*ḥāsîdîm*) during that troubled period. Note also Ps 116.16: 'Precious in the sight of the Lord is the death of his *ḥāsîdîm*' followed immediately by the psalmist's declaration 'Lord, I am your servant; I am your servant, the son of your handmaiden'.

those Servants of the Lord who survived the disaster give expression in prayer to their attachment to the city as the place in which their God had chosen to live and the focus of their aspirations for the future:

> You, Lord, are enthroned for ever,
> your fame endures for all generations.
> You will arise and have compassion on Zion,
> for it is time to take pity on her,
> the appointed time has come.
> Her stones are dear to your servants,
> even her dust moves them to pity
> When the Lord rebuilds Zion
> he will appear in his glory.
> He will hear the prayer of the destitute,
> he will not despise their prayer. (Ps 102.14–18)

The same psalm concludes with the assurance that, at some point in the future, after they themselves have passed from the scene, the descendants of the 'Servants of the Lord' will occupy a rebuilt and restored Zion:

> The children of your servants will dwell in security,
> their offspring will be established in your presence.

Similar assurance is voiced at the conclusion of Ps 69:

> God will deliver Zion
> and rebuild the cities of Judah.
> His people will live there and possess it,
> the descendants of his servants will inherit it,
> and those who love his name will live there.

The Servants of the Lord therefore see themselves, or their descendants, as the destined inhabitants of the future Zion, as God's restored and purified people, but so far there is no suggestion that they formed a distinct, identifiable group. In Book V, the situation is different. The designation 'Servants of the Lord' in this fifth and last book is relatively rare, occurring only in three psalms in the plural with a specifically religious connotation. In Ps 134, the servants stand – that is, take their station – by night in the temple where they are to bless, sing hymns of praise, and lift their hands in prayer, all of which is the responsibility of the temple singers and instrumentalists. A nocturnal liturgical service conducted by the singers is explicitly attested by the author of Chronicles, who refers to 'the singers ... living in the chambers of the temple free of other service, for they were on duty day and night' (1 Chr 9.33); and this practice can also be deduced from allusions in several psalms in addition to Ps 134.[4] Ps 135, which is without introductory rubric, issues the same injunction to Servants of the Lord who 'stand [i.e. take their station] in the house of the Lord, the courts of the house of our God'. They are to praise the Lord and sing psalms to his name. There is admittedly an element of indeterminacy in this designation and the others like it we have been discussing, but it seems from usage in Book V that the temple musicians could be referred to with this title of honour, which is hardly surprising since David, founder of the guilds of temple musicians, is the prototypical Servant of the Lord throughout the book of Psalms.[5]

Book V has been subjected to particularly intense scrutiny in the expectation of obtaining further insight into the formation of the collection as a whole.[6] The expectation would be especially lively with respect to the Great Hallel of Pss 146–150, understood to be the last addition to the book. We find the *saddîqîm/rěšā'îm* dichotomy there (Ps 146.8–9), and Ps 148 concludes with praise for the *hāsîdîm*, which connects with the 'assembly of the devout' (*qěhal hāsîdîm*) at the beginning of Ps 149. Since the early modern period, and still today, no consensus exists on the 'situation in life' of Ps 149, described by one commentator as 'a nasty psalm' ('ein garstig Lied'), presumably on account of its bellicose tone and

---

[4] Pss 42.9; 88.2–3; 92.2–3.
[5] See note 218.
[6] For a recent survey of opinion on the formation of the book as a whole and the fifth book in particular, see Susan E. Gillingham, 'The Levites and the Editorial Composition of the Psalms', in *The Oxford Handbook of the Psalms*, ed. William P. Brown (Oxford: University Press, 2014), 201–13.

religiously inspired fantasy of domination.[7] Since early times, the origin of this psalm, and perhaps of the entire series 146–150, has been located in the Maccabean period, among the conventicles of the Asidaeans, descendants of the biblical *ḥāsîdîm* who were as prominent at that time as they are in Ps 149. A Maccabean date for this psalm appears to be no longer in favour, but perhaps should not be dismissed out of hand.[8] When we first encounter them, in 1 Macc 2.42, the Asidaeans give the impression that they had been in existence for some time, and the *sunagōgē asidaiōn* will bring to mind the *qĕhal ḥāsîdîm* ('the assembly of the devout') of Ps 149.1. Whatever time frame is chosen, the close association of the devout and their assembly (vv. 1, 5, 9) with language and activities associated with the temple singers is unmistakable, at least in the first half of the psalm: the praise of God with singing and dancing accompanied with tambourine and lyre; all of this in an abandon of ecstatic joy.[9] On the troubling question of the two-edged sword in the hands of God's faithful ones (Ps 149.6), we might recall that, on their first appearance in the texts, the Asidaeans are presented as 'mighty warriors of Israel' (1 Macc 2.42). All this will provide another reminder that, in Psalms more so than in Isaiah – in which *ḥāsîdîm* do not feature, not directly at any rate – there is a fair degree of indeterminacy in the use of these designations and titles. It will also raise again the possibility of a connection between those who served God, who acted as Servants of the Lord, by music and song in the temple service and the Servants of the Lord whom we encounter in the book of Isaiah.

---

[7]Notger Füglister, 'Ein garstig Lied – Ps 149', in *Freude an der Weisung des Herrn. Beiträge zur Theologie der Psalmen. Festgabe zum 70. Geburtstag von H. Gross*, ed. E. Haag and F. L. Hossfeld (Stuttgart: Katholisches Bibelwerk, 1986), 81–105. He tells us that this characterization of the psalm goes back to Goethe.
[8]A Maccabean date was argued initially by Friedrich Baethgen, *Die Psalmen übersetz und erklärt* (Göttingen: Vandenhoeck & Ruprecht, 1897), 434–5 and Bernhard Duhm, *Die Psalmen erklärt* (Freiburg: Mohr, 1899), 482–4. At the other chronological extreme a pre-monarchy date was advanced by Hans Schmidt, *Die Psalmen* (Tübingen: Mohr, 1934), 257 and Anthony R. Ceresco, *Psalm 149: Poetry, Themes (Exodus and Conquest) and Social Function*, Bib 67 (1986): 177–94.
[9]All these activities certainly did not take place on their couches, as NRSV. For MT *miškĕbôtām* ('couches' 'beds', v. 5) read miškĕnôtām ('dwellings' or, better, 'dwelling'), cf. Ps 84.2 for another 'plural of extension' (*miškĕnôtêka*, 'your dwelling', that is, the temple).

Servants of the Lord and related titles in Isaiah

In the first of the three major sections of the book (Isa 1–39), *'ebed* (servant) refers to everyday social realities including slaves (14.2; 24.2) and state officials (22.20; 36.9; 37.5, 24). It also serves as expressive of deferential self-reference, whether genuine or feigned (36.11). The prophet is introduced as servant of the Lord in carrying out a symbolic, mimetic act predictive of the fate of Egyptian and Nubian rebels against the Assyrian emperor Sargon II in about 714 B.C.E., a time of great crisis involving also Philistines and Judaeans (Isa 20.1–6). To be a servant of the Lord therefore denotes instrumentality; it means serving as the instrument or agent of God's purposes. A few years later, in the course of a greater crisis for Judah and Jerusalem, Isaiah reassured Hezekiah, under siege from Sennacherib son of Sargon, that the Lord would rescue Jerusalem for his own sake and that of his servant David (Isa 37.33–35). This reassurance will bring to mind the thanksgiving prayer of David, the prototypical Servant of the Lord, after his rescue from Saul and other enemies (Ps 18).

In the first part of Deutero-Isaiah (chapters 40–48) reference to the servant of the Lord is much more deliberately in the service of a theological agenda. In the first address to a Servant of the Lord (42.1–4), the addressee appears to be the Persian ruler Cyrus rather than a prophetic figure, since the commission to establish a just order and the rule of law for the nations of the world is a task for a ruler not a prophet.[10] Elsewhere in this section, the servant of the Lord does designate the prophet who predicts the rebuilding and repopulation of Jerusalem (Isa 44.26), but the emphasis is more often on the people as a whole living in a collapsed world and in need of redemption, and generally referred to as Israel or Jacob.[11] In the second part of Deutero-Isaiah (49–55), after the failure of Cyrus to fulfil his commission, the focus is on an individual prophetic figure called to carry out a mission

---

[10]This identification is defended in my *Isaiah 40-55. A New Translation with Introduction and Commentary* (AB 19A; New Haven and London: Yale University Press, 2002), 207–12.

[11]Isa 41.8–9; 42.9; 43.10; 44.1–2, 21; 45.4; 48.20.

of renewal for Israel and the world, a mission which ended with his rejection and death (49.1–6; 50.4–11; 52.13–53.12). Isaiah 55 serves to recapitulate Isa 40–54, which therefore begins and ends with the theme of return from exile (Isa 40.3–5; 55.12–13a). It appears to have been added after the original conclusion in the preceding chapter which consists in an apostrophe addressed to Zion holding out the prospect of renewal and redemption (54.1–17a), followed by a brief final statement assuring 'the servants of the Lord' that the rebuilt and repopulated city Zion will be for their benefit and will make up for past sufferings (54.17b). This entire chapter can be understood as editorial linkage with the principal theme of Isa 56–66: Zion, city of light, and the Servants of the Lord who will have rights of citizenship in it.

Servants of the Lord in Trito-Isaiah (Isaiah 56–66)

Third Isaiah opens with a prophetic oracle which reassures foreigners and eunuchs, threatened with ostracism or banishment, of their good standing in the community (Isa 56.1–8). The foreigners in question are described as follows (56.6–7):

> they are attached to the Lord God
> they are to minister to him
> they love the name of the Lord
> they are to be his servants
> they are to observe sabbath and the covenant in general
> they are promised access to Zion, God's holy mountain, which they will co-inherit
> they will experience joy in the temple, now described as 'the house of prayer' for all people
> their burnt offerings and sacrifices will be acceptable to God.

It is clear that these are not just any foreigners, but who are they? Before we can answer this question some clarification of terms is called for. The first qualification listed – attachment to the Lord God – is not self-explanatory, but the Hebrew verb *lwh* (Niphal/Passive, 'attach') is used to create a derivation for the name Levi, ancestor of all priests and Levites including the temple musicians (Gen 29.34). According to the ordinances about temple personnel in Num 18.1–7, Levites are 'attached' to the priests – using the same verb – in a subordinate status, as those responsible for the temple liturgy of which music with singing was an indispensable element. This hint of an association with temple personnel is confirmed by the second qualification – they are to minster to God – which refers to ministry of different kinds, sacred and secular, but predominantly temple service including the service of Levites and Levitical singers.[12] These foreigners are therefore being assured that they qualify to serve in different liturgical ministries in the temple. The love of the Name, which means love of God,[13] is explained by the belief that God's real abode is in heaven (Isa 57a.15; 66.1), but that he is represented by his name in the temple (2 Chr 6.18–21) – a theme prominent in Deuteronomy.[14] Name therefore means presence and God is present in the temple. The psalmist prays:

> may all who take refuge in you rejoice,
> may they ever sing for joy;
> spread your protection over them
> so that those who love your name may exult in you. (Ps 5.12)

Here, too, the language – joy, singing, exultation – is strongly suggestive of the temple musicians. Psalm 69 concludes as follows:

> God will deliver Zion,
> he will rebuild the cities of Judah;
> his people will live there and possess it,
> the descendants of his servants will inherit it,
> those who love his name will live there. (Ps 69.36–37)

Those who love the name of the Lord God – most frequently 'Lord of Hosts' in Isaiah and Psalms – are also the Servants of the Lord

---

[12] The verb *šārēt* refers specifically to temple musicians in 1 Chr 6.17 and 2 Chr 31.2, and to Asaphite singers in 1 Chr 16.37.

[13] Compare 'the Name' (*ha-šēm*) as a reverential substitute for YHWH in Orthodox Jewish usage.

[14] On the temple as the location of the Name, see Deut 12.2, 11, 21; 14.23–24, and so on.

God, the future restored people of Zion. The promise is repeated in Trito-Isaiah:

> I shall bring forth descendants from Jacob,
> from Judah inheritors of my mountain;[15]
> my chosen ones shall inherit it,
> my servants shall settle there. (Isa 65.9)

The Servants of the Lord will therefore include foreign proselytes and, together with them, will constitute the core of the restored community in Zion, the renewed and rebuilt city, the city of light. This reassuring word reiterates in more idealistic terms the prediction in Ps 69.36–37:

> God will deliver Zion,
> he will rebuild the cities of Judah;
> his people will live there and possess it,
> the descendants of his servants will inherit it,
> those who love his name will live there.

The remarkably eirenic and welcoming statement at the beginning of Third Isaiah concludes by anticipating the experience of joy in the service of the temple, now described as a house of prayer (*bêt těpillāh*) for all peoples (56.7). From our reading of psalms, it has become increasingly clear that joy in the service of the temple is expressed pre-eminently in music and song. The expression 'house of prayer', found only here, reflects an enhanced esteem for prayer in the temple service commensurate with the decline of confidence in the value and efficacy of the prescribed daily sacrifices controlled by the temple priesthood, a subject which will claim our attention in the following chapter. The prayers which had always accompanied sacrifice, and which had been the primary responsibility of the temple musicians, had come to be more highly appreciated than the sacrifice itself.

---

[15] Reading *hārî* ('my mountain') for *hāray* ('my mountains'), consistent with *wîrēšûhāh*, fem. suffix with reference to the servants of the Lord settling in the Zion of the future – more likely than settling on mountains.

The Servants as a distinct minority

As we read on through Third Isaiah, it becomes evident that these Servants of the Lord constitute a distinct minority living among a people corrupted by idolatry. The author describes their situation with the figure of a few good grapes in a bunch that is rotten (65.8), and locates the metaphor meaningfully between two grim accounts of idolatrous practices, apparently also involving elements of the temple priesthood (65.1–7, 11–12). These servants form the remnant of which the prophets spoke of old, the nucleus of a renewed and purified community for the future Zion (65.9–10). Their destiny is set out in starkly contrasting and characteristically sectarian terms of eschatological reversal:

> My servants will eat while you go hungry,
> my servants will drink while you go thirsty,
> my servants will rejoice while you are put to shame,
> my servants will exult with heartfelt joy
> while you cry out with heartache and wail with anguish
>   of spirit. (Isa 65.13)

The designation 'ăbādîm is not, therefore, a title in the same way as the Asidaeans of the Maccabean age or the early Christian Ebionites (the Poor), but it serves nevertheless to describe an identifiably distinct group, or groups, with acknowledged sectarian characteristics. And, finally, our reading of Trito-Isaiah in the light of psalms suggests that this title may also have been assigned to members of the singers and musicians guilds in the service of the temple.

The Servants of the Lord of Trito-Isaiah are also related to or indistinguishable from a group referred to as 'those who trembled at the word of God' (Isa 66.2, 5). We come upon these 'Tremblers' (hărēdîm) at a time when they had enough social visibility to be expelled from the community by their fellow Jews:

> Hear the word of the Lord, you who tremble at his word!
> Your brethren who hate you,
> who cast you out for my name's sake have said:
> 'May the Lord reveal his glory, that we may witness your joy!'
> But it is they who will be put to shame. (Isa 66.5)

Outcasts in their own society, they were nevertheless accepted in the sight of God together with the poor and the afflicted in spirit:

On these I look with favour;
the poor, the afflicted in spirit
and those who tremble at my word. (Isa 66.2)

There is more to these terms than meets the eye. The poor (*'ăniyyîm*), those of low status, are in evidence in Psalms (twenty-seven times) and in Isaiah (thirteen times) as a religiously significant as well as a purely social category. The afflicted in spirit are probably those identified elsewhere as penitents (*šābîm*). The third title – *hārēd*, *hărēdîm* – occurs elsewhere only in the account of Ezra's activity after his return to the Persian province of Yehud. There it attaches to members of the religious leadership within Ezra's golah group. They are therefore, so to speak, a conventicle within a conventicle. In his autobiographical account Ezra relates how 'all who trembled at the words of the God of Israel on account of the infidelity of the golah gathered around me while I sat appalled until the evening sacrifice' (Ezra 9.4). What caused the dismay of Ezra and these *hărēdîm* was the discovery that members of the golah had contracted marriage with women from outside the group. To remedy this situation, a certain Shecaniah, one of the leaders of the group and certainly himself *hārēd*, proposed the drastic solution of dismissing these 'foreign' wives and their children, adding that this should be done according to Ezra's counsel and that of 'those who tremble at the commandment of our God' (Ezra 10.3).[16] Whether there is any historical link between these *hărēdîm* who were at least temporarily in control of their own destiny and those outcasts upon which the God of Israel looked with favour in Isa 66.2 we do not know. The 'Tremblers' of Ezra and Shecaniah are leaders in their own society while those of Trito-Isaiah are an excluded and reviled group. The latter were also known, and by some mocked, for their eschatological and probably apocalyptic beliefs, which reflects a development later than the time of Ezra. In any case, it is only

---

[16] Was Ezra himself a *hārēd*? Probably, to judge by his extreme reaction to the bad news about intermarriage – tearing his tunic and mantle, and remaining for some time in a catatonic state (*měšômēm*, Ezra 9.3–4), a condition which also affected Ezekiel (Ezek 3.18) and Daniel (Dan 8.27) after a vision.

by chance that we have this information about groups and group formation from the time of Ezra's activities in the mid-fifth century B.C.E. The history of these and other such self-segregating or coercively segregated groups remains for the most part unknown.[17] At any rate, we hear no more of these *hărēdîm* after their brief appearance in Ezra 9–10 and Isaiah 66, though the title is still in use among the Haredi Orthodox Jews, and similar designations (Quakers, Shakers) have appeared in the history of Christianity from time to time.

Postscript

One of the dominant themes in Psalms is the contrast between the righteous and the unrighteous, *saddîqîm* and *rĕšā'îm*, enunciated in Ps 1, elaborated at length in Pss 34 and 37, and present throughout the collection. It will lead eventually to the situation in which the righteous and devout can fulfil their religious goals only by segregation from the social environment, in other words, by the formation of distinct and distinctive religious conventicles or sects.[18]

---

[17] Among recent studies of these issues which focus on the servants of the Lord in Trito-Isaiah, I mention Willem A. M. Beuken, 'The Main Theme of Trito-Isaiah. "The Servants of YHWH",' *JSOT* 47 (1990): 67–87; Ulrich Berges, *Das Buch Jesaja. Komposition und Endgestalt* (Freiburg: Herder, 1998), 481–534; idem, 'Die Ziontheologie des Buches Jesaja', *Est. Bibl.* LVIII 2 (2000): 167–98. On the early second temple origins of sectarianism see my 'Interpretation and the tendency to sectarianism: An aspect of Second Temple history', in *Jewish and Christian Self-Definitioni*, ed. E. P. Sanders (Philadelphia: Fortress, 1981), 1–26; 'The Servants and the Servant in Isaiah and the formation of the book', in *Writing and Reading the Scroll of Isaiah: Studies of an Interpretive Tradition. Vol.I*, ed. C. C. Broyles and C. A. Evans (Leiden: Brill, 1997), 155–75; 'The Development of Jewish Sectarianism from Nehemiah to the Hāsîdîm', in *Judah and the Judeans in the Fourth Century B.C.E.*, ed. O. Lipshits and Gary Knoppers (Winona Lake, Indiana: Eisenbrauns, 2007), 385–404.

[18] In view of the ambiguities of current usage, it should be added that the term 'sect' is not pejorative. On the definition and description of the term as a voluntarist rather than an ascriptive body in the context of Jewish and Christian history, see Max Weber's *Economy and Society*, 4th edn, edited by G. Roth and C. Wittich (Berkeley and Los Angeles: University of California Press, 1978), II 1204–11, and his *Ancient Judaism* (New York: The Free Press, 1952), 385–91. On Weber's understanding of sectarianism, see Peter L. Berger, 'The Sociological Study of

It is acknowledged that a decisive impulse towards sect formation in early Judaism was the impact of Hellenistic culture on traditional beliefs and practices. This is so, but by then the tendency was well underway and, as we have seen, the potential for this outcome was already discernible in the contrast between the conclave of sinners (*'ăsat hattā'îm*) and the assembly of the righteous (*'ădat saddîqîm*) in Ps 1.

A further point, conflict within the ranks of the temple personnel, especially between the priestly administration of the temple and lower-order temple personnel, namely, Levites, including the guilds of singers and instrumentalists, may help to explain the frequent reference in psalms to enemies and their machinations directed against the psalmists speaking in the first person. Experience teaches that hostility and conflict of this kind can lead to the self-segregation of those deprived of power, and this may have happened to the temple singers as well as to the Servants of the Lord and those who trembled at his word. This issue calls for further research, but we have seen that some aspects of its history can be reconstructed from a close reading of Isaiah and Psalms. In the following chapter, we shall discuss one factor in generating this situation as it is reflected in Isaiah and Psalms.

Sectarianism', *Social Research* 21 (1954): 467–71; J. A. Holstean, 'Max Weber and Biblical Scholarship', *HUCA* 46 (1975): 159–79.

10

The repudiation of sacrifice in Isaiah and Psalms

Introductory observations

For most if not all peoples in the ancient world, including Israel and the Judaism, which grew from it, sacrifice was the quintessential act of public worship. It is attested in all periods of Israel's history from the beginnings to the Roman period; it was the principal occupation of the temple priesthood, contributing substantially to their maintenance; and its detailed regulation occupies a considerable amount of space in the Pentateuch. It is therefore understandable that the destruction of the temple by the Romans in 70 C.E., which brought the sacrificial ritual to an end, would have the most profound and far-reaching consequences. From it emerged rabbinic Judaism which survived by developing forms of public worship possible in the absence of a temple and priesthood. Destined for revival in a distant future, possibly in the last days, sacrifice served as a potent metaphor and was internalized and individualized in the practice of personal piety, observance of written commandments, and prayer in praise, petition, and thanksgiving.[1] But the destruction of the temple was not the only reason for the crisis of sacrifice in Late Antiquity. For those who embraced the Christian faith, the representation of the death of Jesus as the one all-sufficient sacrificial act rendered the sacrifices of the older covenant superfluous, a position set out with rhetorical force in the Epistle

---

[1] b.Ber, 15a.b, 33a; Sukkah 45a; Ta'an 26a; Meg. 31a.

to the Hebrews. The death of those Christians who refused to take part in the official, civic sacrifices, which signified renouncing their faith – Ignatius of Antioch, Perpetua and Felicity, and others – was considered sacrificial, in that respect no different from those who perished during the interdiction of the Jewish faith by Antiochus IV many years earlier. One of the youths in the fiery furnace, a story familiar from the Old Greek version of the book of Daniel, prayed that 'with a contrite heart and humble spirit we may be accepted as though with burnt offerings of lambs and bulls ... and that our sacrifice this day may be acceptable in your (God's) sight' (*Prayer of Azariah* 1:17). Before being burnt alive, Polycarp offered himself to God as a burnt sacrifice (*Martyrdom of Polycarp* 14).

But loss of confidence in the efficacy of sacrifice was not confined to Judaism. In the Graeco-Roman world in general, the eclipse of sacrifice, an essential element in maintaining civic functioning and social coherence, also had important consequences, and came to be seen as one aspect of a profound transformation, inaugurating a second axial age long before 70 C.E.[2] The corrosive effect of the teaching in the philosophical schools on the practice of animal sacrifice had long been apparent. Indifference to or outright rejection of sacrifice is most clear in evidence in the Pythagorean and Orphic communities, which practised different forms of asceticism including vegetarianism, a practice inconsistent with animal sacrifice. Jewish intellectuals active under the Hellenistic empires could hardly have been unaware of these tendencies. Some admittedly remote echoes may be heard in the didactic writings of the sages, for example in Prov 15.8, which contrasts the sacrifice of the wicked with the prayer of the upright. Qoheleth's advice on religious observances including sacrifice goes further: 'Be on your guard when you enter the house of

---

[2] See the fascinating study of Guy G. Stroumsa, *The End of Sacrifice. Religious Transformations in Late Antiquity*, trans. Susan Emanuel (Chicago and London: University of Chicago Press, 2009); also, along the same lines, Peter Jackson and Anna-Pya Sjödin (eds), *Philosophy and the End of Sacrifice* (Sheffield and Bristol: Equinox, 2016). On the theology and sociology of sacrifice in general, see Gary A. Anderson, *Sacrifices and Offerings in Ancient Israel. Studies in their Social and Political Importance* (Atlanta: Scholars Press, 1987); Robert T. Beckwith and Martin J. Selman (eds), *Sacrifice in the Bible* (Grand Rapids: Baker Book House, 1995); David Janzen, *The Social Meaning of Sacrifice in the Hebrew Bible. A Study of Four Writings* (Berlin: de Gruyter, 2004).

God. Obedience to God is more acceptable than the sacrifices of fools' (Qoh 4.17). For the Qumran sectarians, the Jerusalem priesthood, which was neither Zadokite nor Aaronite, was illegitimate, and illegitimacy deprived the temple sacrifices of authenticity and value. What was almost worse, the temple priesthood celebrated the festivals according to the wrong calendar. As far as we know, the Qumran sectarians did not themselves sacrifice but regarded their common practice of prayer and meditation as the equivalent of the temple sacrifices, described in a curious phrase as 'the offering of the lips' (tĕrûmat śĕpātayîm, 1QS ix 4–5). An even more curious formulation occurs in the Jewish morning prayer (birkôt ha-šahar), which laments the loss of the temple and its sacrificial liturgies in place of which 'we offer the bullocks of our lips' as an acceptable alternative to sacrifice.[3] In the Temple Scroll (11Q19), the War Scroll (1QM), and other texts, the Qumran sectarians made up for the lack of sacrifice by the collective projection of an imagined future: a purified city with a rebuilt temple and the daily sacrifices restored to their pristine state as prescribed in the laws.[4]

It is also significant in this respect that the earliest designation for the synagogue as surrogate temple is not *sunagoge* but *proseuchē*, '(house of) prayer', as we learn from Graeco-Jewish texts from the time of the Ptolemies and surviving inscriptions, including one from a Samaritan synagogue on the island of Delos.[5]

Sacrifice in Isaiah

The crisis of sacrifice therefore came to a head in the period from the first century B.C.E. to the second or third century C.E., but signs

---

[3] The expression *pārîm śĕpātēnû* ('the bullocks of our lips') is taken from Hos 14.3; the original text may, however, have read *pĕrî śĕpātēnû*, 'the fruit of our lips' as in the Old Greek version and, in consequence, Hebr 13.15: *karpon cheileōn*.
[4] Joseph M. Baumgarten, 'Sacrifice and Worship among the Jewish sectarians of the Dead Sea (Qumran) scrolls', *HTR* 46 (1953): 141–59; Lawrence H. Schiffman, 'The Sacrificial System of the *Temple Scroll* and the Book of Jubilees', in *SBL Seminar Papers*, ed. Kent H. Richards (Atlanta: SBL, 1985); Jacob Milgrom, 'SACRIFICE', *EDSS* 2: 807–12.
[5] Emil Schürer, *The History of the Jewish People in the Age of Jesus Christ* (revised and edited by G. Vermes et al. (Edinburgh: T. & T. Clark, Vol. II, 1979), 424–6.

of discontent and lack of confidence in the efficacy of sacrifice can be detected much earlier. The second discourse in the first chapter of Isaiah (1.10–20) opens with an indictment of the ruling classes which would have included the temple priesthood.[6] It continues with a passage which reads like a repudiation of sacrifice expressed in the most disdainful and dismissive language (1.10–17). However, the repudiation can hardly be absolute and comprehensive since otherwise the festivals and prayer would also be repudiated (vv. 14–15), which is highly unlikely. The usual explanation is that the ritual is rendered null and void by the immoral life or at least the inadequate disposition of the ones offering the sacrifices. This is certainly the case, as we see in the exhortation to do good and to seek justice on behalf of the disadvantaged (1.16–17), and in similar polemic about sacrifice in other prophetic writings (e.g. Amos 5.21–24 and Mic 6.6–8). But emphasis on the right disposition does not exclude other factors. The indictment begins by referring to sacrifices in general (*zĕbāḥîm*) but goes on to express dissatisfaction with burnt offerings or whole offerings: *'ôlôt*, a term which applies in the first instance to the prescribed daily sacrifice of animals, the central and essential ritual in temple worship and the principal responsibility of the priesthood (Isa 1.11).[7] The indictment goes on to present a fairly comprehensive list of the animals suitable for sacrifice – rams, well fed cattle, bulls, lambs, and goats. It seems, therefore, that criticism is focussed on the prescriptive temple sacrifice and directed in the first place against the temple priesthood included among the ruling classes under indictment.

One of the many parallels between the beginning and end of the book of Isaiah is the repudiation of false ideas about the temple with which the last chapter of the book begins:

Heaven is my throne, earth is my footstool.
What kind of house could you build for me?
What kind of place for my abode?
Did not my hand make all of these,

---

[6] In Mic 3.9–11, as in Isa 1.10, the term *qesînîm*, 'rulers', includes priests who 'give rulings for payment', in other words, use their office for personal gain.
[7] Both translations, 'burnt offering' and 'whole offering', are in use. They are combined in *holocautōma*, the LXX translation of *'ōlāh*.

and all these things came to be?
On these I look with favour:
the poor, the afflicted, and those who tremble at my word. (66.1–2)

This statement would seem to be a repudiation of the temple in keeping with polemic against 'temples made with hands' in Late Antiquity: for example among the Pythagoreans, in Apollonius of Tyana, and the speech of Stephen the Deacon in Acts 7.48–49. But here, too, the rejection cannot be absolute since it would then contradict what is said about the temple, 'the holy and beautiful house', elsewhere in these last chapters (60.7; 64.11). This statement is, however, followed by a verdict pronounced not on the practice of sacrifice itself but on the sacrificers:

The one who slaughters an ox is the one who kills a man.
The one who sacrifices a sheep is the one who wrings a dog's neck.
The one who makes a cereal offering is the one who presents
    pig's blood.
The one who makes a memorial offering with incense is the one
    who pronounces a blessing over an idol. (66.3)

The presence of eight active participles in this brutal indictment indicates that the emphasis is on the agents rather than the act, which is to say on the sacrificing priests rather than the ritual.[8] The acrimony and rancour about sacrifice here and in the first chapter suggest that there was much at stake in this polemic. In the first chapter, it is the ruling class, and the temple priesthood in particular, who are condemned as rebels and sinners and – in the last section of the chapter (1.27–28) – it is the penitents (*šābîm*) who will survive the judgement. In the final chapter, the sacrificing priests are the main target and the penitents include 'the servants of the Lord' (*'ăbādîm*, 65.6–10, 13–16) and 'those who tremble at the word of God' (*hărēdîm*, 66.2, 5). These are to be the nucleus of the penitent and redeemed community of the future. Indications in all three major sections of Isaiah support this interpretation of the commination addressed to 'the rulers of Sodom and the people of

---

[8] The lack of a *kaph comparationis* in the Hebrew is supplied by the equivalent in LXX, Vulgate, the Targum and 1QIsaᵃ.

Gomorrah' in Isa 1.10–17. In Deutero-Isaiah, Yahweh complains that his people have not brought him their sheep for burnt offerings and have not honoured him with their sacrifices (43.23). In one of the last additions to the Isaian corpus, foreign proselytes are assured that even in the 'house of prayer' their burnt offerings and sacrifices will be acceptable to God (56.6–8); and in one of a series of glosses about the Egyptian diaspora appended to an early oracle against Egypt, it is predicted that 'the Egyptians will come to know the Lord on that day, and will worship with sacrifice and burnt offering' (19.21). Animus therefore appears to be directed more against the sacrificing priests rather than against the practice itself.

Sacrifice in Psalms

It would obviously be of interest to explore this adversarial relationship between priests and Levites further, but first we must take a look at a psalm which has much in common with the first chapter of Isaiah. Psalm 50, the first of those attributed to the Asaph guild which somehow became detached in the course of transmission from the other eleven Asaphite psalms (Pss 73–83), also contains two judgement oracles in first-person discourse of the deity,[9] and in both Isa 1 and Ps 50 they are introduced by a summons to the heavens and the earth to act as witnesses to the justice of the indictments which follow (Ps 50.4–6; Isa 1.1a).[10] In both Isaiah and the psalm the sacrificial cult is repudiated in the absence of the right moral disposition on the part of the one offering the sacrifice. After rejecting current ideas about animal sacrifice, especially sacrifice represented as feeding the deity to whom it is offered as food, the

---

[9] Ps 50.7–15, 16–23 cf. Isa 1.2–9, 10–20.
[10] Cf. Deut 32.1. Appeal to the heavens and the earth, mountains, etc. to act as witnesses to the acceptance of the terms of a solemn agreement, and to the justice of the indictment in the event of their violation, is familiar from surviving texts of international treaties in the Near East. Traces of this practice appear in biblical accounts of covenant-making or covenant-renewal, but this does not oblige us to conclude that Ps 50 belongs to a liturgy of making or renewing a covenant, pace Artur Weiser, *The Psalms. A Commentary* (OTL; Philadelphia: Westminster, 1962), 393; Peter C. Craigie and Marvin E. Tate, *Psalms 1-50* (WBC; 2nd edn, Nashville: Nelson, 2004), 363.

author of the psalm goes on to recommend in its place a thanksgiving offering (*tôdāh*) in fulfilment of a vow previously made (Ps 50.14).[11] The first hemistich of v. 14, *zĕbah lēlohîm tôdāh*, is ambiguous since *tôdāh* connotes either a thanksgiving offering or the psalm of thanksgiving which accompanies the ritual. If one translates 'offer to God a sacrifice of thanksgiving' (as REB and NRSV), the psalmist is recommending a voluntary offering as more acceptable to God than participation in the official prescribed sacrificial ritual. If the preference is for 'make thanksgiving [i.e. a thanksgiving psalm] your sacrifice to God' (an alternative translation in NRSV), the sense would be that true value inheres in the prayer of thanksgiving and praise which accompanied the sacrifice rather than the sacrifice itself. In either case, thanksgiving expressed in prayer and song is preferred to sacrifice; it is the essence and *raison d'être* of the ritual.[12] The preceding rhetorical question 'Do I eat the flesh of bulls or drink the blood of goats?' suggests further that it is the official, daily animal sacrifice under the control of the priesthood which the author of this radical critique has in mind, not the voluntary offerings of the faithful. The first half of the concluding verse of Ps 50 should therefore be rendered, 'Those who honour me are those who offer a sacrifice of thanksgiving.'

Needless to say, but we will say it, questions remain to be answered about the attitude to sacrifice in these prophetic and psalmodic texts. What did their authors really think about the sacrificial ritual which, like all rituals, retained much of the magical and mythic thinking of its origins, reflecting the needs and exigencies out of which it arose ages before Isaiah and the Asaphites? Did they really think that their deity needed feeding? To judge by Isa 1.10–20 and Ps 50, they had moved beyond this common understanding of animal sacrifice but without abandoning or significantly modifying either the ritual itself

---

[11]For the thanksgiving offering see Lev 7.12–15; 22.29–30. It is one of several *voluntary* offerings, usually in fulfilment of a vow, which are distinct from the *prescriptive* temple sacrificial ritual (2 Chr 29.31–32; 33.16; Jer 17.26; Amos 4.4–5).
[12]Ps 56.13: 'I am bound by a vow made to you, God, / and will redeem it with a thanksgiving offering to you'. In Ps 22.26–27: 'From you comes my praise in the great congregation/ my vows I will fulfil in the presence of those who fear him' is followed by the participation of the poor ('*ănāwîm*) in the festive meal associated with this kind of sacrifice.

or the language in which they represented it.[13] The main point about the whole or burnt sacrifice, the *'ôlāh* is that it is handed over to the deity whole and entire and therefore rendered unavailable to the sacrificers. What happens to the sacrificial victim is described by two verbs: It is 'sent up' to the Lord God (*ha'ăleh*, causative theme of the verb *'ālāh*),[14] and it is 'turned into smoke' (*hiqtîr*, for example, Lev 1.9, 17; Exod 29.18). The same applies to the few examples of human sacrifice, whether contemplated or carried out, recorded in the Hebrew Bible: the near sacrifice of Isaac (Gen 22.2–3, 6–8, 13), the achieved sacrifice of Jephthah's daughter (Judg 11.3), and the sacrifice of the Moabite king's son (2 Kgs 3.27), which are all described as burnt and whole sacrifices. The fact that supernatural visitors are sometimes described as eating, but the Lord God is not, may have encouraged the reinterpretation of the ritual in the sense that what is being 'sent up' is the smoke, or its symbolic equivalent the incense, and it is this which is acceptable to the deity as a 'sweet-smelling odour' in lieu of the animal.[15] This interpretation had the further advantage of making the meat available to the sacrificers, perhaps helping to explain why this interpretation of the ritual came to be accepted as both theologically rational and practically convenient.

The liturgical practice of accompanying the *tôdāh* sacrifice with joyful hymns of praise and thanksgiving made this rite of obvious interest to the temple singers and instrumentalists. Jeremiah predicts that the voices of the singers will be heard again, bringing thanksgiving offerings to the temple (Jer 33.11). Psalm 100 is explicitly identified as a hymn to accompany the thanksgiving offering and, as such, it invites the whole world to join in praise and thanksgiving to God in joyful acclamation and hymns. Likewise Ps 107.22 reads:

> Let them give thanks to the Lord for his steadfast love,
> for the marvellous things he has done for humanity.
> Let them offer sacrifices of thanksgiving,
> telling of his deeds with joyful songs.

---

[13] Other psalms, Pss 40.7–9 and 51.18–21, go as far or further, but not so far as Qoheleth who counsels against offering sacrifices like the fools who are not even aware that they are doing wrong. (Qoh 4.17).

[14] The connection between the verb *'ālāh* and the *'ôlāh* is generally recognized.

[15] A psalmist prays that 'my prayer be counted as incense in your presence/ and the lifting up of my hands (in prayer) as an evening sacrifice' (Ps 141.2).

The essential distinction, therefore, is between voluntary offerings vowed to God by any participant in temple worship and the official prescribed sacrifice under the direct control of the temple priesthood. We shall go on to see that the prescribed daily sacrifice became a bone of contention between priests and Levites, including members of the guilds responsible for liturgical music. It would therefore seem antecedently more probable that the repudiation of sacrifice in Isa 1.10–20 is drawing on the Asaphite Ps 50, and on critical statements about sacrifice in other psalms, rather than the contrary. This hypothesis would not be ruled out by the long tradition of prophetic criticism of the sacrificial system to which Isa 1.10–20 belongs.[16] I am aware that at this point, we are opening up a much larger area of study than can be accommodated here. For the present, all that space permits is to put forward one explanation of the loss of confidence in the value and efficacy of the official sacrificial system in evidence at the beginning and end of Isaiah and in Ps 50, taking into account the point of view and particular concerns of those most closely involved, in the first place the Levites and, among Levites, the temple musician guild members including the Asaphite author of Ps 50.

Bad feelings between priests and Levites

It is not difficult to accept that criticism of the sacrificial system of the Jerusalem temple would derive from Levites and, among Levites, members of the singers guilds. At the most basic level, sacrifice constituted a significant part of the income and emoluments of the temple priesthood. The ritual laws about sacrifices in general specify precisely what is for the use and usufruct of the priests, including grain (Lev 2.3, 10), flour (Lev 5.13), oil, wood, wine (Deut 18.3–5), and meat from cuts of the sacrificed animal (Lev 10.12–15; Num 6.19–20). Sacrificial offerings – a lamb, a measure of wheat or oil, whatever – could also be converted to the equivalent in specie as assessed by the temple authorities, in some cases with the addition of a 20 per cent surcharge (Lev 5.14–16, 25). There was also the tithe. During the governorship of Nehemiah, and no doubt subsequently, collection of the tithe was

---

[16]Amos 4.4–5; 5.21–27; Hos 6.6; Jer 6.20–21; 7.21–26; 17.26–27.

confided to Levites, but Levites under the supervision of a priest (Neh 10.38–39; 12.44). What must have been particularly galling for Levites, including temple musicians, was the requirement that they surrender a tenth of their own tithe to the priests, the so-called tithe of the tithe (Num 18.21–31). In addition, priests controlled the tax for the upkeep of the temple fabric which stood at one third of a silver shekel at the time of Nehemiah (Neh 10.33), but at half a shekel according to the Priestly law in Exod 30.13. Given the inexorable tendency for taxes to increase, this would suggest that the latter is later than the former, though other explanations are possible. Writing much later, Josephus informs us that diaspora Jews were in the habit of paying their two-drachma temple tithe through what was in effect a Syrian bank of deposit.[17] This was the didrachma paid in his own incomparable way by Jesus (Matt 7.24).

The privileges and wealth of the temple priesthood, or at least the upper echelons of the priesthood, help to explain the frequent criticism which priests attracted at all times, from the early monarchy to the 'Wicked Priest' of the Qumran texts, a situation which no doubt contributed to the loss of confidence in the value and efficacy of the prescribed sacrificial rites, most forcefully expressed in prophetic texts.[18] Hostility, even open conflict between priests and Levites, is also reflected in situations and incidents in the account of origins. In a Priestly version of events in the wilderness, the Lord God tells Moses that Levites are to be at the disposal of Aaron (i.e. the Aaronite priesthood) and, by implication, that they are forbidden under penalty of death to aspire to the priestly office (Num 3.5–10). The wilderness was also the scene of the suppression of the rebellion of the Levite Korah against Moses and Aaron (2 Chr 20.19).[19] The rebellion was brought to an abrupt end by a tectonic event and, to make the point even more clearly, there followed a demonstration of the authority of Aaron by the

---

[17] *Ant* 18.313. The term used is *tameion*.
[18] Mic 3.1 (greed), Isa 28.7–8 (inebriation), Jer 5.31 (arbitrary rule), Jer 6.13; 8.10 (greed), 14.18 (ignorance), Mal 1–2 (a whole battery of accusations, including negligence in performing the prescribed sacrifices).
[19] By the time of the Chronicler, Korah, a descendant of Levi, was a prominent member of a temple musicians guild (2 Chr 20.19) to whom eleven psalms are attributed (Pss 42, 44–49, 84–85, 87–88).

miraculous flowering of his staff (Num 17.16–26). On the other side, evidence of anti-Aaronite and pro-Levitical polemic can be discerned in the account of calf worship at Sinai (Exod 32). Aaron's absurd excuse for initiating this idolatrous cult did not absolve him from responsibility; he was spared, but Moses turned to Levites to purge the idolators, with the result that three thousand of them were put to death on the same day.

The rebuilt Jerusalem temple, like other temples throughout the Persian empire, evolved into a wealthy, multifunctional institution in which the prestige and assets of the high priest and his associates would have given rise to resentment and hostility among the lower ranks of temple personnel. The Jerusalem temple drew its wealth not only from the sources mentioned but from ownership and rental of land holdings enlarged by donations and confiscations of real estate governed by ritual law.[20] Temples, including the Jerusalem temple, also offered financial services including loans, providing further occasions for abuse and contributing further to the secularization and commercialization of the senior priesthood, a process well advanced under Persian rule. During his years, as governor of the Persian province of Yehud, Nehemiah expended a great deal of energy in a not entirely successful attempt to control the temple and its considerable assets. He took vigorous action against an alliance between Tobiah, member of a wealthy aristocratic family, and the priest Eliashib, a relative of Tobiah, who had secured him a residence in the temple precincts and no doubt associated privileges (Neh 13.4–14). Nehemiah also had to remedy the lack of provisioning for the Levites which had led them to abandon the temple, walk off the job, and return to their family homes (Neh 13.10). Levites, including musicians and gatekeepers, were among Nehemiah's most valuable supporters. We learn from his memoirs that he appointed Levites to a wide range of offices including provincial governor (Neh 3.17), instructor (Neh 8.7–9, 11–13), oversight of the temple treasury (13.10–14), and temple police (13.22). Temple singers

---

[20] Lev 27.14–29; Ezra 10.8; 1 Esd 9.4; Josephus, *Ant* 11.148. J. Blenkinsopp, 'Temple and Society in Achaemenid Judah', in *Second Temple Studies. 1. Persian Period*, ed. Philip R. Davies (JSOTSup 117; Sheffield: Sheffield Academic Press, 1991), 22–53; idem, 'Did the Second Jerusalemite Temple Possess Land?' *Transeuphratène* 21 (2001): 61–8.

played a prominent part in the dedication of the city wall rebuilt by Nehemiah (12.17–43).[21]

The problems affecting the functioning of the temple under Persian rule pale by comparison with later events: the sale of the office of the high priesthood to the highest bidder under Seleucid rule, and the usurpation of the high priestly office by the Hasmonaeans who were neither of Zadokite nor of Aaronite descent. It was probably the conviction that the temple priesthood was irredeemably corrupt and inauthentic that led some temple personnel from among the lower ranks of the priesthood and the Levites, including liturgical singers and instrumentalists, to set up an alternative centre and alternative forms of worship at Qumran.[22] At this point, we enter a new phase in the vicissitudes of the ritual, especially the ritual killing of animals as a form of worship. Even long before the destruction of the temple by the Romans in 70 C.E, new ways of thinking about religion and ritual, in part under the influence of Greek philosophy, were leading in the direction of an interiorization and spiritualization of sacrificial ritual, or even to outright rejection. Something of this is already detectable, as I have tried to show, in the closely related attitudes to sacrifice in the books of Isaiah and Psalms.

---

[21]Still of interest on the subject of priest-Levite relations in the Second Temple period are Hermann Vogelstein, *Der Kampf zwischen Priestern und Leviten seit den Tagen Ezechiels: Eine historisch-kritische Untersuchung* (Stettin: Friedrich Nahel (Paul Niekammer) 1889); R. Meyer, 'Levitische Emanzipationsstrebungen in nachexilischer Zeit', *Orientalische Literaturzeit* 12 (1938): 721–8.

[22]See Joseph M. Baumgarten, 'Sacrifice and Worship among the Jewish Sectarians of the Dead Sea (Qumran) Scrolls', *HTR* 46 (1953): 141–59; Martin Hengel, *Judaism and Hellenism: Studies in their Encounter in Palestine during the Early Hellenistic Period. Volume One* (Philadelphia: Fortress, 1974), 175–81; Emil Schürer, *The History of the Jewish People in the Age of Jesus Christ. Volume II*, revised and edited by Geza Vermes et al. (Edinburgh: T. & T. Clark, 1979), 583–90; Jacob Milgrom, 'Sacrifice', *EDSS* 2:807–12; Robert A. Kugler, 'PRIESTS', *EDSS* 2:688–93; L. H. Schiffman, 'The Sacrificial System of the Temple Scroll and the Book of Jubilees,' in *SBL Seminar Papers*, ed. K. H. Richards (Atlanta: Society of Biblical Literature, 1985).

11

The beauty of holiness

The temple as the place of encounter with God

In the early seventeenth century, the phrase serving as title for this last chapter, as also for the book, was a byword among both the supporters and detractors of William Laud, archbishop of Canterbury. The phrase encapsulated the archbishop's resolve to restore the traditional liturgy to its central place in the life of the English church at the expense of the pulpit. His strenuous efforts to achieve this goal were opposed by the Puritans, then a strong presence in the religious life of the country, for whom preaching was the primary and indispensable element. They eventually succeeded in winning the support of the weak and temporizing Charles I, and the eclipse of the monarchy under Cromwell's Covenanters left Laud's programme in indefinite suspension. As it turned out, Laud was beheaded at Tyburn on 10 January 1645 and Charles followed him to the scaffold four years later.

The archbishop's motto, taken from the first half line of Ps 96.9 in the Book of Common Prayer and the King James Version, 'O worship the Lord in the beauty of holiness,'[1] may serve as a

---

[1] The KJV version of Ps 96.9 (LXX 95.9) is contested. LXX, *proskunēsate tō kuriō en aulē hagia autou* ('worship the Lord in his holy court') followed by Jerome's Vulgate, *adorate Dominum in atrio sancto eius*, seems to have read *běhadrat-qōdeš* ('in the holy court') for *běaderet qōdeš*, 'in the splendour/beauty of holiness') perhaps on account of parallelism with *lěhasrôtâw*, '(come) into his courts' in the previous verse. I take it that both terms, *heder* and *hasēr*, refer to enclosed spaces in the temple

fitting summary of what the temple singers, and the author of this anonymous psalm in particular, aimed to achieve in their participation in the temple liturgy. The essential part of their task consisted in offering praise (*těhillāh*) and thanksgiving (*tôdāh*) to God in music and song. They performed this service primarily as accompaniment to both the prescribed daily sacrifices and the voluntary offerings of the laity but, as the psalms themselves attest, their service of thanksgiving and praise continued by day and night. A Korahite singer attests that 'at night his song is with me, a prayer to the God of my life' (Ps 42.9). A psalm for recital on Sabbath reads:

> It is good to give thanks to the Lord,
> to sing psalms of praise to your name, Most High;
> to declare your love in the morning,
> and your faithfulness every night. (Ps 92.2–3)

And one of the pilgrim psalms invites the singers to

> come bless the Lord,
> all you, his servants,
> who minister night after night
> in the house of the Lord. (Ps 134.1)[2]

To respond to the invitation was, it seems, no burden on the temple singers and instrumentalists. Their hymns reflect the conviction that to cross the threshold into the temple, to enter 'the courts of the Lord', was to pass from the everyday world into a space qualitatively different, a space of light and ecstatic joy in which one might in some degree experience the power, goodness, and beauty of the Lord God:

---

precincts, especially the larger space, the *hêkāl*, between the entrance porch and the inner sanctum – the 'holy of holies' – where thanksgiving vows were fulfilled with voluntary offerings (Pss 96.8; 100.4; 116.19) and the temple musicians performed (Pss 65.5; 84.3,11; 135.1–2). In Ps 100.4, the faithful are urged to 'enter his gates with thanksgiving, his courts with praise'.
[2]Compare the dispositions in the Qumran *yahad* for night watches for the reading and study of the book of the law (1QS VI 6–7).

One thing I ask of the Lord,
it is the one thing I seek:
that I may dwell in the house of the Lord
all the days of my life,
to gaze on the beauty of the Lord
and to seek him in his temple. (Ps 27.4)

Lord of Hosts,
How lovely is your dwelling place!
I pine and faint with longing
for the courts of the Lord's temple;
my whole being cries out with joy
to the living God. (Ps 84.1–2)

In his monograph *Sinai and Zion* Jon Levenson made the same point apropos of Isaiah's vision in the temple (Isa 6.1–13):

This Temple is an institution common to the heavenly and the terrestrial realms; they share it. It is the place where a mere mortal, even a man who had uttered slander (Isa 6:5), can make contact with the realm of overpowering holiness, where he can hear the language of angels and respond to it.[3]

In all parts of the ancient world, the distinctive character of temples is in evidence, signified by rites of dedication and insistence on the appropriate disposition on the part of the one entering and participating in the rituals, as in Pss 15 and 24. Temples were often built on mountains as a way of representing the link between heaven and earth and providing an appropriate abode for deities, as Mount Olympus in Greece, the Mons Capitolinus in Rome, and Mount Zaphon in the far reaches of the north, the place of assembly for the Canaanite deities to which, as we have seen, the temple on Mount Zion was assimilated (Ps 48.3 cf. Isa 14.13). One aspect of the close relation between Psalms and Isaiah is the frequency with which holy temple and holy mountain are identified. In Third Isaiah, 'my holy mountain' is identical with 'my house of prayer' (Isa 56.7),

---

[3]Jon D. Levenson, *Sinai and Zion. An Entry into the Jewish Bible* (Minneapolis: Winston Press, 1985), 123.

and the same association is implicit in the reference throughout the Isaianic compilation to Zion as 'the holy mountain',[4] to the temple as 'the mountain of the house of God' (Isa 2.2), and to the mountain as the place where the Lord of Hosts dwells (Isa 8.18 cf. Ps 74.2). The temple is also the centre of the universe, the *axis mundi*, like the Ekur shrine of Enlil, supreme deity of the Sumerians, in his holy city Nippur, or the great temple of Marduk in holy Babylon represented in the epic *enuma elish* as a copy of a heavenly prototype.[5]

This aspect is not explicit in Laud's psalm, Ps 96, but the call to worship the Lord in the beauty of holiness is addressed to all the earth (v. 1, 9), and all the nations are to acknowledge the marvellous works of the God of Israel and his concern for all creation (vv. 2–3, 10–13). In Isaiah, likewise, people from all nations will converge on 'the mountain of the Lord's house' for instruction on how to build a world in which justice reigns, disputes are settled by arbitration, and war has become obsolete (Isa 2.2–5). In addition, the proclamation of the kingship of the Lord God among all the nations (Ps 96.10) will inevitably bring to mind the messenger in Isa 52.7 who announces the reign of God in Zion:

> How welcome on the mountains are the feet of the herald,
> the bringer of good news,
> announcing deliverance,
> proclaiming to Zion, 'Your God has begun his reign'.

There are also links between Ps 96 and Isa 42.10–13, one of the psalms or psalm fragments in Second Isaiah discussed in an earlier chapter. Like Ps 96, this psalm is presented as a new song, and it extends the offer of salvation to all peoples and indeed to all creation,

---

[4] Isa 11.9; 27.13; 57.13; 65.11,26; 66.20. Compare Ps 2.6; 15.1; 99.9.
[5] *Enuma elish* V 119–30; *ANET* 503. On Sumerian temples, see S. N. Kramer, *The Sumerians. Their History, Culture, and Character* (Chicago: University of Chicago Press, 1963), 135–44; idem, 'The Temple in Sumerian Literature', in *Temple in Society*, ed. M. V. Fox (Winona Lake, IN: Eisenbrauns, 1988), 1–16. On Greek temples, see W. Burkert, 'The Temple in Classical Greece', in Fox, *Temple in Society*, 27–47 with bibliography. On Israelite temples, including the so-called high places, see Menahem Haran, *Temples and Temple Service in ancient Israel* (Winona Lake, IN: Eisenbrauns, 1985), 1–57.

land and sea, in the same way and sometimes with the same words as the psalm. *It is in the book of Psalms and the book of Isaiah that the idea of a religion for all humanity is first clearly enunciated.*

In both Psalms and Isaiah, the temple offers security: for many, then and now, the beginning if not the whole of salvation. In our contemporary world, this is not a difficult concept to grasp. The idea that a holy place should offer security lived on in the practice of sanctuary. From mediaeval times, the great cathedrals of England and Europe served to shelter those accused of certain crimes who sought sanctuary in them and were thereby temporarily exempt from capture and possible execution.[6] In the Middle Ages, this custom was already ancient, and some hints of it can be found in biblical texts. Adonijah escaped imminent death by grasping the horns of the altar in Solomon's temple (1 Kgs 1.49–53). The priest Jehoiadah forbade his men from killing Queen Athaliah in the temple, but she was put to death at their hands once outside the building (2 Kgs 11.15; 2 Chr 23.14). Perhaps, too, the idea of sanctuary is in the background in Cain's complaint to the Lord that, in consequence of his crime, he is hidden from the face of God and anyone who meets him can kill him (Gen 4.14). The Jerusalem temple and other shrines in the land no doubt served this purpose, perhaps in the context of the Cities of Refuge, but the temple on Mount Zion was a source of security in a more fundamental sense. It was the place where one could experience the presence of God, where one could in some sense see the face of God (e.g. Pss 11.7; 17.15). In psalms, the temple offers security and protection under the shadow of the Almighty, the outstretched wings of God.[7] In welcoming Ruth, Boaz expresses the assurance that she will have a reward from the God of Israel under whose wings she had come seeking refuge (Ruth 2.12). In Isaiah, Zion is more often than not named as the place of refuge[8] but the temple is at the centre of Zion, in some respects not unlike Babylon and other

---

[6]In the case of Durham Cathedral, for example, the applicant for sanctuary grasped the knocker on the great door of the building which features a dragon holding the knocker ring in its teeth, whereupon a monk would at once open the door, allowing the applicant thirty-seven days of immunity. The practice of sanctuary was abolished in England in 1624.
[7]Pss 17.8; 36.8; 57.2; 61.5; 63.8; 91.1, 4.
[8]Isa 14.32; 28.16; 33.20–22; 51.3.

Mesopotamian cities in which the temple was the focal institution of the city, and local power was vested in temple personnel under the control of the *šatammu*, the temple administrator.⁹

This strange but somehow comforting expression of sheltering under the outstretched wings was suggested by the cherubim, the two composite animal figures, part-leonine or bovine and part-aquiline, with a human face, whose outstretched wings reaching from wall to wall overshadowed the cover of the holy ark (*kappōret*) in the inner sanctum, the 'Holy of Holies', the locus of revelation. The cherubim in the wilderness sanctuary were made of, or covered with, hammered gold by the artificer Bezalel (Exod 32.17–22; 37.7–9), modelled on the deities, likewise composite and theriomorphic, on guard at the entrance to Mesopotamian temples and palaces. Cherubim in the Jerusalem temple served as a decorative motif on walls and doors, but also, and more importantly, as protective covering for the ark which represented the throne of the invisible God, to judge by the expression 'enthroned on the cherubim' (*yōšēb hakkěrûbîm*).¹⁰ Here, under those mighty pinions, was the place of encounter with the Enthroned One (Exod 25.22).¹¹

Seeing and not seeing God in the temple

The temple is the house of God.¹² To be in God's house is therefore to be in the presence of God. Several psalms attempt to communicate something of what it means to encounter God in the temple as either a visitor or an active officiant in the temple liturgy. In doing

---

⁹R. J. van der Spek, 'The Babylonian City', in *Hellenism in the East: The Interaction of Greek and non- Greek civilizations from Syria to Central Asia after Alexander*, ed. Amélie Kuhrt and S. Sherwin White (London: 1987), 57–74; Heinz Kreissig, 'Eine beachtenswerte Theorie zur Organisation altvorderorientalischer Tempelgemeinden im Achämenidenreich,' *Klio* 66 (1984): 35–9; S. N. Kramer, 'The Temple in Sumerian Literature', in *Temple in Society*, ed. Michael V. Fox (Winona Lake: Eisenbrauns, 1988), 1–16.

¹⁰1 Sam 4.4; 2 Sam 6.2; 2 Kgs 19.15 = Isa 37.16; 1 Chr 13.6; Ps 99.1.

¹¹More on the cherubim in Menahem Haran, *Temple and Temple Service in Ancient Israel*, 247–59.

¹²Ps 23.6; 27.4; 42.5; 52.10; 65.5; 66.13; 84.5; 92.14; 116.19; 118.26; 122.1; 135.2; Isa 2.2,3; 14.31; 37.1; 38.20, 22.

so, these psalms speak of seeking or seeing the face of God, and of the overwhelming effect of the experience:

> One thing I ask of the Lord,
> it is the one thing I seek:
> that I may dwell in the house of the Lord
> all the days of my life,
> to gaze on the beauty of the Lord
> and to seek him in his temple...
> Come, I say to myself: seek God's face;
> your face, Lord, I seek; do not hide your face from me!
>   (Ps 27.4, 8)

The Hebrew word *pānîm* ('face') also means 'presence', understandably since it is by the face that we recognize that we are in the presence of a person rather than an object. The language of seeking and seeing the face, turning the face towards or away from someone, hiding the face, lifting up the face, and other expressions of the kind, of frequent occurrence in psalms, corresponds at one level to the language of court protocol in the ancient Near East. Abimelech, ruler of Tyre, requests an audience with Pharaoh Akhenaton, his overlord, in the conventional formulaic way, 'When shall I see the face of the king, my lord?' Another Egyptian vassal, Abdi-Hepat (or Puti-Hepat) of Jerusalem, makes a similar request: 'Let me enter into the presence of the king, my lord, and let me see the two eyes of the king, my lord.' A ruler of the city of Gezer attempts to ingratiate himself with the same Pharaoh following the same pattern: 'I have looked this way and I have looked that way, but it was not bright. I looked towards the king, my lord, and it was bright.'[13]

The use of such a stylized form of address is understandable, but in order to grasp what the psalmists mean by seeing God in the temple, we must go further and, in the first place, take account of the actual temple environment. We should ask, first

---

[13]For these citations from the Amarna Letters (fourteenth century B.C.E.), see William L. Moran, *The Amarna Letters* (Baltimore and London: Johns Hopkins University Press, 1992), 233 (EA 147), 326 (EA 286), 335 (EA 292) or, in the same order, in *ANET* 484, 487, 489.

of all, what would have been visible to one present in the *hêkāl*, the central court facing the inner sanctum, the 'Holy of Holies' – for example, to a temple singer or a member of the congregation bringing a thanksgiving offering. Following the Priestly account of the wilderness sanctuary and the report of the dedication of Solomon's temple, the individual in question would have seen the following: the holy ark (*'ărôn*) made of acacia wood with gold overlay (Exod 25.1–16; 1 Kgs 8.6–9); the *kappōret* or 'mercy seat' (more properly, 'atonement seat') which covered the ark (Exod 25.17, 21); the cherubim flanking both ark and *kappōret* (Exod 25.18–20); a table for offerings, incense, and the 'bread of the presence'; a golden lampstand (*měnōrāh*) with its seven lamps (Exod 25.31–39). The function, and therefore the configuration of the central object, the holy ark, is obscured by the conflation of two irreconcilably different traditions about it. According to the Priestly version, Moses was commanded to make the ark of wood and put it in the wilderness sanctuary (Exod 25.10–16), and it was subsequently constructed by the artisan Bezalel together with the *kappōret* and the cherubim (Exod 35.12; 37.1–9). According to the Deuteronomic version, Moses was commanded to make an ark, that is, a wooden chest, to hold the tablets of the law, and he himself did so (Deut 10.1–5). A tradition more primitive than both, however, holds that the ark was a palladium on which the safety of the early Israelites in battle and the survival of the sanctuary of Shiloh depended. It was taken into battle against the Philistines, captured by them, eventually recovered, and, after many vicissitudes, placed in the inner shrine of Solomon's temple (1 Sam 4–6; 2 Sam 6; 1 Kgs 8.1–14). The title *yōšēb hakkěrûbîm* ('enthroned on the cherubim') is consistent with the idea that the ark, however configured, represented a throne, and was therefore symbolic of the kingship of Yahweh God of Israel.[14] These objects, all of central importance to the temple cult, carried associations which gave substance to the religious experience of the worshipper. What difference they made may be assessed by comparing the canonical psalms with the

---

[14] 1 Sam 4.4; 2 Sam 6.2; 1sa 37.16; Ps 99.1; 1 Chr 13.6. Apart from usage in these sources, *'ărôn* occurs only with reference to the coffin of the patriarch Joseph (Gen 50.26) and the receptacle for depositing contributions and dues for the temple (2 Kgs 12.10–11; 2 Chr 24.8, 10–11).

apocryphal psalms from Qumran composed by authors who, as far as we know, had notional knowledge but no personal experience of the temple and its liturgies.[15]

The prototype for all claims or disavowals with respect to seeing the face of God is Moses. The tradition holds that the Lord God spoke to Moses from above the *kapporet*, between the cherubim in the wilderness sanctuary (Exod 25.22; Num 7.89), and it was therefore at that place that God was present but hidden in a cloud and therefore invisible and unapproachable (Lev 16.2). The instructions for the performance of the cult in the wilderness sanctuary confirm this tradition and no doubt reflect the dispositions for worship in the second and perhaps also in the first temple. During the sacrifice, Aaron is to take a thurible with live coals from the fire and add incense to it, so that 'the cloud of the incense' covers the *kappōret* (Lev 16.12–14). We hear of this cloud again at the dedication ceremony for Solomon's temple when, we are told, 'the priests were unable to continue to minister because of the cloud, for the glory (*kābôd*) of the Lord filled the house of the Lord' (1 Kgs 8.10–11). The presence of God during the liturgy is therefore known not by an actual visual experience but by the numinous cloud, represented by incense, and the awe inspired by the liturgy itself. At this point there is a significant difference between the account of the experience of divine presence in the temple presented above and the vision of Isaiah in the temple (Isa 6.1–13). Isaiah's vision describes a temple liturgy in the course of which the seer has a *visual* experience of the Lord God seated on a throne which resulted in Isaiah fearing that he was doomed. This experience can be explained by the combination of a temple vision with a prophetic commissioning similar to that of the prophet Micaiah ben Imlah who also claimed to have seen the Lord God on his throne surrounded by attendants, though in the royal court rather than the temple (1 Kgs 22.19–22). To a lesser extent, the scenario of Isaiah's vision may be compared and contrasted with Ezekiel's phantasmagoric vision of 'something like a human form' (*dĕmût kĕma'rēh 'ādām*, Ezek 1.26) surrounded by 'four living

---

[15] 11Q Apocryphal Psalms. See most recently Peter W. Flint, '"Apocryphal" Psalms in the Psalms Scroll and in Texts Incorporating Psalms', in *The Oxford Handbook of the Psalms*, ed. W. P. Brown (Oxford: The University Press, 2014), 621–9.

creatures' which the prophet or members of his 'school' describe in great detail (Ezek 1.5–14).

In all these different expressions of the proximity and in some way visible presence of God in the temple, Moses is in one way or another the paradigm. In the incident of the rebellion of Miriam and Aaron against his authority, Moses is said to have spoken with God face to face, unlike prophets with whom God communicates through visions and dreams (Num 12.6–9). This affirmation of the unique status of Moses is made against the background of the well-attested belief that no one can see God and live. Hagar in the wilderness (Gen 16.13) and Jacob at Peniel (the name means 'Face of God', Gen 32.30) are surprised that they are still alive after seeing a deity. Gideon is in a panic after seeing an angel of the Lord face to face (Judg 6.22), and after a vision with an angelic being, Manoah, Samson's father, tells his wife that they would surely die (Judg 13.15–23). We have just seen that Isaiah himself thinks he is doomed after his eyes have looked on the King, the Lord of Hosts (Isa 6.5). But even Moses' unique privilege of encounter with God face to face is not always maintained. In the Sinai revelation, Moses hid his face for fear of seeing God (Exod 3.6) and the people kept their distance, unable to penetrate the thick smoke and darkness (Exod 20.18–21).[16] When Moses asks God for a revelation of the divine $k\bar{a}b\hat{o}d$ he is told, 'You cannot see my face, for no one can see me and live.' The solution involved Moses being placed in a cleft of the rock, whereupon God covers Moses' face with his hand while crossing in front of him, so that he sees God only from the rear, after he has passed by (Exod 33.17–23).

In view of all this, it is not surprising that whenever psalms refer to seeing the face of God, or the power, goodness, and beauty of God in the temple (Pss 11.7; 17.15; 27.4; 63.3), the verb used – $h\bar{a}z\bar{a}h$ rather than $r\bar{a}'\bar{a}h$ – denotes a visionary experience, an experience

---

[16]The description of the event – the smoke, the numinous awe of those present, the prohibition of coming up the mountain imposed on the people – may reflect a temple service, the mountain corresponding to the temple and its summit to the 'Holy of Holies'.

in a state of transformed consciousness.[17] One example must suffice. The prayer (*těphillāh*) in Ps 17 is a petition for vindication of one falsely accused of wrongdoing. The petitioner, praying in the court facing the inner sanctum, is moved by the sight of the cherubim to ask God to hide him in the shadow of his wings (v. 8). He claims that God has watched, assayed, and tested him all night long, perhaps while the petitioner was performing a nocturnal vigil, and has found no fault in him (v. 3). He concludes by asserting the justice of his cause, and therefore prays that he might behold the face of God and be fully satisfied on awakening by a visionary experience. Use of the verb *hāzāh* ('see in vision') implies that this is more than a formal request for an interview with the Lord of Hosts, King of Israel, in keeping with accepted protocol. There is much at stake here as we see from the conclusion of the psalm:

> My plea is just: may I see your face
> and be blest with a vision of you when I awake. (Ps 17.15)

The anticipation of a vision, on awakening, of the *těmuûnāh* of God – an indeterminate term meaning the form, manifestation, in some way perceptible appearance of God – may simply be another and more intense way of praying for a vision of the face of God in the morning, the favoured time for revelation after the night vigil.[18] I leave it to the reader to consult the literature offering explanations in psychological terms of these types of extreme psychic and religious experience.

---

[17] Pss 11.7; 17.15; 27.4; 63.3. On the characteristics of the visionary (*hōzeh*) especially in the Judaean tradition, see Robert R. Wilson, *Prophecy and Society in Ancient Israel* (Philadelphia: Fortress, 1980), 254–95; David L. Petersen, *The Roles of Israel's Prophets* (Sheffield: JSOT Press, 1981), 51–69; Joseph Blenkinsopp, *Sage, Priest, Prophet, Religious and Intellectual Leadership in Ancient Israel* (Louisville: Westminster, 1995), 115–29; idem, *A History of Prophecy in Israel* (2nd edn, Louisville: Westminster, 1996), 26–30.

[18] On the widely differing interpretations of Ps 17.15, including reference to the beatific vision and to a solar theophany, see, in addition to the commentaries, Mark S. Smith,' 'Seeing God' in the Psalms': The Background to the Beatific Vision in the Hebrew Bible,' *CBQ* 50 (1988). Apart from its appearance in this verse, *těmûnāh* is used of idolatrous images (Deut 4.12–29), and even for a ghost (Job 4.16). Moses is said to be the only one who sees the divine *těmûnāh* (Num 12.8). More on this word in KB I 1746–47.

Once again, Isaiah's vision in the temple (Isa 6.1–13)

At this point, we return to Isaiah's inaugural vision, reported in the first person by the prophet himself and represented as taking place in the temple (Isa 6.1–13). The term *hêkāl* (v. 1) is ambiguous since it can also refer to the royal palace, but not when combined with *habbāyit*, 'the house' (v. 4), namely, the house of God, and not in view of its occupants and the activities in which they are engaged. Here, the prophet is drawing freely on liturgical hymns composed for worship in the temple. At the centre is the One seated on a throne raised up on high, as in one of the Korahite psalms:

> Seated on his holy throne,
> God reigns over the nations. (Ps 47.9)

In the vision, he is the King of Glory (*melek hakkābôd*, cf. Ps 24.8–10), Lord of Hosts (cf. Ps 24.10; 59.6; 84.2, 4, 9, 13), the Holy God (cf. Pss 22.4; 99.3, 5; 111.9). The Enthroned One is surrounded not by the cherubim, as in psalms (Pss 80.2; 99.1), but by seraphim, the incandescent ones, who use their wings to cover their faces, as the face of Moses was covered in the presence of God (Exod 33.17–23).[19] This the prophet himself failed to do, which merited reproof from some rabbinic readers of the vision narrative.[20] There is also the smoke produced by the incense (cf. Lev 16.11–14; 1 Kgs 8.10–11). A liturgy is in progress in which the seraphim intone

---

[19] It is not clear why Isaiah replaced the cherubim in the Jerusalem temple with seraphim (*sĕrāpîm*). Elsewhere (Num 21.6; Deut 8.15), the seraph is a poisonous snake whose bite served to punish the Israelites in the wilderness for complaining. Isaiah 14.29 and 30.6 refer to a flying serpent like the seraphs in the vision report who use their wings to remain aloft. In keeping with the meaning of the corresponding verb, the seraphs may have been thought of as fiery creatures. See *KB* 3:1360–61. There may also be a connection with the bronze serpent image made by Moses to heal those suffering from snake bites (Num 21.8–9). Known as Nehushtan, the minor deity represented by this image was incorporated into the Judaean Yahweh cult until destroyed by king Hezekiah (2 Kgs 18.4). See Lowell K. Handy, 'SERPENT BRONZE', *ABD* V 1117.

[20] b.Yev. 49b, b.Sanh. 103b, y.Sanh. 10.2.

antiphonally (*zeh'el-zeh*, 'one to the other', v. 3) the praise of the Enthroned One:

Holy, holy, holy, is the Lord of Hosts,
all the earth is full of his glory!

The intonation of the seraphim could have been taken from Ps 99 which proclaims the holiness of the Lord God three times (vv. 3, 5, 9). Psalm 24 also praises the Lord of Hosts as the King of Glory, and several psalms declare that 'all the earth is full of the glory of God' (Pss 57, 72, 108). The threefold praise of the Holy God – the origin of the Sanctus, the Trisagion, and the Kedushah – is therefore essentially a distillation of the praise of God in these and other psalms.

In parenthesis: there has been much discussion about the authenticity and formation of this vision report. Practically all exegetes hold that 6.13b, *zera' qōdeš massabtāh* ('the holy seed is its stump') is post-exilic (cf. Ezra 9.2), and a majority argue that vv. 12–13, which predict exile and the devastation of the land and in which Yahweh is referred to in the third person, are also additions to the core narrative.[21] At the least, we can say that the report is not the spontaneous transcription of an experience. It is a constructed narrative which not only represents a combination of different genres, as we have seen, but reflects an acquaintance with much in the book of Isaiah which post-dates the death of Uzziah, perhaps 734 B.C.E., and much in the psalms with which it shares a profound regard for the temple.

The invocation of the Lord of Hosts in Isaiah's vision brings us back to the theme most central to Psalms and Isaiah, to Zion

---

[21]C. F. Whitley, 'The Call and Mission of Isaiah,' *JNES* 18 (1959): 38–48, was among the first to hold that the entire incident is a post-exilic creation dependent to a considerable extent on Ezekiel. Among those who consign only vv. 12–13 to the post-disaster period are O. Kaiser, *Der Prophet Jesaja. Kap. 1-12* (2nd edn, Göttingen: Vandenhoeck & Ruprecht, 1963); Eng. Tr. *Isaiah 1-2. A Commentary* (Philadelphia: Westminster, 1972), 71–86; J. Vermeylen, *Du Prophète Isaïe à l'Apocalyptique. Isaïe I – XXXV. Tome I* (Paris: Gabalda, 1977), 187–97; H. Wildberger, *Isaiah 1-12* (Minneapolis: Fortress, 1991), 246–78; U. Berges, *Das Buch Jesaja. Komposition und Endgestalt* (Freiburg im Breisgau: Herder, 1998), 94–104; W. A. M. Beuken, *Jesaja 1-12* (Freiburg im Breisgau: Herder, 2003), 158–82.

where the Lord of Hosts is enthroned. The original impetus for the concentration on Zion as a focus of shared desires and a way of envisaging a future different from the unsatisfactory present was the return of expatriates in the early Persian period, an event which was in process from the reign of Cyrus II to that of Darius I, and which continued at a reduced rate for long after that time.[22] In Psalms, this return is conceived as a procession to Zion, for which the so-called Psalms of Ascent (Pss 20–34) were composed, perhaps with some additions and subtractions, by the temple singers either before or shortly after their repatriation. But this procession also replicates the original transfer of the ark from Shiloh via Kiriath-jearim to Zion where it served as the *hieros logos* for the liturgy of Solomon's temple, a strong echo of which can be heard in Ps 132 and, to a lesser extent, in the Asaphite Ps 78 and the Korahite Ps 84. In Psalms, the emphasis is more on Zion as a present reality: Jerusalem-Zion destroyed (Ps 74.2), the city and temple awaiting rebuilding and restoration of the temple liturgies (Pss 51.20; 53.7; 69.36; 102.14, 17), the hope for a reversal of fortune and a return of the deportees (14.7), the sadness of exile (Ps 137), and finally the realization of the hope, the joyful fulfilment of the dream (Ps 126.1). The desire, the energy, the intensity of feeling recur throughout the psalms collection, especially in the psalms originating in the guilds of Asaph and Korah. The Zion of Isaiah, in all three major sections, is for the most part an object of aspiration, an eschatological goal.

A final summation

The Hebrew Bible is commonly associated with a religion of the written word: the commanding word of the law, the challenging word of prophecy. Yet the temple singers, with their close contacts with the circles which carried forward and contributed to the

---

[22] The best known of these later 'goings up' from Babylon is that of Ezra and his group including temple singers (Ezra 7–8; 7.7). For the Babylonian origins of the Essenes, see Jerome Murphy-O'Connor, 'Damascus' in *EDSS* 1:165–166; Philip R. Davies, 'The Birthplace of the Essenes: Where Is "Damascus?"', *Revue de Qumrân* 14 (1990): 503–19, reprinted in *Essays on Qumran and Related Topics* (Atlanta: Scholars Press, 1996), 95–111. On exile in the history of the interpretation of Isaiah, see my *Opening the Sealed Book* (Grand Rapids: Eerdmans, 2006), 222–50.

traditions eventuating in the book of Isaiah, demonstrated that the word is not incompatible with other modalities of religious experience and expression, affective and even mystical, given personal and social enactment in joyful liturgies, song, dance, ritual prayer, and lament. The beauty of the psalms resounds throughout the book of Isaiah, and the Isaian vision of the Creator God, Lord of nature and history beyond the bounds of Israel, is echoed and joyfully proclaimed by the psalmists.

SUBJECT INDEX

Aaronite priesthood 144
    (*see also* priesthood)
Aaronite-Zadokite
    priesthood 14, 92
    (*see also* priesthood)
Abdi-Heba (Hurrian prince) 87
Abimelech (ruler of Tyre) 153
Abraham 109, 121
Achaemenid period 20
Ahab ben Kolaiah 66
Ahaz (king of Judah) 53
akitu New Year festival 13
Amarna period 87
Amaziah of Judah, king of
    Judah 24
Amos (one of Twelve Minor
    Prophets) 32
  at Bethel 34–5
  curt dismissal of liturgical
    singing 19
  Elisha (prophet) and 32
  gender issue and 19
  Kingdom of Samaria and 32,
    35 n.20
animal sacrifice 136, 140–1
    (*see also* sacrifice)
Antiochus IV 100 n.26, 122, 136
Aramaic texts 34, 113
    (*see also* texts)
architecture of
    Isaiah 40-55, 57–61
Asaphite guilds 11, 40
  destruction of Jerusalem
    and 122

God abandoning his dwelling
    in Shiloh 90
  as Heman group 29 n.5
  psalms of 93, 96–8
Asaphite musicians 43
Asaphite singers 17, 43, 66, 96
asceticism 136
Asidaeans (*asidaioi*) 116–17,
    117 n.26
Asidaeans, of Maccabean age 130
Assyrians 12, 97, 101
Athaliah (female Judaean
    ruler) 15

Baal (Syrian god) 87
    Babylonian *nāru* 12
Babylonians 12, 19, 66, 72,
    101, 122
Bach, Johann Sebastian 7
'benevolent deeds' 81–2
Berges, Ulrich 65, 67, 99 n.23
biblical texts 1, 8, 20, 22, 25, 65
    n.14, 82, 103, 114, 117,
    151 (*see also* texts)
Book of Isaiah 1–2, 6, 8, 27,
    31, 53, 57, 63–4, 67,
    98, 101–2, 114, 117,
    125, 138, 151, 159–61
    (*see also* Isaiah)
'Book of Meditation' 111
British Museum 60

Canaanite deities 149
Canaanite-Jebusite mythology 41

canonical psalms 28, 43, 48–52, 54, 69–71, 77–8, 80–2, 110, 114, 154
Catholic charismatic movement 7
Charles I of England 147
Chenaniah (precentor and master-musician) 14
cherubim
 Enthroned One and 158
 in Jerusalem temple 152
 replaced in Jerusalem temple 158 n.19
 in the wilderness sanctuary 152, 155
Christian faith 135–6
Christianity 107, 132
Christians 136
Chronicles 6, 11, 13–14, 16 n.9, 17–18, 24, 28, 31–4, 34 n.18, 89, 93, 97, 124
cult prophet hypothesis 31–5
Cyrus Cylinder 60
Cyrus II of Persia 17, 61, 65, 69, 96, 160

Damascus sect 65 n.14, 113
Darius I, king of Persian Achaemenid Empire 17, 19, 65, 77, 160
Demetrios I Soter, King 116
'The Destiny of the Nations in the Book of Isaiah' (Davies) 64
Deutero-Isaiah 2, 3, 57, 58–9, 61–7
Deuteronomistic History 1, 7, 28
Deuteronomists 5
Deuteronomy 77, 128
devout (*ḥāsîdîm*)
 Isaiah 114–17
 psalms 114–17

Didache ('The Teaching of the Twelve Apostles') 107

early Christian communities 29
early Christian Ebionites (the Poor) 130
Ebedlieder 59–60, 62, 71
ēdāh (LXX *sunagōgē*) 112–13
Edomite clan 20–5, 21
Edomite Korahites 23
Edomite singers 22 n.22
Egyptian execration texts 87 (*see also* texts)
Egyptians 12, 140
Elijah (Israelite prophet) 6, 31–2
Enlil (supreme deity of the Sumerians) 150
Ezrahite 11, 21–2
Ezra-Nehemiah 11
 Chronicles and 16 n.9, 17–18, 34
 singers and instrumentalists in 17–18, 34
 temple musicians in 17–18

Garden of Eden 88
God (*see also* specific entries)
 as Creator 73
 Ephraimites and 5
 as Father and the Merciful One 5
 obedience to 137
 Qedushah and 38
 Sanctus and 38
 seeing and not seeing 152–7
 temple as the place of encounter with 147–52
 Trisagion and 38
God of Israel 2, 45, 67, 69, 131, 150–1 (*see also* 'Lord of the Hosts')
'God of Sinai' 4 (*see also* 'The One of Sinai' (*zeh sinai*))
God of Zion

SUBJECT INDEX

Asaphite psalm 76 and 97
   titulature of 102–5
Graeco-Jewish texts 137 (see also texts)
Graeco-Roman period 108
Greek philosophy 146

Haredi Orthodox Jews 132
hasde YHWH 82
hāsîd 114–15
Hasidic movement 7
hāsîdîm 45, 114–17
hāsîd in Isaiah 117–19
Hasmonaean Janneus 49
Hebrew Bible 1, 61, 91, 121, 142, 160
Hellenistic culture 133
Hellenistic empire 136
Hellenistic period 9, 18, 20, 108, 122
Hittites 12
holiness
   Isaiah's vision in the temple 158–60
   seeing and not seeing God in the temple 152–7
   temple as the place of encounter with God 147–52
'the Holy One of Israel' 44, 103–4
Holy Spirit 29
human sacrifice 142 (see also sacrifice)
Hurrians 12

identity of Isaiah 56-66 75–7
Isaiah
   devout (*hāsîdîm*) 114–17
   hāsîd in 117–19
   postscript 132–3
   repudiation of sacrifice in 135–46
   righteous (*saddîqîm*) 108–10

saddîq in 117–19
'Servant of God/the Lord' in 126–7
two ways in 107–19
vision in the temple 158–60
Zion as reality and symbol in 87–105
Isaiah 40-48 68–71
Isaiah 40-55 57–75
   architecture of 57–61
   Prophecy and Psalmody in 57–75
   Psalm elements in 67–8
Isaiah 49-55 71–4
Isaiah 56-59 77–85
   two laments 79–85
   two prophetic judgements 78–9
Isaiah 56-66
   identity of 75–7
   structure of 75–7
Islam 7
Israel 1
   Amos and 19
   Bethel 19
   Judaean monarchy and 14
   liturgical music in 11–25
   temple musicians and singers in 13
   Transjordanian kingdoms and 30
Israel-Jacob 60, 121

Jahaziel ben Zechariah 30
Jebel'el-Aqra 88
Jehoash (ruler of northern Israelite kingdom) 24
Jehoshaphat, King of Judah 15, 30
Jerusalem 8
   Assyrian army, siege by 99
   destruction of 8, 73, 122
   fall and sack of 61 n.4, 65, 98, 122 n.3

Mesopotamian temples and   20
pre-Israelite   87, 89
rebuilding and repopulation of   126
Sennacherib's Assyrians and   97–8
temple cult   32
Jerusalem priesthood   137
(*see also* priesthood)
Jerusalem temple   145
Baals and   35
canonical psalms and   82
cherubim in   152, 158 n.19
Cities of Refuge and   151
Edomites and   25
financial services offered by   145
Joel and Habakkuk (prophets) and   32
rebuilding   145
sacrificial system of   143
second   35
throne of the Lord of Hosts in   38, 103
wealth of   145
Jewish Scripture   2
Jews   95–6, 130, 132, 144
Judaean monarchy   14
Judahite genealogy   22
Judaism   7, 107, 133, 135
rabbinic   135
Second Temple   109

'King of Glory'   90–1
Kohathite Levitical singers   30
Kohathite singers   30
Korahite guilds   11, 40
Edomite origins of   93
God of Jacob and   104
psalms of   93–6
Korahite Levitical singers   30, 94
Korahite musicians   43
Korahite psalms   41, 45

Korahite singers   43, 94, 148

Lamentations   7, 65
Late Antiquity   135
legal formalism   8 (*see also* prophetic pessimism)
Levites
Athaliah (female Judaean ruler) and   15
bad feelings between priests and   143–6
Court of the Israelites and   91 n.7
Court of the Women and   91 n.7
liturgical role of   16–17
Mesopotamian temples and   18
origins of   105
rebuilding Jerusalem   66–7
sacrifice and   143–6
singers and instrumentalists and   12, 14
singers guilds and   8
temple musicians as   15, 128, 133, 143
temple singers   92, 96
Levitical genealogy   22
Levitical singers   84, 92, 105, 128
liturgical music
in Israel   11–25
Levitical leaders and   15
in Near East   11–25
in Solomon's temple   18–20
liturgical musicians   15, 17–18, 21, 23–4, 29
liturgical psalms   8
Lord of Hosts (*YHWH sĕbāʾôt*)   89
'The Lord of Hosts enthroned upon the cherubim'   102–3
'Lord of the Hosts'   45, 100
(*see also* God of Israel)

Maccabean period 33, 116
Maccabean revolt 109
Marduk (Babylonian
 deity) 60, 150
Mesopotamia 18, 34 n.18, 42,
 96, 113
Mesopotamian temples 18, 20
Micah ben Imlah 38
Micaiah ben Imlah (prophet) 62,
 90, 155
Middle Ages 151
Mons Capitolinus, Rome 149
moral teaching 107
Mosaic-Sinaitic law 1
Moses (prophet in the Abrahamic
 religions) 2, 4–6,
 23, 27–9, 113, 121,
 144–5, 154–8
Mount Olympus, Greece 149
Mount Zaphon 41, 45,
 87–8, 149
Mount Zion 72–3, 90, 97–9,
 149, 151
music
 liturgical (see liturgical music)
 worship and 12
musicians
 Asaphite 43
 in Israel 13
 Korahite 43
 liturgical 15, 17–18, 21,
  23–4, 29
 temple 15, 17–18

Near East
 court protocol in 153
 dance as part of religious
  celebration in 23
 liturgical music in 11–25
 professional musicians in 12
 role of music in worship and
  public ceremony in 12
 texts of international treaties
  in 140 n.10

Negative Confessions in the
 Egyptian Books of the
 Dead 51
Neo-Babylonian period 20
New Jerusalem 84
New Testament 109
'The One of Sinai' (*zeh sinai*) 4
 (*see also* 'God of Sinai')

Orpheus, son of Apollo 27
Orphic communities 136
orthodox Lutheran theology 7

Pentecostal movement 7
Persian-Achaemenid empire 2
Persian empire 145
Persian period 108
personal piety 135
Pharaoh 87, 153
pilgrimage 91, 100
pilgrim psalms 91–2 (*see also*
 'Psalms of Ascent')
pre-Israelite Jerusalem 87, 89
priesthood 144 (*see also* priests)
 Aaronite 144
 Aaronite-Zadokite 14, 92
 animal sacrifice under the
  control of 141
 Jerusalem 137
 preponderant role of 23
 rebellion of Levites against
  Moses and Aaron
  and 23
 secularization and commercialization of
 senior 145
 temple 129, 130, 135, 137–9,
  143–4, 146
priests (*see also* priesthood)
 bad feelings between Levites
  and 143–6
 sacrifice and 143–6
prophecy (*see also* psalmody)
 in Isaiah 40-55 57–75

in Isaiah 56-66   75–85
psalmody and   27–31
prophetic books   54, 61
prophetic judgements   78–9
prophetic pessimism   8 (*see also* legal formalism)
prophets
  cult prophet hypothesis and   31–5
  Israelite   31
  local hill sanctuaries and   30
  small colonies of self-sustaining   30
  teaching to posterity   2
  and temple worship   31–5
  and the *torat YHWH*   2
  watchman as   63
Proto-Isaiah   57
Psalm 1   108, 110–12
psalmody (*see also* prophecy)
  in Isaiah 56-66   75–85
  prophecy and   27–31
  temple   67
psalmody in Isaiah 1-39   37–56
  Isaiah 1-12   37–44
  Isaiah 13-27   44–50
  Isaiah 28-35   50–3
  Isaiah 36-39   53–6
psalmody in Isaiah 40-55   57–75
psalms
  of the Asaphite guild   96–8
  canonical   28, 43, 48–52, 54, 69–71, 77–8, 80–2, 110, 114, 154
  devout (*ḥasîdîm*)   114–17
  elements in Isaiah 40-55   67–8
  of the Korahite guild   93–6
  pilgrim   91–2
  postscript   132–3
  repudiation of sacrifice in   135–46
  re-reading isaiah in the light of   1–9

  righteous (*saddîqîm*)   108–10
  'Servant of God/the Lord' in   121–5
  terms for self-segregating conventicles   112–13
  and their authors   11–25
  two ways in   107–19
  wisdom   6
  Zion as reality and symbol in   87–105
'Psalms of Ascent'   91, 160
  (*see also* pilgrim psalms)
Ptolemies   137
public worship   135
Puritans   147
Pythagorean communities   136

Quakers   132
Queen Athaliah   151
Qumran Isaiah scroll   49
Qumran Psalms Scroll   29
Qumran sect   111
Qumran texts   144
  (*see also* texts)

rabbinic Judaism   135
  (*see also* Judaism)
religious poem   11
righteous (*saddîqîm*)
  in Isaiah   108–10
  in psalms   108–10
Romans   12, 135, 146

Sabbath   148
sacrifice
  animal   136, 140–1
  bad feelings between priests and Levites   143–6
  human   142
  introductory observations   135–7
  in Isaiah   137–40
  Levites and   143–6
  priests and   143–6

SUBJECT INDEX

in Psalms 140–3
sacrificial offerings 13, 143
saddîq in Isaiah 117–19
Sargon II (Assyrian
    emperor) 126
Second Temple Judaism 109
    (*see also* Judaism)
Second Temple period 33
sect 132 n.18
    Damascus 65 n.14, 113
    formation in early
        Judaism 133
    from Hasmonaean
        periods 114
    Qumran 111
    from Roman periods 114
self-segregating conventicles
    terms 112–13
Sennacherib (Assyrian king) 53
'Servant of God/the Lord'
    as a distinct minority 130–2
    in Isaiah 126–7
    postscript 132–3
    in psalms 121–5
    in Trito-Isaiah (Isaiah
        56-66) 127–9
Shakers 132
Sinai 2–6, 31, 145, 149, 156
Sinai and Zion (Levenson) 149
singers (*see also* specific types)
    Asaphite 17, 43, 66, 96
    Edomite 22 n.22
    female 20
    in Israel 13
    Kohathite 30
    Korahite Levitical 30, 94
    Levitical 84, 92, 105, 128
    temple 8, 13, 19–20, 32, 34,
        38, 64–7, 70, 84, 92, 96,
        98, 102, 111–12, 114,
        124–5, 142, 145–8, 160
Solomon's temple
    Edomite connection 20–5
    liturgical music in 18–20

'the Song at the Papyrus Sea' 44
southern Mesopotamia 18, 34
    n.18, 66
'the Strong One of
    Jacob' 104–5
structure of Isaiah 56-66 75–7
Sufi orders (*tariqas*) 7
Sumerians 12, 150

temple
    Isaiah's vision in 158–60
    as place of encounter with
        God 147–52
    seeing and not seeing God
        in 152–7
temple musician guilds 13–14
temple musicians 15
    in Ezra-Nehemiah 17–18
temple priesthood 129, 130,
    135, 137–9, 143–4, 146
    (*see also* priesthood)
temple singers 8, 13, 19–20, 32,
    34, 38, 64–7, 70, 84, 92,
    96, 98, 102, 111–12,
    114, 124–5, 142,
    145–8, 160
temple worship
    cult prophet hypothesis 31–5
    David as founder of 14
    origins of 90
    prophets and 31–5
    sacrifice of animals and 138
terms for self-segregating
    conventicles 112–13
texts (*see also* specific texts)
    Aramaic 34, 113
    biblical 1, 8, 20, 22, 25,
        65 n.14, 82, 103, 114,
        117, 151
    Egyptian execration 87
    Graeco-Jewish 137
    Qumran 144
Third Isaiah 99, 103, 114,
    129–30, 149

titulature of the God of
    Zion   102–5
tôdāh sacrifice   142
torah   1–2
torat YHWH ('the law of the
    LORD')   2
Torrey, Charles Cutler   80
Transjordanian
    kingdoms   30
Trito-Isaiah (Isaiah
    56-66)   58, 59
  'Servant of God/the Lord'
    in   127–9
'Two Spirits in the Qumran
    Community Rule'   107

University of Altdorf   57
Urusalim   87

vegetarianism   136
'the Vineyard Song'   41

William Laud, Archbishop of
    Canterbury   147

'wisdom psalms'   6
worship
    music and   12
    public   135
    temple (*see* temple worship)

Yahweh (warrior-God)   3, 14, 39,
    62, 68–70, 76, 78, 89,
    91, 140
Yahweh God of Israel   69,
    103, 154

Zedekiah ben Maaseiah   66
Zion   3
    in Isaiah   98–102
    in psalms   91–2
    as reality and symbol in
        Isaiah   87–105
    as reality and symbol in
        psalms   87–105
Zionism   98
Zion theology   38
Zion traditions, origins of   7,
    87–91

AUTHOR INDEX

Ackroyd, Peter R.   53 n.43
Albright, William Foxwell
   16 n.10, 21 n.20
Amir, Yehoshua   4 n.8
Anderson, Gary A.   136 n.2
Assmann, Jan   13 n.3
Avigad, N.   34 n.18

Badali, Enrico   13 n.3
Barton, John   12 n.2, 66 n.17
Baumgarten, Joseph M.   137 n.4,
   146 n.22
Beaulieu, Paul-Alain   60 n.2
Beckwith, Robert T.   136 n.2
Begrich, Joachim   33 n.13
Bellinger, W. H.   35 n.21
Bellinger, W. H., Jr.   34 n.16
Berger, Peter L.   132 n.18
Berges, Ulrich   45 n.16, 50 n.30,
   53 n.43, 61 n.4, 65, 65 n.15,
   67, 67 n.19, 68 n.20, 99 n.23,
   102 n.30, 122 n.2, 132 n.17,
   159 n.21
Bergmeier, Roland   110 n.10
Beuken, Willem A. M.   132 n.17,
   159 n.21
Boda, M. J.   112 n.17
Braun, J.   13 n.3
Bremer, J.   67 n.19, 102 n.30
Briggs, C. A.   95 n.17, 122 n.3
Briggs, E. G.   95 n.17, 122 n.3
Bright   103 n.33
Brown, William P.   12 n.2, 124
   n.6, 155 n.15

Broyles, C. C.   41 n.6, 81 n.12,
   132 n.17
Burkert, W.   150 n.5
Buss, M. J.   24 n.27

Ceresco, Anthony R.   125 n.8
Chilton, Bruce D.   51 n.34
Clausen, W.   42 n.12
Clements, Ronald E.   2 n.3,
   89 n.3, 101 n.28
Coats, George W.   23 n.26
Cogan, Mordechai   21 n.19
Craigie, Peter C.   140 n.10
Cromwell, Oliver   137
Cross, Frank Moore   62 n.5

Dandamaev, Muhammad A.
   65 n.14
Danker, Frederick W.   109 n.5
Davies, Graham I.   64, 64 n.13
Davies, Philip R.   145 n.20,
   160 n.22
Day, John   35 n.21, 51 n.33
de Geus, C. H. J.   22 n.22
Dekker, Jaap   3 n.6
de Vaux, Roland   21 n.20, 22
   n.22, 31 n.8, 35 n.21
de Vries, Simon   17 n.11, 29 n.4
Döderlein, Johann Christoph   57
Driver, Samuel Rolles   16 n.10
Duhm, Bernhard   45, 45 n.17,
   58–9, 58 n.1, 75, 76 n.2, 104,
   104 n.34, 125 n.8
Dybwad, Jacob   64 n.9

AUTHOR INDEX

Eaten, John 23 n.25
Eaton, John H. 64 n.10
Emanuel, Susan 136 n.2
Evans, C. A. 41 n.6, 81 n.12, 132 n.17

Fischer, Irmtraud 3 n.6
Flint, Peter W. 119 n.30, 155 n.15
Fohrer, Georg 46 n.18
Fox, Michael V. 150 n.5, 152 n.9
Frank, H. T. 22 n.22

Galpin, F. W. 13 n.3
Gerhardt, Paul 7
Gese, Helmut 16 n.11, 18 n.14
Gesenius, Wilhelm 58
Gillingham, Susan E. 12 n.2, 112 n.17, 124 n.6
Gosse, Bernard 38 n.1
Goulder, Michael D. 24 n.27
Gunkel, Hermann 33, 33 n.13, 52, 52 n.37

Haag, E. 125 n.7
Haldar, Alfred 33 n.12
Handy, Lowell K. 158 n.19
Hanson, Paul D. 118 n.30
Haran, Menahem 150 n.5, 152 n.11
Hayes, John H. 101 n.28
Hengel, Martin 114 n.23
Holstean, J. A. 133 n.18
Hossfeld, Frank-Lothar 5 n.14, 67 n.19, 90 n.5, 93 n.13, 102 n.30, 122 n.3, 125 n.7

Jackson, Peter 136 n.2
Janzen, David 136 n.2
Japhet, Sara 16 n.9
Jeanrond, Werner G. 101 n.27
Jenkins, A. K. 45 n.16
Jensen, Joseph 2 n.4

Johnson, Aubrey R. 33, 33 n.16, 35
Jones, D. R. 64 n.10

Kaiser, O. 34 n.16, 159 n.21
Kant, Immanuel 4
Kapelrud, Arvid 33 n.12
Kilmer, A. D. 13 n.3
Kleer, Martin 29 n.4
Kleinig, J. W. 14 n.6, 16 n.11
Knoppers, Gary 132 n.17
Koch, Klaus 109 n.5
Körting, Coriana 101 n.28
Kramer, S. N. 150 n.5, 152 n.9
Kratz, Reinhard G. 60 n.3, 112 n.17
Kraus, Hans-Joachim 33 n.15, 74 n.27, 89 n.3
Kreissig, Heinz 152 n.9
Kugler, Robert A. 146 n.22
Kuhrt, Amélie 152 n.9

Lau, Wolfgang 118 n.30
Levenson, Jon D. 89 n.4, 101 n.28, 149, 149 n.3
Levin, Christoph 12 n.1, 109 n.7
Lewis, I. M. 31 n.7
Lichtheim, Miriam 51 n.36
Lindblom, J. 46 n.18
Lipshits, O. 132 n.17
Loewe, R. 29 n.4

Mare, W. H. 89 n.3
Matthews, V. H. 13 n.3, 14 n.6
Mayes, Andrew D. H. 101 n.27
Mays, James L. 29 n.4
McCarter, P. Kyle, Jr. 24 n.28
McConville, J. G. 2 n.3
McEwan, Gilbert J. P. 13 n.3
McKane, William 103 n.33
Melugin, Roy F. 2 n.2, 3 n.6, 62 n.5
Meyer, R. 93   n.11, 146 n.21

AUTHOR INDEX

Milgrom, Jacob   146 n.22
Mohr, J. C. B.   74 n.27
Möller, Karl   2 n.3
Montague, J.   14 n.6
Moran, William L.   87 n.2, 153 n.13
Mowinckel, Sigmund   32-3, 32 n.11, 35, 64, 74 n.27
Murphy-O'Connor, Jerome   160 n.22
Myers, Jacob M.   16 n.10

Nasuti, Harry P.   5 n.14
Niekammer, Paul   93 n.11

Ollenburger, Ben C.   74 n.27, 89 n.4, 101 n.28

Pauritsch, K.   81 n.12
Pedersen, Johannes   33 n.12
Petersen, David L.   16 n.9, 34 n.16, 157 n.17
Pfeiffer, Robert H.   16 n.10
Plöger, Otto   47 n.21, 50 n.31
Porton, Gary G.   114 n.23
Prinsloo, W. S.   68 n.22
Provan, Ian   112 n.17

Quell, G.   35 n.21

Reed, W. L.   22 n.22
Richards, Kent H.   137 n.4, 146 n.22
Rimmer, J.   14 n.6
Roberts, J. J.   89 n.4
Roth, G.   132 n.18
Rowley, H. H.   33 n.12, 34 n.16, 35 n.21
Roy, M. Lee   112 n.17
Rudolph, W.   33 n.15, 103 n.33
Rupprecht, K.   89 n.3

Sanders, E. P.   132 n.17
Sanders, J. A.   29 n.3

Sarna, Nahum   29 n.4
Schiffman, Lawrence H.   137 n.4, 146 n.22
Schmidt, Hans   125 n.8
Schürer, Emil   114 n.23, 137 n.5, 146 n.22
Seitz, Christopher R.   58 n.1, 62 n.5, 101 n.28
Sekine, S.   81 n.12
Selman, Martin J.   136 n.2
Seybold, Klaus   24 n.27, 93 n.12
Sheppard, Gerald T.   2 n.2
Siebeck, Mohr   60 n.3
Sjödin, Anna-Pya   136 n.2
Skinner, John   22 n.23
Smart, James D.   118 n.30
Smith, Henry Preserved   24 n.28
Smith, Mark S.   157 n.18
Snaith, N. H.   112 n.17
Steck, Odil H.   60 n.3
Steiner, T. M.   67 n.19, 102 n.30
Stern, S.   29 n.4
Stroumsa, Guy G.   136 n.2
Sweeney, Marvin A.   2 n.2, 3 n.6

Tate, Marvin E.   140 n.10
Torrey, Charles Cutler   16 n.10, 51 n.35, 81 n.11
Tournai, R. J.   116 n.25
Tov, Emanuel   119 n.30

Vanderkam, James C.   119 n.30
van der Spek, R. J.   152 n.9
Van Ruiten, J.   68 n.22, 89 n.3, 101 n.28
Verlag, Ludwig Reichert   65 n.14
Vermes, Geza   114 n.23, 137 n.5, 146 n.22
Vermeylen, Jacques   38 n.1, 45 n.16, 159 n.21
Vervenne, M.   68 n.22, 89 n.3, 101 n.28
Vincent, J. M.   64 n.10

Vogelstein, Hermann 92, 92 n.11, 146 n.21
von Rad, Gerhard 33 n.15, 103 n.31

Wanke, Günther 24 n.27, 93 n.12, 95 n.17, 101 n.28
Weber, Max 132 n.18
Weil, Simone 48
Weiser, Artur 95 n.17, 103 n.33, 140 n.10
Westermann, Claus 13 n.3, 64, 64 n.11, 68 n.20
White, S. Sherwin 152 n.9
Whitley, Charles F. 38 n.1, 159 n.21
Wildberger, Hans 38 n.1, 50 n.29, 51 n.33, 101 n.28, 159 n.21
Willi, Tomas 17 n.11, 101 n.28
Williamson, Hugh G. M. 16 n.9, 16 n.10, 51 n.33, 52 n.37, 53 n.43, 62 n.5, 64 n.12, 81 n.13
Willis, John T. 41 n.6
Wilson, Robert R. 157 n.17
Wittich, C. 132 n.18
Wolff, H. W. 89 n.4
Würthwein, E. 34 n.16

Zenger, Erich 5 n.14, 24 n.27, 90 n.5, 93 n.12, 93 n.13, 122 n.3

www.ingramcontent.com/pod-product-compliance
Lightning Source LLC
Chambersburg PA
CBHW060954230426
43665CB00015B/2199